MW01011923

The Preschool
Inclusion Toolbox

The Preschool Inclusion Toolbox

How to Build and Lead a High-Quality Program

by

Erin E. Barton, Ph.D., BCBA-D
Vanderbilt University
Nashville, Tennessee

and

Barbara J. Smith, Ph.D.
University of Colorado Denver

with invited contributors

Baltimore • London • Sydney

Paul H. Brookes Publishing Co.
Post Office Box 10624
Baltimore, Maryland 21285–0624

www.brookespublishing.com

Typeset by Scribe Inc., Philadelphia, Pennsylvania.
Manufactured in the United States of America by
Sheridan Books, Inc., Chelsea, Michigan.

Cover images ©istockphoto/Rawpixel/vtwinpixel/WestLight/Aneese/leisuretime70/jenifoto/Bozena_Fulawka

Library of Congress Cataloging-in-Publication Data
The Library of Congress has cataloged the print edition as follows:

Library of Congress Cataloging-in-Publication Data
Barton, Erin Elizabeth.
    The preschool inclusion toolbox : how to build and lead a high-quality program / Erin E. Barton, Barbara J. Smith ; foreword by Christine L. Salisbury.
        pages   cm
    Includes bibliographical references and index.
    ISBN 978-1-59857-667-2 (paperback) — ISBN 978-1-59857-842-3 (epub ebook) — ISBN 978-1-59857-845-4 (pdf ebook)
    1. Children with disabilities—Education (Preschool) 2. Inclusive education. 3. Education, Preschool—Administration.
I. Smith, Barbara J. II. Title.
    LC4019.2.B37 2015
    371.9'046—dc23   2014041803

British Library Cataloguing in Publication data are available from the British Library.

2019   2018   2017

10   9   8   7   6   5   4   3   2

Contents

About the Downloads

Purchasers of this book may download, print, and/or photocopy Appendixes IA, IB, IC, and 3A and Forms 1.1, 2.1, 2.2, 2.3, 2.4, 3.1, 4.1, 7.1, and 7.2 for educational use. PowerPoint slides for Chapters 1–7 are also available for course or professional development use. To access these materials, please visit **http://www.brookespublishing .com/barton/materials.**

About the Authors

Erin E. Barton, Ph.D., BCBA-D, Assistant Professor, Department of Special Education, Peabody College, Vanderbilt University, 230 Appleton Place, Nashville, Tennessee 37203

Dr. Barton teaches courses in early childhood special education on evidence-based assessment and intervention practices for young children with disabilities and their families and single-case research design. She is a Board Certified Behavior Analyst and has worked with children and families in homes, schools, and clinics. Her research interests include early intervention practices for young children with or at risk for disabilities in natural settings and professional development with early childhood practitioners. She directs research projects related to evidence-based practices for young children and professional development systems. Dr. Barton serves on several editorial boards and is an active scholar, with more than 40 publications in major journals and multiple chapters related to early intervention for young children with disabilities. Dr. Barton is currently President Elect of the Division for Early Childhood of the Council for Exceptional Children.

Barbara J. Smith, Ph.D., Research Professor, School of Education and Human Development, University of Colorado Denver, 1380 Lawrence Street, Denver, Colorado 80204

Dr. Smith received her master's degree in early childhood special education and her doctorate in special education and public policy from the University of North Carolina at Chapel Hill. Her areas of interest include early childhood special education/early intervention policies, systems, and program development; leadership and collaboration; and the scaling up of evidence-based practices.

Dr. Smith has held early childhood and early childhood special education positions since 1974, including early childhood teacher, executive director of the Division for Early Childhood (DEC) of the Council for Exceptional Children (CEC); policy specialist at CEC; and program specialist at the Office of Special Education Programs (OSEP), U.S. Department of Education. She has served as a consultant on state and national early childhood policy and an expert witness in right-to-treatment litigation, prepared and delivered legislative testimony to Congress as well as state legislatures, and worked with many parent and professional groups in their state policy efforts.

In an effort to help shape high-quality inclusive early childhood environments for all children, including those with special needs, she has worked closely for many years with the National Association for the Education of Young Children (NAEYC) and other early childhood leadership organizations, including serving on the National Association for the Education of Young Children (NAEYC) Commission on Early Childhood Program Standards and Accreditation Criteria, to develop the current program accreditation criteria. Dr. Smith has authored more than 20 peer-reviewed journal articles and 15 books and chapters, one of which was the first book for administrators on preschool inclusion:

The Administrator's Policy Handbook for Preschool Mainstreaming (Brookline Books, 1993). She also chaired the most recent effort to establish the *DEC Recommended Practices in Early Intervention/Early Childhood Special Education 2014* (Division for Early Childhood, 2014) to help guide the field in improving services for young children with special needs, their families, and those who work with them.

She is currently a coprincipal investigator of an OSEP-funded doctoral program at the University of Colorado Denver in early intervention and early childhood special education policy and collaborative leadership and is involved in the OSEP-funded national Early Childhood Technical Assistance Center. She is the recipient of several awards and honors.

About the Contributors

Debbie Cate, M.S., Technical Assistance Specialist, Early Childhood Technical Assistance Center, CB 8040, University of North Carolina, Chapel Hill, North Carolina 27599

Ms. Cate is a technical assistance specialist at the Early Childhood Technical Assistance Center and the former National Early Childhood Technical Assistance Center in the Frank Porter Graham Child Development Institute. Her work supports states in their provision of early childhood special education services in accordance with the Individuals with Disabilities Education Act for children birth through Grade 3 and their families.

Ching-I Chen, Ph.D., Assistant Professor, Special Education, School of Lifespan Development and Educational Sciences, 150 Terrace Drive, Kent State University, Kent, Ohio 44242

Dr. Chen has served as a practitioner with young children with special needs and their families and has worked on personnel development in early childhood intervention. Her research interests include developmental screening and curriculum-based assessments as well as personnel development.

Geneva J. Hallett, M.A.Ed., Director, Pyramid Plus: The Colorado Center for Social Emotional Competence and Inclusion, and Doctoral Candidate, School Education and Human Development, University of Colorado Denver, 1380 Lawrence Street, Suite 643, Denver, Colorado 80204

Ms. Hallett is an early childhood educator with more than 30 years of experience. She has taught in and directed early childhood programs, taught early childhood courses at the university level, and trained and coached early childhood professionals. Ms. Hallett has given presentations on various early childhood education topics at the local, national, and international levels.

Jaclyn D. Joseph, M.S.W., BCBA, Doctoral Candidate, School of Education and Human Development, University of Colorado Denver, 1380 Lawrence Street, Denver, Colorado 80204

Ms. Joseph is a doctoral student concentrating in early childhood education/early childhood special education and a research assistant for the Positive Early Learning Experiences Center. Ms. Joseph's professional and research interests include young children with challenging behavior and interventions for improving social emotional competence in young children with disabilities.

Katy McCullough, A.M., Technical Assistance Specialist, Early Childhood Technical Assistance Center, CB 8040, University of North Carolina, Chapel Hill, North Carolina 27599

Ms. McCullough has worked as a technical assistance specialist for more than 10 years, supporting state Part C (early intervention) and Section 619 (preschool special education) systems of the Individuals with Disabilities Education Act in improving programs, practices, and policies that affect young children with disabilities and their families. She lives near Chapel Hill, North Carolina, with her husband and two young children.

Lois M. Pribble, Ph.D., Instructor and Research Associate, Early Intervention Program, University of Oregon College of Education, 901 East 18th Avenue, Eugene, Oregon 97403

Dr. Pribble is an instructor and research associate in the Early Intervention/Early Childhood Special Education (EI/ECSE) Program at the University of Oregon. She teaches methods and applications courses in EI/ECSE with a focus on intervention in naturalistic settings. Prior to becoming a university instructor, Dr. Pribble was an EI/ECSE classroom teacher, consultant, and early childhood screener for 15 years.

Alissa L. Rausch, MA.Ed., Senior Instructor, Early Childhood/Early Childhood Special Education, School of Education and Human Development, University of Colorado Denver, 1380 Lawrence Street, Denver, Colorado 80204

Ms. Rausch is pursuing a doctorate in education with a concentration in early childhood education/early childhood special education at the University of Colorado Denver. Her work in early childhood education began as an occupational therapist on a transdisciplinary team. This early experience has blossomed into 15 years of practice as an early childhood special educator working in inclusive preschool classrooms serving young children with special needs and their families in Colorado and Iowa. Ms. Rausch has also had the privilege of serving children with special needs and their families in their homes and in community settings. Currently, she enjoys teaching preservice practitioners and looks to complete action research focused on inclusive civil discourse and effective policy implementation in the field of early childhood education.

Elizabeth A. Steed, Ph.D., Assistant Professor, Early Childhood Special Education, School of Education and Human Development, University of Colorado Denver, 1380 Lawrence Street, Denver, Colorado 80204

Dr. Steed coordinates the early childhood education master's, licensure, and doctoral programs at the University of Colorado Denver. She has experience working with young children with disabilities and their families in classroom and home-based settings. She has been the principal investigator on several research projects focusing on building partnerships with preschool teachers to prevent the development of challenging behavior in young children. She is on the editorial board of *Topics in Early Childhood Special Education,* and her research has been published in peer-reviewed journals and presented at national conferences. Dr. Steed is the first author of the *Preschool-Wide Evaluation Tool*™ (*PreSET*™; Paul H. Brookes Publishing Co., 2012), an assessment of program-wide positive behavior interventions and support in early childhood settings. She is on Colorado's governor-appointed Interagency Coordinating Council for early intervention; the Colorado Department of Human Services Exploration Work Group; the Colorado Preschool Special Education Advisory Board for the Colorado Department of Education; and the state policy team for the Pyramid Model and Inclusion Practices, where she works collaboratively with Colorado's early childhood special educators, administrators, and policy makers.

Foreword

This book is a unique and bold departure from others that address preschool inclusion. What is striking about its content is how effectively it integrates capacity-building strategies with indicators of program quality in formats that are easily consumed by administrators and other school leaders alike. Capacity building is a complex and fundamental aspect of program improvement, and leveraging change is often dependent on the interplay of the four *P*s—policies, procedures, practices, and progress. Each of these core elements is covered in this book. From beginning to end, *The Preschool Inclusion Toolbox* delivers essential information in a series of well-designed chapters that help us understand what it takes to develop high-quality preschool programs so that *all* children can learn. Erin Barton and Barbara Smith have pooled their collective experiences and expertise to pack important process and content information into a valuable guidebook that deconstructs the complexities of how one goes about building capacity in schools. Each section of the book contains helpful templates, checklists, sample documents, reflective questions, and case studies that give readers the necessary tools to promote change in their local contexts. Although *The Preschool Inclusion Toolbox* cannot provide all the answers, what it does offer is a blueprint for change, process and content information, and a wide array of practical tools that can be used to develop high-quality inclusive preschool programs. Each chapter is grounded in evidence-based and recommended practices, and each provides guidance that will address both immediate and long-term needs of administrators and other school leaders. Although Barton and Smith suggest that the primary audiences for this book are school leaders and inclusion teams, I believe graduate students in special education and educational leadership may also find this book's content valuable.

The first section of the book anchors the information that follows by covering policy and procedural foundations of inclusive preschool programs. In a series of three chapters, Barton, Smith, and their colleagues characterize quality inclusion; present national survey data that identify policy, attitude, and resource challenges to preschool inclusion; and outline strategies for designing policies and procedures to address these challenges. The research-based Preschool Inclusion Self-Checklist offers a particularly efficient way to begin a conversation among stakeholders about where program changes may be needed. Included in this section are handouts, sample policy and research briefs, and a template for constructing an issue brief. These tools are nicely integrated into the chapters so the reader can understand how they can be applied to local priorities and issues.

The second section of *The Preschool Inclusion Toolbox* presents two levels of information that are relevant to those involved in developing or expanding inclusion at the local level. In Chapter 4, Steed and Smith focus on what administrators can do to support the development of high-quality preschool inclusion programs. They provide a cogent overview of evidence-based professional development (PD) practices and, in particular, detail how administrators can support capacity building using a range of PD formats. The graphics, checklists, and forms provide administrators, other school leaders, and inclusion teams with useful tools that should help enhance their efforts to support the growth of inclusion in their schools. In providing information about how practice-based coaching can be used to enhance program quality, Steed and Smith have added a unique dimension to this chapter and given school leaders important tools for building individual and school capacity. In Chapter 5, Barton, Pribble, and Joseph offer readers a comprehensive overview of evidence-based instructional practices that educators should know and do to ensure that young children with a range of support needs benefit from placement in an inclusive classroom setting. The information in this chapter ties directly back to Chapter 4, as it represents what can and should be covered in a well-designed professional development program. The intersection of content with Division for Early Childhood (DEC) Recommended Practices offers inclusion teams a rich base of information from which to continue their program improvement journey.

The final section of this book includes three chapters that focus on different aspects of how districts can not only move the capacity-building process forward but also ensure that they do so with quality. In Chapter 6, Chen, Barton, and Hallett discuss the importance of monitoring changes at the classroom level, the progress of children, and the perceptions of key stakeholders. The authors provide an overview of several measures and checklists that inclusion teams can use to make sure the quality of programs is monitored, all children's engagement in typical preschool classrooms is meaningful, and programs produce positive learning outcomes. Chapter 7 provides an applied discussion of how child progress data can be used to inform placement decisions within the individualized education program (IEP) process. Barton and her colleagues provide policy examples from several states and offer recommendations for how families and professionals may weigh program options in making their decisions. The two case studies included in this chapter are particularly helpful in tying the chapter's points to these families' IEP decisions. *The Preschool Inclusion Toolbox* concludes in Chapter 8 with a forceful call to action by Barton. She argues that we have the laws, research, and professional organization support needed to continue expanding inclusive opportunities for all preschool children. I absolutely concur with her that it is now time to do the heavy lifting and make inclusion a reality for *all* children. *The Preschool Inclusion Toolbox* gives administrators and other school leaders the blueprint and the tools for making much-needed progress happen.

Christine L. Salisbury, Ph.D.
Professor
Department of Special Education
College of Education
University of Illinois at Chicago

*To all young children—especially Joseph,
who was born during the book's development*

The Preschool
Inclusion Toolbox

Introduction

TOOLS FROM THE TOOLBOX

- **Appendix IA** Fact Sheet of Research on Preschool Inclusion
- **Appendix IB** Individuals with Disabilities Education Act Provisions Supporting Preschool Inclusion
- **Appendix IC** DEC/NAEYC Joint Position Statement on Inclusion
- **Appendix ID** Lifelong Experiences with Inclusion: A Personal Story

The purpose of this book, which we sometimes refer to as a toolbox, is to provide tools for assisting school districts in developing program-level policies and procedures that promote preschool inclusion and to help change public policies as needed. This book also could serve as a text for graduate students in early childhood special education and early childhood programs. According to the Individuals with Disabilities Education Improvement Act (IDEA) of 2004 (PL 108-446), school districts must ensure that children with disabilities, ages 3–21, are educated with children without disabilities to the maximum extent appropriate. In fact, IDEA asserts a strong preference for the placement of young children with disabilities in settings with typically developing children (see Appendix IB). This toolbox can be used as a self-directed guide for identifying challenges to preschool inclusion and for creating policies and procedures that support the appropriate placement of young children with disabilities in settings with children without disabilities for their special education and related services.

The goals of the toolbox are as follows:

1. To describe high-quality preschool inclusion
2. To identify possible challenges to preschool inclusion as well as supportive policies and procedures
3. To help school district preschool inclusion teams develop and implement an action plan for preschool inclusion

4. To suggest strategies for developing and implementing individualized education programs (IEPs) for high-quality preschool inclusion placements

    The tools in the toolbox include the following:

- Fact sheets summarizing research and IDEA requirements as well as other handouts to be used to build awareness and support
- Templates, checklists, and samples of materials to be used in the process of creating supportive policies and practices
- Boxes and other graphics summarizing typical challenges and possible solutions
- "Tips for Success" from professionals in the field who have succeeded in preschool inclusion efforts
- Reflection questions and application questions
- PowerPoint slides that can be used with the other tools in professional development and awareness activities

    For items that are reproducible, please use and disseminate them!

WHY THIS TOPIC?

Research consistently demonstrates that high-quality, inclusive environments are associated with positive outcomes for young children, which is described in more detail in Chapter 1 (Camilli, Vargas, Ryan, & Barnett, 2010; Espinosa, 2002; Pianta, Barnett, Burchinal, & Thornburg, 2009). Inclusion has been at the heart of policy, professional standards, and research for decades. For more than 35 years, IDEA and other federal mandates concerning early childhood (EC; e.g., Head Start) have encouraged educational services for children with disabilities to be delivered where education is needed. In 2012, across all states, a total of 42.5% of children ages 3–5 years served under IDEA received their special education and related services in a regular EC classroom (US Department of Education, 2014). During 1984–1985, this same measure was 36.8% (US Department of Education, 1987).

While the definitions of settings and reporting methods by states have changed over time, comparing the 1985 data to the 2012 data, the practice of providing special education and related services to children with disabilities ages 3–5 years in regular EC settings appears to have increased by only 5.7%. These numbers are deplorable, given research *and* laws support preschool inclusion. It is alarming and indefensible that more children are not educated alongside their typically developing peers. These numbers were the impetus for this book.

The sluggish growth rate of preschool inclusion suggests that school districts need more support. Districts need help understanding the developmental importance of making inclusive placement decisions for young children with disabilities. Districts also need evidence-based strategies for designing services, implementing systems, and crafting policies and procedures that result in the full inclusion of young children with disabilities into high-quality EC settings.

FIELD RESEARCH

This toolbox is the result of research, our professional experiences, and information obtained from a 2014 survey. The survey focused on the following overarching research questions: Are there challenges affecting the inclusion of young children with disabilities, and if so, what are the challenges and what are possible solutions? This mixed methods study combined qualitative and quantitative approaches for data collection and analysis. The online survey instrument (Barton & Smith, 2014b) consisted of 11 items regarding demographics (3), policy challenges related to inclusion (5), general challenges to inclusion (2), and value/attitude challenges to inclusion (1). The challenges were derived from a previous survey (Rose & Smith, 1993, 1994; Smith, Salisbury, & Rose, 1992) and allowed for an "other" category. The previous survey (Smith & Rose, 1993) yielded the following eight categories of possible challenges to inclusion: differences in program quality, personnel issues, fiscal issues, transportation, approval of private/nonpublic agencies, conflicting policies across public and nonpublic schools, curricula difference, and values/attitudes. The 2014 survey instrument consisted of multiple-choice, yes/no, and open-ended questions.

The survey was sent via e-mail in January 2014 to 619 state education agency (SEA) preschool coordinators in the U.S. states and territories. The survey e-mail asked the recipients to send the survey link to other preschool administrators and program directors in their states or territories. The wealth of information gained from more than 200 respondents across 33 states and territories was compiled and analyzed and has been embedded throughout this toolbox. In light of these survey results and recent reports about the numbers of children included with their peers (Smith, 2013; U.S. Department of Education, 2012), it is clear that there are significant challenges to inclusion. Specific challenges are discussed in more detail in Chapter 2.

Based on our findings, this book is timely, necessary, and important. Preschool inclusion is compelling for three main reasons: 1) research supports preschool inclusion, 2) laws support preschool inclusion, and 3) national professional organizations support preschool inclusion.

Research Supporting Preschool Inclusion

Decades of research have shown that high-quality early education and developmental services for young children with disabilities can "(a) ameliorate, and in some cases, prevent developmental problems; (b) result in fewer children being retained in later grades; (c) reduce educational costs to school programs; and (d) improve the quality of parent, child, and family relationships" (Salisbury, 1990). Furthermore, this research has shown that high-quality early services in inclusive settings are beneficial for all young children (Guralnick, 2001; National Professional Development Center on Inclusion, 2009; Strain & Bovey, 2011). Positive outcomes, including social and communication skills and academic achievement, accrue to children with and without disabilities in high-quality inclusive settings. This is described in more detail in Chapter 1. Please refer to Appendix IA for a summary of this research.

Laws Supporting Preschool Inclusion

In addition to the research findings on the efficacy of inclusive service delivery for preschoolers with disabilities, special education placement options are driven by the least restrictive environment (LRE) requirement of Part B of IDEA. In fact, multiple laws support preschool inclusion (e.g., the Americans with Disabilities Act [ADA] of 1990 [PL 101-336], IDEA). An IDEA fact sheet is provided in Appendix IB, which lists, verbatim, the provisions from the regulations in Part B (34 CFR §300) regarding LRE placements. In addition, following the provisions of IDEA, this fact sheet includes the most recent policy letter from the U.S. Department of Education's Office of Special Education and Rehabilitative Services clarifying that the IDEA LRE provisions apply to preschool children with disabilities. According to the policy letter, "These requirements state IDEA's strong preference for educating students with disabilities in regular classes with appropriate aids and supports" (Musgrove, 2012, p. 1).

National Professional Organizations Supporting Preschool Inclusion

In 2009, two prominent EC organizations, the Division for Early Childhood (DEC) of the Council for Exceptional Children (CEC) and the National Association for the Education of Young Children (NAEYC), jointly developed and published a statement advocating for and supporting preschool inclusion. This statement offers a definition of EC inclusion and provides recommendations for implementing preschool inclusion. They define inclusion in terms of access, participation, and supports. Inclusion means children are given access to a range of experiences and provided the supports they need to fully participate alongside their typical peers in the general education classroom. Thus, the outcomes of high-quality preschool inclusion are full membership, ongoing friendships and positive relationships, and enhanced development and independence. The outcomes of inclusion do not end with placement in a general education classroom. Placement in typical early childhood settings is a critical part of inclusion. However, inclusion also embodies the authors' values, vision, philosophy, leadership, and commitment so that inclusion becomes ubiquitous and the typical way of doing things. One local administrator said it best during our interviews: "Inclusion is simply the way we do things. We wouldn't think of educating children any other way."

Here is a link to the joint position statement: http://www.dec-sped.org/papers. This statement is provided as Appendix IC, described in more detail in Chapter 1, and referred to throughout the toolbox.

BOOK OVERVIEW

This toolbox is designed with readily accessible examples of policies, procedures, and strategies for implementation. Full-scale implementation of inclusion requires attention to effective policies, professional development (PD), and evidence-based practices (EBPs) within the classroom. Thus, there are chapters on identifying typical challenges (Chapter 2), creating new policies and procedures to address those challenges (Chapter 3), establishing effective PD approaches (Chapter 4), and implementing EBPs for inclusive preschool classrooms (Chapter 5). We recognize that many school district personnel and families are committed to preschool inclusion, and we hope this toolbox provides the resources needed to achieve your preschool inclusion goals.

The first step in expanding preschool inclusion from a systems change perspective is to establish a team of people to provide expertise and garner support. In this toolbox, this team is referred to as a *preschool inclusion team*. The preschool inclusion team will find answers to the following types of questions in this toolbox:

- What is effective inclusion?
- What tools do the preschool inclusion team need to effectively implement quality inclusion?
- How can the preschool inclusion team comply with the law regarding the inclusion of young children with disabilities into regular EC programs?
- How can the preschool inclusion team advocate for inclusion with families, stakeholders, and legislators?

The preschool inclusion team differs from the IEP team in focus and outcomes. The preschool inclusion team's focus is at the policy, procedure, and system level, with the outcome of their work being facilitative procedures for preschool inclusion. The IEP team's focus is on using the systems and procedures developed by the preschool inclusion team to make appropriate inclusive placement decisions for individual children.

Key Terms

The following key terms are defined for the purposes of this toolbox:

- *Public policies* are laws, regulations, and other legal requirements enacted by public institutions such as Congress and federal and state departments of education.
- *Procedures* and *program-level policies* are written guidelines and plans that do not carry the weight of laws or regulations. For instance, school district procedures or policies would include guidance for delivering PD or writing memoranda of agreement with a local child care center to serve as an inclusive placement for a child with an IEP.
- *Preschool children with disabilities* are children ages 3–5 years who are eligible for a free appropriate public education (FAPE) under Part B of IDEA.

Format of This Book

This is a self-guided toolbox containing basic information ranging from what high-quality preschool inclusion looks like to effective PD and EBPs that support it. We designed the toolbox to be used by a school district's preschool inclusion team to create and implement an action plan to develop and monitor policies and procedures within individual programs and agencies. This toolbox is arranged in three major sections. The first section of the toolbox provides background knowledge and resources related to preschool inclusion. Chapter 1 describes high-quality preschool inclusion and the current state of preschool inclusion in the United States. Chapter 2 provides information on the policies and procedures that are barriers or disincentives to preschool inclusion, the attitude or value challenges to preschool inclusion, as well as options for addressing these barriers and challenges. Chapter 3 provides an overview of the systems and structures for revising and designing policies and procedures to support high-quality preschool inclusion. This chapter provides recommendations from effective school-reform efforts and suggestions given to us by people around the country who have succeeded in establishing inclusive preschool programs in their school districts.

The second section of the toolbox describes EBPs for implementing high-quality preschool inclusion. Chapter 4 describes effective PD practices and feasible strategies for implementing effective PD systems within inclusive programs. Chapter 5 describes EBPs for increasing access, participation, and supports for children with disabilities.

The third section of the toolbox supports the school district's preschool inclusion team in ensuring quality inclusion placement decisions. Chapter 6 describes quality indicators of inclusion and guides preschool inclusion teams and IEP teams in developing and sustaining quality inclusion. Chapter 7 provides guidance and tools for IEP teams for making individual child placement decisions. Chapter 8 wraps up the text with a brief summary of the next steps to help preschool inclusion teams achieve their goals.

This toolbox includes PowerPoint slides for use in PD activities, fact sheets and handouts to distribute widely, and templates and forms to guide decision making. In addition, there is a Resources list to support your inclusion efforts.

Setting the Tone for the Toolbox and for Preschool Inclusion

To set the stage for this book, we share a personal account of inclusion from a parent of a young adult with a disability (see Appendix ID). This personal account provides realistic examples of the hurdles families face when they seek inclusion for their children. However, it also reflects the hopefulness we want readers to embrace as they begin this important endeavor. It is our belief that inclusion is for *all* young children. Because research, laws, and professional organizations support inclusion, we are optimistic that inclusion for all can become a reality.

APPENDIX IA

Fact Sheet of Research on Preschool Inclusion

1. In 27 years, the practice of providing special education and related services in regular early childhood (EC) settings to preschoolers with disabilities has increased only 5.7%, and many young children with disabilities continue to be educated in separate settings.

   U.S. Department of Education. (2014). *2012 IDEA part B child count and educational environment.* Retrieved from https://explore.data.gov/Education/2012 -IDEA-Part-B-Child-Count-and-Educational-Envir/5t72-4535
   Summary: In 2012, across all states, a total of 42.5% of children ages 3–5 years served under IDEA received their special education and related services in a regular EC classroom.

   U.S. Department of Education. (1987). *Annual report to congress on the implementation of the Education of the Handicapped Act.* Washington, DC: U.S. Department of Education.
   Summary: During 1984–1985, across all states, a total of 36.8% of children ages 3–5 years served under IDEA received their special education and related services in a regular EC classroom.

2. Inclusion benefits children with and without disabilities.*

   Buysse, V., Goldman, B.D., & Skinner, M.L. (2002). Setting effects on friendship formation among young children with and without disabilities. *Exceptional Children, 68,* 503–517.
   Summary: Typically developing children in specialized classrooms had more friends than their peers with disabilities. However, typically developing children in child care programs did not have more friends than their peers with disabilities. The authors noted that when children with disabilities have access to multiple playmates, they have more opportunities to develop social and play skills. Also, child care teachers in this study reported that young children with disabilities in inclusive settings had friends who were typically developing.

   Cross, A.F., Traub, E.K., Hutter-Pishgahi, L., & Shelton, G. (2004). Elements for successful inclusion for children with significant disabilities. *Topics in Early Childhood Special Education, 24,* 169–183.
   Summary: The authors examined the teacher practices and parent beliefs related to inclusion of several young children with disabilities. The authors found that peers of children with disabilities in inclusive classrooms were helpful. Parents and teachers reported the peers were learning compassion and empathy. Furthermore, the authors noted that individualized instruction was specifically related to learning and achieving goals for the children with disabilities.

   Holahan, A., & Costenbader, V. (2000). A comparison of developmental gains for preschool children with disabilities in inclusive and self-contained classrooms. *Topics in Early Childhood Special Education, 20,* 224–235.

Summary: The authors examined outcomes for children with disabilities in inclusive versus segregated settings. The authors found that children with higher social-emotional skills performed better in inclusive settings than segregated ones. Children with lower social-emotional development performed equally well in both types of settings.

Odom, S.L., Zercher, C., Li, S., Marquart, J., Sandall, S., & Brown, W. (2006). Social acceptance and social rejection of young children with disabilities in inclusive classes. *Journal of Educational Psychology, 98,* 807–823.

Summary: The authors found that a substantial number of children with disabilities are accepted by their peers in inclusive preschool settings. However, at least equal numbers of children with disabilities are not accepted by their peers. The authors highlight the importance of early identification and interventions focused on social competence and the development of friendships among children with and without disabilities.

Strain, P.S., & Hoyson, M. (2000). The need for longitudinal, intensive social skill intervention: LEAP follow-up outcomes for children with autism. *Topics in Early Childhood Special Education, 20,* 116–122.

Summary: Follow-up data at age 10 for six children who participated in inclusive preschool programs indicate positive outcomes, including reduced autism severity, average IQ, positive rating of social behaviors by parents, levels of social interactions similar to typically developing peers in the same settings, and participation in general education classrooms for five of the six children.

3. The quality of preschool programs including at least one student with a disability was as good as or better than that of preschool programs without children with disabilities. However, traditional measures of EC program quality might not be sufficient for assessing the quality of programs that include children with disabilities.*

Buysse, V., Wesley, P.W., Bryant, D.M., & Gardner, D. (1999). Quality of early childhood programs in inclusive and noninclusive settings. *Exceptional Children, 65,* 301–314.

Summary: The authors examined factors that affected program quality in EC settings. They found that programs that included at least one child with a disability scored significantly higher on measures of program quality (i.e., Early Childhood Environment Rating Scale [ECERS]; Harms, Clifford, & Cryer, 1998) than programs that did not include children with disabilities. The authors provided multiple explanations for this finding, including 1) parents of children with disabilities might seek higher quality programs for their children with unique learning needs, 2) programs for children with disabilities might attract or seek better resources and more funding, and 3) programs for children with disabilities might seek more qualified and experienced staff.

Soukakou, E.P. (2012). Measuring quality in inclusive preschool classrooms: Development and validation of the Inclusive Classroom Profile (ICP). *Early Childhood Research Quarterly, 27*(3), 478–488.

Summary: The author examined an observational measure, the Inclusive Classroom Profile, which was developed based on current research regarding inclusion and using quality indicators that were applicable to groups of children with disabilities. This measure correlated with other, more traditional measures of classroom quality (ECERS; Harms, Clifford, & Cryer, 1998) and provided additional information regarding the quality of adaptations, supports, and instruction for children with disabilities.

4. Children with disabilities can be effectively educated in inclusive programs using specialized instruction.*

Division for Early Childhood. (2014). *DEC recommended practices in early intervention/early childhood special education 2014.* Retrieved from http://www.dec-sped.org/recommendedpractices

Summary: The DEC Recommended Practices were developed to provide guidance to practitioners and families about the most effective ways to improve the learning outcomes and promote the development of young children, birth through 5 years of age, who have or are at risk for developmental delays or disabilities. The DEC Recommended Practices are based on the best available empirical evidence as well as the wisdom and experience of the field.

Odom, S.L., DeKlyen, M., & Jenkins, J.R. (1984). Integrating handicapped and nonhandicapped preschoolers: Developmental impact on the nonhandicapped children. *Exceptional Children, 51,* 41–48.

Summary: The authors found that children in segregated and inclusive settings had similar outcomes and followed a similar trajectory.

Rafferty, Y., Piscitelli, V., & Boettcher, C. (2003). The impact of inclusion on language development and social competence among preschoolers with disabilities. *Exceptional Children, 69,* 467–479.

Summary: The authors found that children with severe disabilities in inclusive settings had higher scores on assessments of their language development than children in segregated settings. Preschoolers with less severe disabilities made similar gains across both inclusive and segregated settings.

Strain, P.S., & Bovey, E.H. (2011). Randomized, controlled trial of the LEAP model of early intervention for young children with Autism Spectrum Disorders. *Topics in Early Childhood Special Education, 31,* 133–154.

Summary: The authors provide empirical support that children with disabilities (i.e., children with autism, in this study) can make significant progress in inclusive, public school classrooms with teachers implementing evidence-based practices with high fidelity. In this study, children with autism in classrooms with teachers implementing LEAP with 90% fidelity or higher did better than children with autism in programs with low fidelity. Furthermore, social validity ratings indicated that teachers found the LEAP program to be feasible and related to positive outcomes for their students.

5. Parents and teachers influence children's values regarding disabilities.*

Diamond, K.E., & Huang, H.-H. (2005). Preschoolers' ideas about disabilities. *Infants and Young Children, 18,* 37–46.

Summary: The authors provide a comprehensive review of the literature and suggest that participation in inclusive preschool programs by children with typical development might positively affect their attitudes regarding children with disabilities. Further, they provide multiple examples of ways in which teachers can promote positive attitudes about disabilities.

Innes, F.K., & Diamond, K.E. (1999). Typically developing children's interactions with peers with disabilities: Relationships between mothers' comments and children's ideas about disabilities. *Topics in Early Childhood Special Education, 19,* 103–111.
Summary: The authors found that children's comments regarding pictures of young children with Down syndrome were similar to their mother's comments about the same pictures.

Okagaki, L., Diamond, K.E., Kontos, S.J., & Hestenes, L. (1998). Correlates of young children's interactions with classmates with disabilities. *Early Childhood Research Quarterly, 13,* 67–86.
Summary: The authors found that a child's acceptance of people with disabilities was related to his or her parents' beliefs about disability.

6.   Individualized embedded instruction can be used to teach a variety of skills, including those related to early learning standards, and promote participation in inclusive preschool programs to children with and without disabilities.*

Daugherty, S., Grisham-Brown, J., & Hemmeter, M.L. (2001). The effects of embedded skill instruction on the acquisition of target and nontarget skills in preschoolers with developmental delays. *Topics in Early Childhood Special Education, 21,* 213–221.
Summary: The authors found that children with disabilities could be taught to count objects during typical classroom activities. Furthermore, one child learned nontarget information (i.e., colors).

Grisham-Brown, J., Schuster, J.W., Hemmeter, M.L., & Collins, B.C. (2000). Using an embedding strategy to teach preschoolers with significant disabilities. *Journal of Behavioral Education, 10,* 139–162.
Summary: Teachers used embedded instruction to teach two children with disabilities multiple IEP goals during typical classroom activities. Furthermore, teachers implemented the embedded instructional procedures with fidelity.

Grisham-Brown, J., Pretti-Frontczak, K., Hawkins, S.R., & Winchell, B.N. (2009). Addressing early learning standards for all children within blended preschool classrooms. *Topics in Early Childhood Special Education, 29,* 131–142.
Summary: In a series of studies, the authors found that embedding intensive instruction into daily activities is effective and efficient for teaching individual skills to children with and without disabilities.

Robertson, J., Green, K., Alper, S., Schloss, P.J., & Kohler, F. (2003). Using a peer-mediated intervention to facilitate children's participation in inclusive childcare activities. *Education & Treatment of Children, 26,* 182–197.
Summary: The authors found that a peer-mediated intervention that embedded songs, fingerplays, visuals, and peer verbal cues into typical daily routines

was related to increases in on-task behaviors, play skills, and participation in circle time for two children with disabilities.

Venn, M.L., Wolery, M., Werts, M.G., Morris, A., DeCesare, L.D., & Cuffs, M.S. (1993). Embedding instruction in art activities to teach preschoolers with disabilities to imitate their peers. *Early Childhood Research Quarterly, 8,* 277–294.
Summary: The authors found that children with disabilities could be taught to imitate their peers during an art activity using progressive time delay. Furthermore, results generalized to fine motor activities (i.e., children with disabilities imitated their peers across settings and activities).

7. Families of children with and without disabilities generally have positive views of inclusion.*

Kasari, C., Freeman, S.F.N., Bauminger, N., & Alkin, M.C. (1999). Parental perspectives on inclusion: Effects of autism and Down syndrome. *Journal of Autism and Developmental Disorders, 29,* 297–305.
Summary: Authors surveyed parents of children with Down syndrome and autism regarding their current placement and their desire to change their placement. Results indicated that parents of children with Down syndrome were most likely to endorse inclusive settings, whereas parents of children with autism were more likely to endorse at least part-time inclusion with peers. Parents of young children and parents who had children in inclusive settings were most likely to have positive views of inclusion.

Rafferty, Y., & Griffin, K.W. (2005). Benefits and risks of reverse inclusion for preschoolers with and without disabilities: Perspectives of parents and providers. *Journal of Early Intervention, 27,* 173–192.
Summary: The authors surveyed parents of children with and without disabilities and teachers from an inclusive EC program. Results indicated that parents of children with and without disabilities as well as teachers viewed inclusion favorably and considered it to be beneficial for children with and without disabilities.

8. Inclusion is not more expensive than having separate programs for children with disabilities.*

Odom, S.L., Hanson, M.J., Lieber, J., Marquart, J., Sandall, S., Wolery, R., . . . Chambers, J. (2001). The costs of preschool inclusion. *Topics in Early Childhood Special Education, 21,* 46–55.
Summary: The authors found that six of the nine inclusive programs they studied were less expensive than self-contained special education placements. The authors also identified specific cost features of inclusive programs.

Odom, S.L., Parrish, T., & Hikido, C. (2001). The costs of inclusion and noninclusive special education preschool programs. *Journal of Special Education Leadership, 14,* 33–41.
Summary: The authors examined the costs of different models of inclusion and traditional special education preschool programs located in five different

From Barton, E.E., & Smith, B.J. (2014). *Fact sheet of research on preschool inclusion.* Denver, CO: Pyramid Plus: The Colorado Center for Social Emotional Competence and Inclusion. Retrieved from http://www.pyramidplus.org/sites/default/files/images/Inclusion%20Fact%20Sheet%202014.pdf
In *The Preschool Inclusion Toolbox: How to Build and Lead a High-Quality Program* by Erin E. Barton and Barbara J. Smith (2015, Paul H. Brookes Publishing Co.)

states. Inclusion was defined as classrooms in which children with disabilities and typically developing children participate together for more than 90% of the time. The authors found lower costs associated with more inclusive programs across public schools, community programs, and Head Start programs. Furthermore, the inclusive preschool models were less expensive for school districts than segregated models.

9. Successful inclusion requires intentional and effective collaboration and teaming.**

   Division for Early Childhood. (2014). *DEC recommended practices in early intervention/early childhood special education 2014.* Retrieved from http://www.dec-sped.org/recommendedpractices

10. The individual outcomes of preschool inclusion should include access, membership, participation, friendships, and support. Children with disabilities do not need to be ready to be included; programs need to be ready to support all children.**

    DEC/NAEYC. (2009). *Early childhood inclusion: A joint position statement of the Division for Early Childhood (DEC) and the National Association for the Education of Young Children (NAEYC).* Chapel Hill: University of North Carolina, FPG Child Development Institute.

REFERENCES

Buysse, V. (2011). Access, participation, and supports: The defining features of high-quality inclusion. *Zero to Three, 31*(4), 24–29.

Buysse, V., & Hollingsworth, H.L. (2009). Research synthesis points on early childhood inclusion: What every practitioner and all families should know. *Young Exceptional Children, 11,* 18–30.

DEC/NAEYC. (2009). *Early childhood inclusion: A joint position statement of the Division for Early Childhood (DEC) and the National Association for the Education of Young Children (NAEYC).* Chapel Hill: University of North Carolina, FPG Child Development Institute.

Division for Early Childhood. (2014). *DEC recommended practices in early intervention/early childhood special education 2014.* Retrieved from http://www.dec-sped.org/recommendedpractices

Lieber, J., Hanson, M.J., Beckman, P.J., Odom, S.L., Sandall, S.R., Schwartz, I.S., . . . Wolery, R. (2000). Key influences on the initiation and implementation of inclusive preschool programs. *Exceptional Children, 67,* 83–98.

National Professional Development Center on Inclusion. (2009). *Research synthesis points on early childhood inclusion.* Chapel Hill: University of North Carolina, FPG Child Development Institute. Retrieved from http://npdci.fpg.unc.edu

Odom, S.L. (2000). Preschool inclusion: What we know and where we go from here. *Topics in Early Childhood Special Education, 20*(1), 20–27.

Odom, S.L., & Bailey, D.B. (2001). Inclusive preschool programs: Classroom ecology and child outcomes. In M. Guralnick (Ed.), *Early childhood inclusion: Focus on change* (pp. 253–276). Baltimore, MD: Paul H. Brookes Publishing Co.

Odom, S.L., Buysse, V., & Soukakou, E. (2011). Inclusion for young children with disabilities: A quarter century of research perspectives. *Journal of Early Intervention, 33,* 344–357.

Odom, S.L., Vitztum, J., Wolery, R., Lieber, J., Sandall, S., Hanson, M.J., . . . Horn, E. (2004). Preschool inclusion in the United States: A review of research from an ecological systems perspective. *Journal of Research in Special Educational Needs, 4,* 17–49.

---

* A sample of empirical citations are provided for each fact. Thus, this fact sheet does not provide a comprehensive list of the references. The citations were intentionally identified to include recent references, representation across disabilities when possible, and studies using rigorous methods.
** These facts are based on principles guiding the field of EC special education, recommended practices, and our collective knowledge and experiences.

From Barton, E.E., & Smith, B.J. (2014). *Fact sheet of research on preschool inclusion.* Denver, CO: Pyramid Plus: The Colorado Center for Social Emotional Competence and Inclusion. Retrieved from http://www.pyramidplus.org/sites/default/files/images/Inclusion%20Fact%20Sheet%202014.pdf
In *The Preschool Inclusion Toolbox: How to Build and Lead a High-Quality Program* by Erin E. Barton and Barbara J. Smith (2015, Paul H. Brookes Publishing Co.)

Purcell, M.L., Horn, E., & Palmer, S. (2007). A qualitative study of the initiation and continuation of preschool inclusion programs. *Exceptional Children, 74,* 85–99.

Sandall, S., Hemmeter, M.L., Smith, B.J., & McLean, M.E. (Eds.). (2005). *DEC Recommended Practices: A comprehensive guide for practical application in early intervention/early childhood special education.* Missoula, MT: Division for Early Childhood.

U.S. Department of Education. (1987). *Annual report to congress on the implementation of the Education of the Handicapped Act.* Washington, DC: U.S. Department of Education.

U.S. Department of Education. (2014). *2012 IDEA part B child count and educational environment.* Retrieved from https://explore.data.gov/Education/2012-IDEA-Part-B-Child-Count-and-Educational-Envir/5t72-4535

Suggested Citation:

Barton, E.E., & Smith, B.J. (2014). *Fact sheet of research on preschool inclusion.* Denver, CO: Pyramid Plus: The Colorado Center for Social Emotional Competence and Inclusion. Retrieved from http://www.pyramidplus.org

Individuals with Disabilities Education Act Provisions Supporting Preschool Inclusion

The following lists, verbatim, the provisions from the regulations governing Part B of IDEA (CFR Part 300) regarding LRE placements. In addition, following the provisions of IDEA, this appendix includes the most recent policy letter from OSEP clarifying that the IDEA LRE provisions apply to preschool children with disabilities.

§ 300.114 LRE requirements.

(a) *General.*

(1) Except as provided in § 300.324(d)(2) (regarding children with disabilities in adult prisons), the State must have in effect policies and procedures to ensure that public agencies in the State meet the LRE requirements of this section and §§ 300.115 through 300.120.

(2) Each public agency must ensure that—

(i) To the maximum extent appropriate, children with disabilities, including children in public or private institutions or other care facilities, are educated with children who are nondisabled; and

(ii) Special classes, separate schooling, or other removal of children with disabilities from the regular educational environment occurs only if the nature or severity of the disability is such that education in regular classes with the use of supplementary aids and services cannot be achieved satisfactorily.

§ 300.42 Supplementary aids and services.

Supplementary aids and services means aids, services, and other supports that are provided in regular education classes, other education-related settings, and in extracurricular and nonacademic settings, to enable children with disabilities to be educated with nondisabled children to the maximum extent appropriate in accordance with §§ 300.114 through 300.116.

§ 300.115 Continuum of alternative placements.

(a) Each public agency must ensure that a continuum of alternative placements is available to meet the needs of children with disabilities for special education and related services.

(b) The continuum required in paragraph (a) of this section must—

(1) Include the alternative placements listed in the definition of special education under § 300.38 (instruction in regular classes, special classes, special schools, home instruction, and instruction in hospitals and institutions); and

(2) Make provision for supplementary services (such as resource room or itinerant instruction) to be provided in conjunction with regular class placement.

15

§ 300.116 Placements.

In determining the educational placement of a child with a disability, including a preschool child with a disability, each public agency must ensure that—

(a) The placement decision—

    (1) Is made by a group of persons, including the parents, and other persons knowledgeable about the child, the meaning of the evaluation data, and the placement options; and

    (2) Is made in conformity with the LRE provisions of this subpart, including §§ 300.114 through 300.118;

        (b) The child's placement—

            (1) Is determined at least annually;

            (2) Is based on the child's IEP; and

            (3) Is as close as possible to the child's home;

        (c) Unless the IEP of a child with a disability requires some other arrangement, the child is educated in the school that he or she would attend if nondisabled;

        (d) In selecting the LRE, consideration is given to any potential harmful effect on the child or on the quality of services that he or she needs; and

        (e) A child with a disability is not removed from education in age appropriate regular classrooms solely because of needed modifications in the general education curriculum.

§ 300.119 Technical assistance and training activities.

Each SEA must carry out activities to ensure that teachers and administrators in all public agencies—

(a) Are fully informed about their responsibilities for implementing § 300.114; and

(b) Are provided with technical assistance and training necessary to assist them in this effort.

§ 300.208 Permissive use of funds.

(a) *Uses.* Notwithstanding §§ 300.202, 300.203(a), and 300.162(b), funds provided to an LEA under Part B of the Act may be used for the following activities:

    (1) *Services and aids that also benefit nondisabled children.* For the costs of special education and related services, and supplementary aids and services, provided in a regular class or other education-related setting to a child with a disability in accordance with the IEP of the child, even if one or more nondisabled children benefit from these services.

From Assistance to States for the Education of Children With Disabilities and Preschool Grants for Children With Disabilities (2006).
In *The Preschool Inclusion Toolbox: How to Build and Lead a High-Quality Program* by Erin E. Barton and Barbara J. Smith (2015, Paul H. Brookes Publishing Co.)

UNITED STATES
DEPARTMENT OF EDUCATION

OFFICE OF SPECIAL EDUCATION
AND REHABILITATIVE SERVICES

FEB 29 2012

Dear Colleague:

The purpose of this letter is to reiterate that the least restrictive environment (LRE) requirements in section 612(a)(5) of the Individuals with Disabilities Education Act (IDEA) apply to the placement of preschool children with disabilities.[1] The LRE requirements have existed since passage of the Education for all Handicapped Children Act (EHA) in 1975 and are a fundamental element of our nation's policy for educating students with disabilities (the EHA was renamed the IDEA in 1990). These requirements state the IDEA's strong preference for educating students with disabilities in regular classes with appropriate aids and supports. Under section 612(a)(5) of the IDEA, to the maximum extent appropriate, children with disabilities, including children in public or private institutions or other care facilities, must be educated with children who are not disabled. Further, special classes, separate schooling, or other removal of children with disabilities from the regular educational environment may occur only when the nature or severity of the disability of a child is such that education in regular classes with the use of supplementary aids and services cannot be achieved satisfactorily.

The LRE requirements in section 612(a)(5) of the IDEA apply to all children with disabilities who are served under Part B of the IDEA, including preschool children with disabilities aged three through five, and at a State's discretion, two-year old children who will turn three during the school year.[2] The statutory

---

[1]Although not discussed here, other Federal laws apply to preschool-aged children with disabilities as well. These laws include section 504 of the Rehabilitation Act of 1973, as amended (Section 504) and Title II of the Americans with Disabilities Act of 1990 (ADA). The Department 's Office for Civil Rights (OCR) enforces Section 504 and pursuant to a delegation by the Attorney General of the United States, OCR shares (with the U.S. Department of Justice) in the enforcement of Title II of the ADA. Section 504 is designed to protect the rights of individuals with disabilities in programs and activities that receive Federal financial assistance from the Department. 29 U.S.C. § 794, 34 CFR §104.4(a). Section 34 CFR 104.38 of the Section 504 regulations specify that recipients of Federal financial assistance from the Department who provide preschool education may not on the basis of disability exclude qualified persons with disabilities, and must take into account the needs of these persons in determining the aid, benefits, or services to be provided. Title II prohibits discrimination on the basis of disability by public entities, including public schools regardless of whether they receive Federal financial assistance. 42 U.S.C. §§ 12131-12134, 28 CFR Part 35 (Title II). Additionally, as applicable, entities providing preschool education must comply with the nondiscrimination requirements set forth in Title ill of the ADA that prohibit discrimination on the basis of disability in places of public accommodation, including businesses and nonprofit agencies that serve the public. The U. S. Department of Justice enforces Title III of the ADA. 42 U.S.C. §§ 12181-12189, 28 CFR Part 36 (Title ill).

[2]Under section 612(a)(l) of the IDEA, a State must make a free appropriate public education (FAPE) available to all children with disabilities residing in the State within the State's mandated age range. If a State's mandated age range includes

400 MARYLAND AVE. S.W., WASHINGTON, DC 20202-2600
www.ed.gov
The Department of Education's mission is to promote student achievement and preparation for global competitiveness by fostering educational excellence and ensuring equal access.

---

provision on LRE does not distinguish between school-aged and preschool-aged children and therefore, applies equally to all preschool children with disabilities. Despite this long-standing LRE requirement and prior policy guidance[3], the U.S. Department of Education (Department) continues to receive inquiries regarding the applicability of the LRE requirements under Part B of the IDEA to preschool children with disabilities.

Statutory and Regulatory Requirements

A preschool child with a disability who is eligible to receive special education and related services is entitled to all the rights and protections guaranteed under Part B of the IDEA and its implementing regulations in 34 CFR Part 300. One of these guaranteed rights is the right to be educated in the LRE in accordance with section 612(a)(5) of the IDEA and 34 CFR §§300.114 through 300.118. The LRE requirements under Part B of the IDEA state a strong preference for educating children with disabilities in regular classes alongside their peers without disabilities. The term "regular class" includes a preschool setting with typically developing peers.[4] In determining the educational placement of a child with a disability, including a preschool child with a disability, the public agency[5] must ensure that each child's placement decision is made in conformity with the LRE provisions in 34 CFR §§300.114 through 300.118. 34 CFR §300.116(a)(2). The child's placement must be based on the child's individualized education program (IEP). 34 CFR §300.116(b)(2). In addition, the IEP must include an explanation of the extent, if any, to which the child will not participate with nondisabled children in the regular class. 34 CFR §300.320(a)(5).

Before a child with a disability can be placed outside the regular educational environment, the group of persons making the placement decision must consider whether supplementary aids and services could be provided that would enable the education of the child, including a preschool child with a disability, in the regular educational setting to be achieved satisfactorily. 34 CFR §300.114(a)(2). If a determination is made that a particular child with a disability cannot be educated satisfactorily in the regular educational environment, even with the provision of appropriate supplementary aids and services, that child then could be placed in a setting other than the regular educational setting. The public agency responsible for providing a free appropriate public education (FAPE) to a preschool child with a disability must make available the full continuum of alternative placements, including instruction in regular

---

children with disabilities aged three through five and two-year-old children who will turn three during the school year, all requirements in Part B of the IDEA, including the LRE requirements in section 612(a)(5), apply to those children.

[3]See OSEP Memorandum 87-17, OSEP—Division of Assistance to States Policy Regarding Educating Preschool Aged Children with Handicaps in the Least Restrictive Environment (June 2, 1987); Letter to Neveldine, 16 LRP 842 (March 23, 1990); Letter to Wessels, 19 LRP 2074 (November 27, 1992); Letter to Neveldine, 20 LRP 2355 (May 28, 1993); Letter to Neveldine, 22 LRP 3101 (January 25, 1995); Letter to Neveldine, 24 LRP 3821 (April I 7, 1996); Letter to Hirsh, 105 LRP 57671 (August 9, 2005); Letter to Anonymous, 108 LRP 33626 (March 17, 2008).

[4]See Assistance to States for the Education of Children with Disabilities and Preschool Grants for Children with Disabilities. Final Rule. Analysis of Comments and Changes, 71 Fed. Reg. 46540, 46666 (August 14, 2006).

[5]The term "public agency" includes the State educational agency, local educational agencies (LEAs), educational service agencies (ESAs), nonprofit public charter schools that are not otherwise included as LEAs or ESAs and are not a school of an LEA or ESA, and any other political subdivisions of the State that are responsible for providing education to children with disabilities. See 34 CFR §300.33.

From U.S. Department of Education Office of Special Education and Rehabilitative Services. (29 February, 2012). *Letter on Preschool (LRE)*. Washington, DC: Author.
In *The Preschool Inclusion Toolbox: How to Build and Lead a High-Quality Program* by Erin E. Barton and Barbara J. Smith (2015, Paul H. Brookes Publishing Co.)

classes, special classes, special schools, home instruction, and instruction in hospitals and institutions, to meet the needs of all preschool children with disabilities for special education and related services. 34 CFR §300.115.

Preschool Placement Options

The public agency responsible for providing FAPE to a preschool child with a disability must ensure that FAPE is provided in the LRE where the child's unique needs (as described in the child's IEP) can be met, regardless of whether the local educational agency (LEA) operates public preschool programs for children without disabilities. An LEA may provide special education and related services to a preschool child with a disability in a variety of settings, including a regular kindergarten class, public or private preschool program, community-based child care facility, or in the child's home.

For data collection purposes, the Department defines a Regular Early Childhood Program as a program that includes a majority (at least 50 percent) of nondisabled children (i.e., children who do not have IEPs) and that may include, but is not limited to:

- Head Start;
- Kindergartens;
- Preschool classes offered to an eligible pre-kindergarten population by the public school system;
- Private kindergartens or preschools; and
- Group child development centers or child care.[6]

If there is a public preschool program available, the LEA may choose to make FAPE available to a preschool child with a disability in the public preschool program. However, many LEAs do not offer, or offer only a limited range of, public preschool programs, particularly for three- and four-year-olds. LEAs that do not have a public preschool program that can provide all the appropriate services and supports for a particular child with a disability must explore alternative methods to ensure that the LRE requirements are met for that child. These methods may include: (1) providing opportunities for the participation of preschool children with disabilities in preschool programs operated by public agencies other than LEAs (such as Head Start or community based child care); (2) enrolling preschool children with disabilities in private preschool programs for nondisabled preschool children; (3) locating classes for preschool children with disabilities in regular elementary schools; or (4) providing home-based services. If a public agency determines that placement in a private preschool program is necessary for a child to receive FAPE, the public agency must make that program available at no cost to the parent.[7]

---

[6]This is the definition that the Department uses in its annual data collection under section 618 of the IDEA on the number of children with disabilities aged three through five served under the IDEA Part B program according to their educational environments.

[7]See Assistance to States for the Education of Children with Disabilities and Preschool Grants for Children with Disabilities. Final Rule. Analysis of Comments and Changes, 71 Fed. Reg. 46540, 46589 (August 14, 2006); and Letter to Anonymous, 108 LRP 33626 (March 17, 2008).

Conclusion

Placement decisions regarding a preschool child with a disability who is served under Part B of the IDEA must be individually determined based on the child's abilities and needs as described in the child's IEP. 34 CFR §300.116(b)(2). State educational agencies and LEAs should engage in ongoing short- and long-term planning to ensure that a full continuum of placements is available for preschool children with disabilities. To achieve this goal, a variety of strategies, including staffing configurations, community collaboration models, and professional development activities that promote expanded preschool options are available. See http://www.nectac.org/ for further information regarding the IDEA and services for preschool children with disabilities.

We hope this information is helpful in clarifying the applicability of LRE requirements to preschool children with disabilities who receive special education and related services under Part B of the IDEA. Thank you for your continued interest in improving results for children with disabilities.

Sincerely,

Melody Musgrove, Ed.D.
Director
Office of Special Education Programs

From U.S. Department of Education Office of Special Education and Rehabilitative Services. (29 February, 2012). *Letter on Preschool (LRE)*. Washington, DC: Author.
In *The Preschool Inclusion Toolbox: How to Build and Lead a High-Quality Program* by Erin E. Barton and Barbara J. Smith (2015, Paul H. Brookes Publishing Co.)

DEC/NAEYC Joint Position Statement on Inclusion
Early Childhood Inclusion

Division for Early Childhood of the Council for Exceptional Children
3415 South Sepulveda Blvd Suite 1100, Los Angeles CA 90034
Phone 406.543.0872 | Fax 406.543.0887
Email dec@dec-sped.org | Web www.dec-sped.org

naeyc®

National Association for the Education of Young Children
1313 L Street NW, Suite 500 | Washington, DC 20005-4101
Phone 202.232.8777 Toll-Free 800.424.2460 | Fax 202.328.1846
Email naeyc@naeyc.org | Web www.naeyc.org

*A Joint Position Statement of the Division
for Early Childhood (DEC) and the National
Association for the Education of Young Children (NAEYC)*

Today an ever-increasing number of infants and young children with and without disabilities play, develop, and learn together in a variety of places—homes, early childhood programs, neighborhoods, and other community-based settings. The notion that young children with disabilities[1] and their families are full members of the community reflects societal values about promoting opportunities for development and learning, and a sense of belonging for every child. It also reflects a reaction against previous educational practices of separating and isolating children with disabilities. Over time, in combination with certain regulations and protections under the law, these values and societal views regarding children birth to 8 with disabilities and their families have come to be known as early childhood inclusion.[2] The most far-reaching effect of federal legislation on inclusion enacted over the past three decades has been to fundamentally change the way in which early childhood services ideally can be organized and delivered.[3] However, because inclusion takes many different forms and implementation is influenced by a wide variety of factors, questions persist about the precise meaning of inclusion and its implications for policy, practice, and potential outcomes for children and families.

The lack of a shared national definition has contributed to misunderstandings about inclusion. DEC and NAEYC recognize that having a common understanding of what inclusion means is fundamentally important for determining what types of practices and supports are necessary to achieve high-quality inclusion. This DEC/NAEYC joint position statement offers a definition of early childhood inclusion. The definition was designed not as a litmus test for determining

21

whether a program can be considered inclusive, but rather, as a blueprint for identifying the key components of high-quality inclusive programs. In addition, this document offers recommendations for how the position statement should be used by families, practitioners, administrators, policy makers, and others to improve early childhood services.

DEFINITION OF EARLY CHILDHOOD INCLUSION

Early childhood inclusion embodies the values, policies, and practices that support the right of every infant and young child and his or her family, regardless of ability, to participate in a broad range of activities and contexts as full members of families, communities, and society. The desired results of inclusive experiences for children with and without disabilities and their families include a sense of belonging and membership, positive social relationships and friendships, and development and learning to reach their full potential. The defining features of inclusion that can be used to identify high-quality early childhood programs and services are access, participation, and supports.

What Is Meant by Access, Participation, and Supports?

Access.   Providing access to a wide range of learning opportunities, activities, settings, and environments is a defining feature of high-quality early childhood inclusion. Inclusion can take many different forms and can occur in various organizational and community contexts, such as homes, Head Start, child care, faith-based programs, recreational programs, preschool, public and private prekindergarten through early elementary education, and blended early childhood education (ECE)/early childhood special education (ECSE) programs. In many cases, simple modifications can facilitate access for individual children. Universal design is a concept that can be used to support access to environments in many different types of settings through the removal of physical and structural barriers. Universal Design for Learning (UDL) reflects practices that provide multiple and varied formats for instruction and learning. UDL principles and practices help ensure that *every* young child has access to learning environments, to typical home or educational routines and activities, and to the general education curriculum. Technology can enable children with a range of functional abilities to participate in activities and experiences in inclusive settings.

Participation.   Even if environments and programs are designed to facilitate access, some children will need additional individualized accommodations and supports to participate fully in play and learning activities with peers and adults. Adults promote belonging, participation, and engagement of children with and without disabilities in inclusive settings in a variety of intentional ways. Tiered models in early childhood hold promise for helping adults organize assessments and interventions by level of intensity. Depending on the individual needs and priorities of young children and families, implementing inclusion involves a range of approaches—from embedded, routines-based teaching to more explicit interventions—to scaffold learning and participation for all children. Social-emotional development and behaviors that facilitate participation are critical goals of high-quality early childhood inclusion, along with learning and development in all other domains.

From DEC/NAEYC. (2009). *Early childhood inclusion: A joint position statement of the Division for Early Childhood (DEC) and the National Association for the Education of Young Children (NAEYC).* Chapel Hill: The University of North Carolina, FPG Child Development Institute. http://www.naeyc.org/positionstatements/ Copyright © 2009 NAEYC®. Reprinted with permission.
In *The Preschool Inclusion Toolbox: How to Build and Lead a High-Quality Program* by Erin E. Barton and Barbara J. Smith (2015, Paul H. Brookes Publishing Co.)

Supports. In addition to provisions addressing access and participation, an infrastructure of systems-level supports must be in place to under-gird the efforts of individuals and organizations providing inclusive services to children and families. For example, family members, practitioners, specialists, and administrators should have access to ongoing professional development and support to acquire the knowledge, skills, and dispositions required to implement effective inclusive practices. Because collaboration among key stakeholders (e.g., families, practitioners, specialists, and administrators) is a cornerstone for implementing high-quality early childhood inclusion, resources and program policies are needed to promote multiple opportunities for communication and collaboration among these groups. Specialized services and therapies must be implemented in a coordinated fashion and integrated with general early care and education services. Blended ECE/ECSE programs offer one example of how this might be achieved.[4] Funding policies should promote the pooling of resources and the use of incentives to increase access to high-quality inclusive opportunities. Quality frameworks (e.g., program quality standards, early learning standards and guidelines, and professional competencies and standards) should reflect and guide inclusive practices to ensure that all early childhood practitioners and programs are prepared to address the needs and priorities of infants and young children with disabilities and their families.

RECOMMENDATIONS FOR USING THIS POSITION STATEMENT TO IMPROVE EARLY CHILDHOOD SERVICES

Reaching consensus on the meaning of early childhood inclusion is a necessary first step in articulating the field's collective wisdom and values on this critically important issue. In addition, an agreed-upon definition of inclusion should be used to create high expectations for infants and young children with disabilities and to shape educational policies and practices that support high-quality inclusion in a wide range of early childhood programs and settings. Recommendations for using this position statement to accomplish these goals include:

1. *Create high expectations for every child to reach his or her full potential.* A definition of early childhood inclusion should help create high expectations for every child, regardless of ability, to reach his or her full potential. Shared expectations can, in turn, lead to the selection of appropriate goals and support the efforts of families, practitioners, individuals, and organizations to advocate for high-quality inclusion.

2. *Develop a program philosophy on inclusion.* An agreed-upon definition of inclusion should be used by a wide variety of early childhood programs to develop their own philosophy on inclusion. Programs need a philosophy on inclusion as a part of their broader program mission statement to ensure that practitioners and staff operate under a similar set of assumptions, values, and beliefs about the most effective ways to support infants and young children with disabilities and their families. A program philosophy on inclusion should be used to shape practices aimed at ensuring that infants and young children with disabilities and their families are full members of the

early childhood community and that children have multiple opportunities to learn, develop, and form positive relationships.

3. *Establish a system of services and supports.* Shared understandings about the meaning of inclusion should be the starting point for creating a system of services and supports for children with disabilities and their families. Such a system must reflect a continuum of services and supports that respond to the needs and characteristics of children with varying types of disabilities and levels of severity, including children who are at risk for disabilities. However, the designers of these systems should not lose sight of inclusion as a driving principle and the foundation for the range of services and supports they provide to young children and families. Throughout the service and support system, the goal should be to ensure access, participation, and the infrastructure of supports needed to achieve the desired results related to inclusion. Ideally, the principle of natural proportions should guide the design of inclusive early childhood programs. The principle of natural proportions means the inclusion of children with disabilities in proportion to their presence in the general population. A system of supports and services should include incentives for inclusion, such as child care subsidies, and adjustments to staff-child ratios to ensure that program staff can adequately address the needs of every child.

4. *Revise program and professional standards.* A definition of inclusion could be used as the basis for revising program and professional standards to incorporate high-quality inclusive practices. Because existing early childhood program standards primarily reflect the needs of the general population of young children, improving the overall quality of an early childhood classroom is necessary, but might not be sufficient, to address the individual needs of every child. A shared definition of inclusion could be used as the foundation for identifying dimensions of high-quality inclusive programs and the professional standards and competencies of practitioners who work in these settings.

5. *Achieve an integrated professional development system.* An agreed-upon definition of inclusion should be used by states to promote an integrated system of high-quality professional development to support the inclusion of young children with and without disabilities and their families. The development of such a system would require strategic planning and commitment on the part of families and other key stakeholders across various early childhood sectors (e.g., higher education, child care, Head Start, public pre-kindergarten, preschool, early intervention, health care, mental health). Shared assumptions about the meaning of inclusion are critical for determining who would benefit from professional development, what practitioners need to know and be able to do, and how learning opportunities are organized and facilitated as part of an integrated professional development system.

6. *Influence federal and state accountability systems.* Consensus on the meaning of inclusion could influence federal and state accountability standards related to increasing the number of children with disabilities enrolled in inclusive programs. Currently, states are required to report annually to the U.S. Department of Education the number of children with disabilities who are participating in inclusive early childhood programs. But the emphasis on

From DEC/NAEYC. (2009). *Early childhood inclusion: A joint position statement of the Division for Early Childhood (DEC) and the National Association for the Education of Young Children (NAEYC).* Chapel Hill: The University of North Carolina, FPG Child Development Institute. http://www.naeyc.org/positionstatements/ Copyright © 2009 NAEYC®. Reprinted with permission. In *The Preschool Inclusion Toolbox: How to Build and Lead a High-Quality Program* by Erin E. Barton and Barbara J. Smith (2015, Paul H. Brookes Publishing Co.)

the prevalence of children who receive inclusive services ignores the quality and the anticipated outcomes of the services that children experience. Furthermore, the emphasis on prevalence data raises questions about which types of programs and experiences can be considered inclusive in terms of the intensity of inclusion and the proportion of children with and without disabilities within these settings and activities. A shared definition of inclusion could be used to revise accountability systems to address both the need to increase the number of children with disabilities who receive inclusive services and the goal of improving the quality and outcomes associated with inclusion.

ENDNOTES

1. Phrases such as "children with special needs" and "children with exceptionalities" are sometimes used in place of "children with disabilities."
2. The term "inclusion" can be used in a broader context relative to opportunities and access for children from culturally and linguistically diverse groups, a critically important topic in early childhood requiring further discussion and inquiry. It is now widely acknowledged, for example, that culture has a profound influence on early development and learning, and that early care and education practices must reflect this influence. Although this position statement is more narrowly focused on inclusion as it relates to disability, it is understood that children with disabilities and their families vary widely with respect to their racial/ethnic, cultural, economic, and linguistic backgrounds.
3. In accordance with the Individuals with Disabilities Education Act (IDEA), children ages 3–21 are entitled to a free, appropriate public education (FAPE) in the least restrictive environment (LRE). LRE requires that, to the extent possible, children with disabilities should have access to the general education curriculum, along with learning activities and settings that are available to their peers without disabilities. Corresponding federal legislation applied to infants and toddlers (children birth to 3) and their families specifies that early intervention services and supports must be provided in "natural environments," generally interpreted to mean a broad range of contexts and activities that generally occur for typically developing infants and toddlers in homes and communities. Although this document focuses on the broader meaning and implications of early childhood inclusion for children birth to eight, it is recognized that the basic ideas and values reflected in the term "inclusion" are congruent with those reflected in the term "natural environments." Furthermore, it is acknowledged that fundamental concepts related to both inclusion and natural environments extend well beyond the early childhood period to include older elementary school students and beyond.
4. Blended programs integrate key components (e.g., funding, eligibility criteria, curricula) of two or more different types of early childhood programs (e.g., the federally funded program for preschoolers with disabilities [Part B-619] in combination with Head Start, public pre-k, and/or child care) with the goal of serving a broader group of children and families within a single program.

APPROVED BY DEC EXECUTIVE BOARD: April 2009

APPROVED BY NAEYC GOVERNING BOARD: April 2009

Suggested citation
DEC/NAEYC. (2009). *Early childhood inclusion: A joint position statement of the Division for Early Childhood (DEC) and the National Association for the Education of Young Children (NAEYC).* Chapel Hill: University of North Carolina, FPG Child Development Institute.

Permission to copy not required—distribution encouraged.

http://www.naeyc.org/files/naeyc/file/positions/DEC_NAEYC_EC_updatedKS.pdf

Acknowledgments

Coordination of the development and validation of this joint position statement was provided by the National Professional Development Center on Inclusion (NPDCI), a project of the FPG Child Development Institute funded by a grant from the U.S. Department of Education, Office of Special Education Programs. NPDCI work group members included Camille Catlett, who directed the validation process, Virginia Buysse, who served as the lead writer, and Heidi Hollingsworth, who supervised the analysis of respondent comments and the editorial process.

DEC and NAEYC appreciate the work of Joint DEC-NAEYC Work Group members who participated in the development of the initial definition and position statement: Terry Harrison, NJ Department of Health and Senior Services; Helen Keith, University of Vermont; Louise Kaczmarek, University of Pittsburgh; Robin McWilliam, Siskin Children's Institute and the University of Tennessee at Chattanooga; Judy Niemeyer, University of North Carolina at Greensboro; Cheryl Rhodes, Georgia State University; Bea Vargas, El Papalote Inclusive Child Development Center; and Mary Wonderlick, consultant. Input from the members of the DEC Executive Board and the NAEYC Governing Board, as well as key staff members in both organizations, also is acknowledged.

APPENDIX ID

Lifelong Experiences with Inclusion
A Personal Story

Linda Frederick

As a teenager, I volunteered at the state home for people with disabilities in 1970. I was a 14-year-old "candy striper" assisting the educational department with 14-year-olds who had Down syndrome. I remember teaching them to catch a giant beach ball for rewards of sticky taffy. Although I enjoyed wearing the striped apron and hat and pretending to be a teacher, I realized that this was an extremely limiting environment. When my second son was born with Down syndrome in 1982, one pediatrician recommended finding an institutional home so that he wouldn't disrupt our family life. From my experiences as a teenager, the one sure thing I knew was that there had to be a better way, and I was determined to find it.

First we had to wake him up! Dan was born with congenital heart defects and slept most of the time. We found one of the first early intervention classes (called "infant stimulation" in those days) that allowed families to join in the fun. The combination of speech, physical, and occupational therapists taught us how to make the most of his waking time with music, movement, and imagination. Parents were taught the basics of child development, and involving siblings and grandparents kept it light and fun. After his heart surgery at 14 months, Dan became stronger and began showing us his lifelong love for music and dancing.

When he turned 3, we had our first choice: continuing at the special preschool program, which was across town, or enrolling Dan in the neighborhood class. We chose to send him to the same school as Carl, Dan's big brother. We knew most of the families from the playground, but a few eyebrows were raised when they saw Dan the first day of school. The teacher was welcoming but hesitant to take him in, because she didn't feel "qualified." As it turned out, a good teacher is a good teacher. She found many ways to include Dan in preschool activities, even though he was mostly using sign language and just learning to walk. His classmates didn't seem to notice his disabilities—he was just "Dan."

When kindergarten time came, public school officials balked at letting Dan into our neighborhood school. They compromised by letting him attend morning class with his friends only if we would send him (by taxi!) to the afternoon special education class in a faraway school. Looking back, I can't believe we agreed to do all this, but Dan ended up sleeping through most of the special education afternoon classes while still having fun and fully participating in the regular morning class. By the time first grade came, I was active in the PTA and good friends with the school principal. I asked her to assign Dan to the most open-minded teachers, so we could work together to figure out the best way to include him. The whole school became part of Dan's learning environment. I remember hearing that the

_____

To set the stage for this book, we would like to share this personal account of inclusion from a parent of a young adult with a disability.

principal would hold Dan's hand and teach him to use alternating feet to walk up and down the school steps. This was not planned but just a need she noticed and problem-solved. Dan was lucky enough to be placed in bilingual classes so that he learned in a classroom of children who were at very different language levels, and these differences were celebrated instead of stifled. Teachers partnered Dan with students who needed extra confidence or who enjoyed helping him do his work. The only downfall was that some treated him more like a class mascot than a classmate. Dan solved this problem himself by preferring to play with the biggest, toughest kids and not the ones who wanted to baby him. As usual, he enjoyed music, and you can imagine how sweet his onstage performances in school concerts were for his family!

Middle school was the next step in Dan's inclusion adventures. Each grade was divided into core groups of students who worked together. These years can be socially hard for anyone, but Dan's special education resource teachers found creative ways to keep him engaged and involved in different activities. He even partnered with the speech therapist to encourage a shy, mostly nonverbal student to talk. Once, his language arts teacher called to report that Dan was writing love notes to her in his journal. She didn't realize that this was the first meaningful communication that Dan ever wrote! She had inadvertently helped him realize the purpose for writing—just as important as Helen Keller's learning that the feeling of water could be communicated by the word for water. To this day, Dan continues to write a daily journal documenting his life.

High school was a mixed bag for Dan. Once again, public school officials were surprised that we wanted full inclusion for our son. Most students with Down syndrome attended a specific school across town. We wanted Dan to attend the high school down the street from our home. We started with very reluctant teachers and lots of fears on all sides. We found a few classes that were somewhat meaningful for Dan's educational levels but most certainly more appropriate than sitting with the special education students doing preschool-level activities in the school basement! Unfortunately, Dan discovered that he could buy Mountain Dew from hallway vending machines. If he didn't have enough money, he borrowed from friends. At one point, he was drinking about six cans a day. He was often distracted by beautiful classmates and age-appropriate hormone levels, as well as too much caffeine. One awesome teacher turned all this around. The speech and drama teacher approached us with his ideas for including Dan on the debate team. This meant that Dan needed to travel with the school team and give speeches at districtwide competitions. Dan never officially "won," but he felt like a winner wearing his suit and tie and competing side by side with a very encouraging teacher and team. He also performed in each year's musical and dramatic productions. His other favorite part of school was hanging out with the football players in the weight-lifting room. They were very protective and helpful. Dan enjoyed going to every dance and prom. On graduation day, Dan proudly received his diploma alongside his friends and fellow students.

At the time, we didn't realize the importance of our decision to include Dan in our neighborhood school at an early age, but a good percentage of his preschool classmates ended up in the same elementary school and some even graduated from high school with him. They formed an invisible circle of support as Dan moved side by side with them through the years in public school. He was invited to birthday parties and sleepovers, and he developed meaningful relationships with friends and teachers over the years. Instead of fighting and forcing schools to include him, we slid in sideways through being involved in the school and neighborhood activities. As parents of two students with special needs (our oldest was labeled as "Talented and Gifted"), we learned to partner with teachers in creative ways to figure out how to challenge and inspire each to find their own way in school.

Dan has now held a job at his neighborhood grocery store for 8 years. His best job skills are showing up on time with a great attitude and being friendly with customers. I believe this comes from learning appropriate social skills from typical kids in typical school classroom environments. Every family has to find their own path, but ours has been full of adventure, fun, and love. We discovered the importance of individualizing education to meet each student's needs while learning alongside neighborhood friends. Full inclusion worked for both our sons and has enabled our family to thrive and grow.

I

Laying the
Groundwork for
Preschool Inclusion

1

What Is Quality Inclusion?

Erin E. Barton and Jaclyn D. Joseph

TOOLS FROM THE TOOLBOX

- **Figure 1.1** National Data on the Slow Progress of Preschool Inclusion
- **Figure 1.2** Preschool Inclusion Framework
- **Figure 1.3** Inclusion For Preschool Children With Disabilities: What We Know And What We Should Be Doing
- **Form 1.1** Preschool Inclusion Self-Checklist

The purpose of this chapter is to provide several important introductory tools for your preschool inclusion toolbox. First, we briefly discuss the state of inclusion in the United States. Then, we discuss our preschool inclusion framework. Finally, as part of our inclusion framework, the empirically supported, effective components of inclusion are presented. As noted in the Introduction, the first step to establishing high-quality preschool inclusion services and systems is to create a preschool inclusion team. Chapter 3 describes specific strategies and logistics for ensuring the preschool inclusion team is focused and effective. One of the first things the team will do is review the data and research on preschool inclusion. This chapter will be helpful in that initial phase of work.

STATE OF PRESCHOOL INCLUSION IN THE UNITED STATES

As shown in Figure 1.1, a comparison of the 2012 IDEA data (which was the most recent information available at the time of printing) to the 1985 IDEA data indicates that the practice of providing special education and related services to children ages 3–5 years old in regular EC settings increased by only 5.7% in 27 years.

The limited improvement from 1985 to 2012 suggests administrators might need support for designing services, implementing systems, and crafting policies that support the inclusion of young children with disabilities in high-quality EC settings.

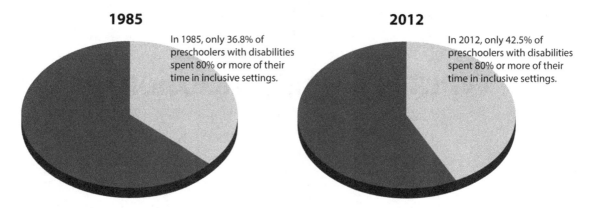

Figure 1.1.   National data on the slow progress of preschool inclusion. (*Sources:* U.S. Department of Education, 1987, 2014.)

EMPIRICAL AND LEGAL SUPPORT FOR PRESCHOOL INCLUSION

Research consistently demonstrates that high-quality and responsive environments are associated with positive outcomes for young children, including for children with disabilities (Camilli et al., 2010; Espinosa, 2002; Pianta, Barnett, Burchinal, & Thornburg, 2009). High-quality inclusive classrooms with adequate ratios of more competent peers, in particular, are related to positive outcomes for children with disabilities (Justice, Logan, Lin, & Kaderavek, 2014). Preschool inclusion has been at the heart of policy, professional standards, and research for decades. For more than 30 years, IDEA and other federal and state policies in EC (e.g., Head Start) have promoted delivering educational services for children with disabilities in which education is delivered for typically developing children. The fact sheet on research support and the fact sheet on IDEA provisions, provided in Appendixes IA and IB, describe the academic and legal foundations for preschool inclusion.

DIVISION FOR EARLY CHILDHOOD/NATIONAL ASSOCIATION FOR THE EDUCATION OF YOUNG CHILDREN JOINT POSITION STATEMENT ON INCLUSION

As noted in the Introduction, the two prominent EC professional associations, DEC and NAEYC, jointly developed and published a statement advocating for and supporting interdisciplinary, inclusive early care and education for all young children. The focus on cross-sector collaboration provides new opportunities at the state and local levels to engage in meaningful dialogue around critical issues for children with disabilities within the broader EC systems (Woods & Snyder, 2009). This is especially important given the fragmented nature of the EC intervention and education system and the need to ensure quality inclusion for young children with disabilities (Buysse & Hollingsworth, 2009; Odom, Buysse, & Soukakou, 2011). The diverse EC systems (e.g., Head Start, child care, public school) need to work together to ensure sufficient support for children with disabilities, their families, *and* the practitioners who work with them (Hayden, Frederick, & Smith, 2003).

APPLICATION QUESTION

You can find state-specific information about preschool inclusion and IDEA at http://www .ideadata.org. What is the percentage of children with disabilities spending 80% or more of their time in inclusive settings in your state? Are you surprised with what you found? Discuss these questions with your preschool inclusion team.

The position statement, provided in Appendix IC, defines EC inclusion and identifies the relevant features and recommendations for developing quality inclusive preschool programs. Their definition of inclusion is as follows (DEC/NAEYC, 2009, p. 2):

> Early childhood inclusion embodies the values, policies, and practices that support the right of every infant and young child and his or her family, regardless of ability, to participate in a broad range of activities and contexts as full members of families, communities, and society. The desired results of inclusive experiences for children with and without disabilities and their families include a sense of belonging and membership, positive social relationships and friendships, and development and learning to reach their full potential. The defining features of inclusion that can be used to identify high quality early childhood programs and services are access, participation, and supports.

Access refers to providing an adequate range of contextually relevant learning opportunities, activities, and settings for every child by enhancing physical accessibility, identifying and eradicating physical or structural barriers, and offering multiple and varied learning opportunities. The goal is to ensure that all children have access to effective learning environments; typical routines, activities, and settings; and general education curricula.

APPLICATION QUESTION

What is your impression of the information presented in the DEC/NAEYC joint position statement? Who would benefit from knowing this information? How will you distribute and use this document? How will you guide discussions about preschool inclusion using this document?

Participation means there is a focus on ensuring all children are active, independent participants in their families, classrooms, and communities. This means adults promote learning and engagement by using a range of instructional practices, from embedded to more explicit, to ensure all children have opportunities to engage, participate, and learn across all domains. Adults use individualized accommodations, modifications, and adaptations to promote active participation and a sense of belonging for all children in typical settings and learning environments. Participation should be driven by the needs of each individual child and his or her family.

Supports refers to broader, infrastructure-level support to the administrators, teachers, staff, and so forth, in providing high-quality programs. This means programs should ensure all adults involved have access to quality PD, effective ongoing follow-up assistance, and support for collaborative teaming. This also requires having effective policies in place that promote and incentivize high-quality preschool inclusion. See Figure 1.2 for a visual representation of the three defining features of inclusion. It is important to note that IDEA includes similar language to ensure participation and success in general education settings. These provisions are "supplementary aids and services" (34 CFR §300.42) and "technical assistance and training activities" (34 CFR §300.119). These provisions are on the IDEA fact sheet in Appendix IB.

EFFECTIVE COMPONENTS OF INCLUSION

Since the 1990s, the term *preschool inclusion* replaced the term *preschool mainstreaming* to promote the full acceptance of each child as an engaged and participating member of his or her family, classroom, and community. The research on inclusion has evolved, and several effective components of preschool inclusion have

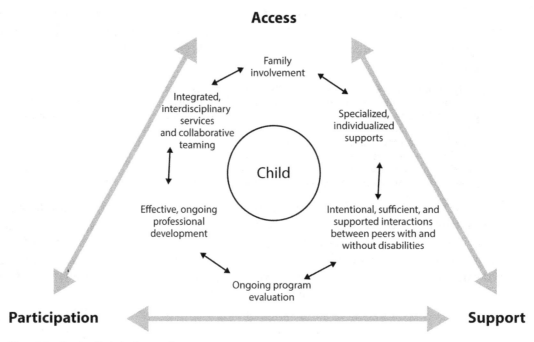

Figure 1.2.   Preschool inclusion framework.

emerged. Figure 1.3 provides a summary of the research supporting preschool inclusion and some guidelines for using the research to get started implementing preschool inclusion (Strain, 2014).

Effective, empirically supported components of inclusion that have been identified in the research include: 1) intentional, sufficient, and supported interactions between peers with and without disabilities; 2) specialized, individualized supports; 3) family involvement; 4) inclusive, interdisciplinary services and collaborative teaming; 5) a focus on critical sociological outcomes; 6) effective, ongoing PD; and 7) ongoing program evaluation (Odom et al., 2011; NECTAC, 2010; Salisbury, 1990). The inclusion self-checklist provided in Form 1.1 can be used to determine where your program is in regard to the implementation of the effective components of inclusion.

The components included in the Inclusion Self Checklist are described in subsequent sections.

Intentional, Sufficient, and Supported Interactions Between Peers with and without Disabilities

Most children learn through interactions with nurturing, responsive adults and peers as well as in quality child care or preschool classrooms. A foremost developmental task of preschoolers is to become an accepted member of a peer group. Children develop relationships over time through a history of interactions with each other. However, some children with disabilities will need more intentional, systematic instruction to learn appropriate social skills. Children with disabilities should have multiple and varied opportunities to interact with typically developing peers, and vice versa. Most young children are quite reciprocal with each other

Handout

Inclusion for Preschool Children with Disabilities: What We Know and What We Should Be Doing

Phillip S. Strain, Ph.D., University of Colorado Denver, 2014

The movement toward inclusion of preschool age children with disabilities originally gained national attention with the passage of Public Law 99-457, the IDEA amendments of 1986. It addressed the inclusion of preschoolers by extending the provisions of the least restrictive environment (LRE) to children with disabilities ages three through five years. The developmental importance of inclusive services for young children with disabilities is clear. Over the last 30 years, the evidence regarding inclusive service delivery for young children with disabilities has accumulated rapidly. Based on scientific evidence, here is what we know:

What We Know

- No study that has assessed social outcomes for children in inclusive versus developmentally segregated settings has found segregated settings to be superior. This is important because one of the things that parents of young children with disabilities most desire for their youngsters is to develop friendships with their same-age, typically developing peers. And if we ask the question, "What developmental outcomes are most likely to lead to successful post-school adjustment?", social skills is always the answer.

- The positive social outcomes attributable to inclusive settings, however, have been seen only when social interaction is frequent, planned, and carefully promoted by teachers.

- Typically developing children have shown only positive developmental, educational and attitudinal outcomes from inclusive experiences.

- There is no evidence that children with particular types or severity of disabilities are poor candidates for inclusion.

- On measures of how well children maintain skills after some initial teaching, segregated settings have been shown to have a poor outcome (i.e. children tend not to use newly-learned skills in segregated settings whereas they are much more likely to use these same skills in inclusive settings).

- Programs that are characterized by inclusive service delivery tend to be state-of-the-art on a variety of other dimensions, including extensive parental involvement; highly-structured scope, sequence, and method of instruction; and attention to repeated outcome assessments.

What We Should Be Doing

How might we translate our empirical findings into an ongoing service delivery model? The results speak to the following programmatic issues: a) child referral to inclusive setting; b) continuum of service; c) personnel training; d) class organization and structure; and e) administrative practices.

Child Referral. *Though there is little scientific evidence available, what exists does not support the notion that less involved children should be preferred for inclusive services while potentially excluding more involved youngsters. When formulating policy and procedures, we must discount this popular belief and recognize that no available data exists upon which to exclude children with severe disabilities from inclusive placements. Further, programs have shown that children with severe disabilities such as autism can be successfully included. Based on the evidence to date, we should screen children away from maximally inclusive options only after these high quality, inclusive options have been tried with fidelity and with supports to the personnel and have failed.*

Continuum of Services. *Policy makers and those who design services are faced with the dilemma that it is possible for practitioners to satisfy the bureaucratic and legal requirements and yet not help, or worse, do potential harm, to the clients.*

The IDEA LRE requirements have evolved into a working definition that describes a continuum of service. This continuum allows requirements to be satisfied by instituting any of a number of options. Yet, scientific evidence shows that inclusive services produce the desired outcomes *only* when young children with disabilities are included at least several days per week into the social and instructional environment with typical peers. Any continuum of permissible services

Figure 1.3. The current state of preschool inclusion. (From Strain, P.S. [2014]. *Inclusion for preschool children with disabilities: What we know and what we should be doing.* Denver: University of Colorado Denver; reprinted by permission. As reprinted at http://www.pyramidplus.org/sites/default/files/images/STRAIN%20PtrYC%20what%20we%20know%20%282%29.pdf)   *(continued)*

Figure 1.3. *(continued)*

that ranges, for example, from a segregated class in a segregated building, through a segregated class in regular building, to a regular class in a regular building, is too broad to be effective and may deny children the opportunity for benefit.

Personnel Training. *A much greater emphasis on the preparation of teachers and other personnel is needed if inclusive service delivery is to fulfill its potential. Attempting any innovation like this with less than the best-prepared staff will likely yield poor services, poor outcomes, and ultimately less inclusion for children with disabilities. Successful teachers and other personnel in inclusive settings must, at a minimum, know how to do the following:*

- Assess the current educational and social needs of all children and plan instruction accordingly.

- Meet the individual goals of all children within a group-teaching format.

- Plan and arrange for daily interactions between children.

- Utilize class peers as instructional agents.

- Frequently monitor child outcomes and use this information to modify instructional procedures, if necessary.

- Communicate effectively with parents and enlist help when needed.

- Plan for child and family transition to the next educational setting.

Classroom Organization and Structure. *As noted, those programs that have been characterized by high quality inclusion and excellent child outcomes have also been state-of-the-art on a variety of other dimensions. To fully realize the potential of inclusive service delivery, programs for young children with disabilities should include:*

- Provisions for early screening, referral, and programming to insure a minimal time delay between problem development and intervention.

- Provisions for the assessment of family strengths and skill needs, and support that is planned accordingly.

- Provisions for repeated curriculum-based assessments and instruction that relates directly to the assessments.

- Provisions for overall program evaluations that include the opinions of consumers (e.g. parents, teachers, administrators).

Policy and Procedures. *To institutionalize quality service delivery, educational practices-not merely personnel-must be certified. We can do this by developing new program standards and using them for scrupulous monitoring, providing technical assistance and training for deficient programs and personnel, and de-certifying programs and personnel that are chronically deficient.*

Administrative Practices. *Any educational innovation, will have little hope for long-term success without the support and vigilance of competent administrators. The administrative practices needed to insure high quality preschool inclusive services include:*

- Eliminating, where necessary, state and local policies and procedures that promote separation rather than integration of all children.

- Providing personnel, time, and fiscal resources needed for necessary training and coaching for all personnel.

- Expanding options for service delivery and staff arrangements to include, for example, team teaching and consulting models.

- Providing professional leadership by encouraging innovative options for including young children with disabilities, and providing specific incentives for other administrators, leaders, and staff to promote high quality inclusive service delivery.

(Guralnick, 2001; Strain, Schwartz, & Bovey, 2007). Children with disabilities in inclusive classrooms who have opportunities to interact with typically developing peers demonstrate higher levels of social competence and better communication skills (Guralnick, Neville, Hammond, & Connor, 2007a). For example, Justice and colleagues (2014) found that children with low language skills in classrooms with more competent peers had better language skills at the end of the school year than children whose classmates had lower skills. This and previous research suggests that children's growth is positively impacted by having more competent peers (Henry & Rickman, 2007; Justice et al., 2014; Mashburn, Justice, Downer, & Pianta, 2009). However, even in inclusive classrooms, children with disabilities demonstrate fewer positive social interactions and are less likely to be included in classroom activities and games than children with typical development (Brown, Odom, Li, & Zercher, 1999; Diamond & Hong, 2010). Their limited social interaction skills might prevent them from having positive interactions with peers and eventually lead to social isolation or rejection. Peer social interactions should be supported to the extent that they occur at sufficient rates to promote the development of friendships. Furthermore, peers provide positive, competent models that allow children with disabilities to learn new skills through imitation.

Preschool Inclusion Self-Checklist

In addition to the three defining features of inclusion (access, participation, and supports) outlined in the Division for Early Childhood/National Association for the Education of Young Children joint position statement on inclusion, research has identified several effective components of quality inclusion. This self-assessment uses these empirically supported qualities of effective preschool inclusive programs. The preschool inclusion team can use this tool to track changes over time. Use a new column for each date of administration, and score how you think your program is doing in terms of its consistent, quality implementation of the inclusion component. If your program is just starting to implement preschool inclusion, expect low scores—that is okay! By completing this evaluation, you are on the road to improvement. Your scores should help you identify your specific strengths and needs, which can be used to plan your next steps. By completing this self-assessment regularly, you will be able to track your program's progress and make necessary adjustments to your plan. Good luck, and remember to enjoy the exciting and rewarding adventure you are about to embark on!

Use this key to score your program:

1	2	3
Not Implemented	Sometimes/ Occasionally Implemented	Fully/Consistently Implemented

		Date:				
	Item				Scores	
Interactions	1. Teachers/staff provide intentional, sufficient, and supported interactions between peers with and without disabilities.					
	2. There are a sufficient number of peer models.					
	3. Teachers/staff provide necessary supports to individual children.					
Specialized Supports	4. Teachers/staff make individual adaptations to all daily activities and routines when necessary for individual children.					
	5. Teachers/staff provide a sufficient number of embedded instructional trials to children to address the complete learning cycle (acquisition, fluency, generalization, and maintenance).					
Families	6. Teachers/staff provide intentional encouragement of family involvement, engagement, and participation in the assessment, intervention, and evaluation processes for children.					
Inclusive Services	7. Relevant individuals involved in each child's service delivery system (including families) are included as members of the child's collaborative team when developing and discussing goals and instructional plans.					
Sociological Outcomes	8. Each child's goals include those that relate to sociological outcomes such as the development of friendships, independent participation, and social acceptance.					
Professional Development	9. Teachers/staff receive administrative supports associated with high-quality implementation (i.e., technical assistance, policies to support evidence-based practice and data-based decision making, coaching, and other supports such as release time for professional development and collaboration).					
Program Evaluation	10. Staff use an evaluation process that measures the implementation fidelity of interventions to ensure that practitioners are using evidence-based practices.					
	11. Professional development systems are informed by program-evaluation data (that include input by consumers and staff).					

Specialized, Individualized Supports

Supports should be provided to children based on their individual needs. Supports should follow each child and be provided in his or her inclusive classroom. A common finding across the research on preschool inclusion is that placement alone is not sufficient to promote learning and development (e.g., McConnell, 2002; Rogers, 2000). Successful placements for young children with disabilities require intentional, specialized instruction and individualized adaptations to daily routines and activities. These are necessary to ensure all children successfully participate and engage in the physical and social environment. In fact, intentional teaching has been described as an integral component of developmentally appropriate practice (DAP; Copple & Bredekamp, 2009). This means teachers plan for and embed a *sufficient number of instructional trials* across the day for those children who need additional instructional support. Teachers systematically and intentionally design the environment and plan what, how, and when to embed learning trials to ensure each child receives multiple, meaningful instructional opportunities.

> **APPLICATION QUESTION**
> Considering the effective components of inclusion, reflect on the percentages of children currently included that were listed earlier in this chapter. What do these numbers tell you about *high-quality* preschool inclusion even for those children with disabilities who are spending more than 80% of their time in inclusive settings? Should the use of quality inclusive preschool practices be measured with these statistics? Discuss this question with your preschool inclusion team.

The first step is to assess each child's functional needs within the context. For example, the team might consider if the child has the language or adaptive skills needed to participate in daily activities and routines. Supports are then individualized to support the child's participation. A range of specialized instructional practices have been examined in inclusive settings and have been identified as EBPs (DEC, 2014; Sandall, Hemmeter, Smith, & McLean, 2005). These are discussed in more detail in Chapter 5.

Family Involvement

A family-centered approach is central to the general philosophy and framework of early intervention/early childhood special education (EI/ECSE) services (DEC, 2014; Sandall et al., 2005). Family plays a key role in the assessment, intervention, and evaluation of services for all young children, and a goal of early intervention is to enhance the family's capacity to promote their child's development. EC programs alone cannot effectively prepare children for school; children need the support of families and communities. To acquire this support, high-quality inclusive preschools intentionally encourage family involvement, engagement, and participation.

Inclusive, Interdisciplinary Services and Collaborative Teaming

The 31st annual report to Congress on the implementation of IDEA revealed increasing trends in percentages of students served under a variety of disability categories (e.g., developmental delay, autism; U.S. Department of Education, 2012). In 2011, 745,349 preschoolers with disabilities were served across 50 states and the

District of Columbia (Data Accountability Center, 2011). In 2011–2012, more children than ever were served in state EC programs. In 2012–2013, although the percentages of children served in these programs stayed the same, 28% of 4-year-olds and 4% of 3-year-olds, the actual number of children enrolled in these programs decreased (Barnett, Carolan, Squires, & Clarke Brown, 2013). Nine thousand fewer 4-year-olds attended state pre-K programs. In 2012–2013, 7% of 3-year-olds and 10% of 4-year-olds were enrolled in Head Start programs. Clearly, EC systems are diverse, fragmented, and complex (Hebbeler, Spiker, & Kahn, 2012).

Research demonstrates that interdisciplinary, coordinated service delivery systems are related to better outcomes for children and families (Harbin, McWilliam, & Gallagher, 2000). No single discipline can meet the needs of the increasingly diverse groups of children and their families (Bricker & Widerstrom, 1996). In addition, children and families reside in communities that vary tremendously in size, demographics, and economic resources. Children with disabilities might be receiving services and supports from multiple practitioners across disciplines. These services are often uncoordinated and have differing definitions, eligibility criteria, and funding requirements. Families of young children with disabilities,

Tip for Success!

Diverse EC systems and services in a community (e.g., school district, child care, Head Start) can establish a *shared* vision statement and action plan focused on high-quality inclusive services for all young children.

particularly those with high needs, interact with many different services and systems (Harbin, Rous, & McLean, 2005). These supports are most effective when they are inclusive and coordinated to ensure the child is making adequate progress.

High-quality inclusive preschools establish a structure and process for collaborative teaming. In fact, Lieber and colleagues (1997) purported that effective collaborative teaming was a critical feature of successful, high-quality inclusive programs. Collaborative teaming requires support from administration, common inclusive philosophy, frequent opportunities for teams and families to meet, shared goals and instructional plans, and clearly identified roles and responsibilities (Hayden, Frederick, & Smith, 2003; Hunt, Soto, Maier, Liboiron, & Bae, 2004). Collaborative teaming can take many different forms, including coaching from an individual with specialized training (e.g., speech-language pathologist, occupational therapist) or coteaching models in which the EC teacher and EC special educator share classroom responsibilities (Odom et al., 2011).

Focus on Critical Sociological Outcomes

Odom and colleagues (2011) call for a focus on both developmental skills and sociological outcomes such as social acceptance, participation, and friendships. This focus on "sociological outcomes" aligns with the DEC/NAEYC joint position statement. High-quality preschool inclusion should result in all children forming positive, meaningful social relationships, independently participating in their classrooms and communities, and having a sense of belonging. Thus, preschool inclusion is more than a placement decision. High-quality preschool inclusion also focuses on the strategies used by the adults in that placement to ensure acceptance, participation, and friendships. Such effective strategies include teaching all children the social skills that help to promote relationships, participation, and belonging. In recognition of the importance of social skills, OSEP identified three outcomes in which states must show progress, and one of the three is positive social emotional skills (including social relationships). For more information on the three outcomes and the measurement systems, go to the web site of the Early Childhood Technical Assistance (ECTA) Center: http://ectacenter.org/eco/pages/faqs.asp. The social skills outcome is defined as "positive social-emotional skills (including social relationships)." ECTA (http://www.ectacenter.org) describes this outcome as follows:

> Positive social-emotional skills refer to how children get along with others, how they relate with adults and with other children. The outcome includes the ways the child expresses emotions and feelings and how he or she interacts with and plays with other children. For toddlers and preschoolers, these skills also include how children follow rules related to interacting with others in group situations such as in a child care center.

Effective, Ongoing Administrative Supports

IDEA calls for scientifically based research to be used to guide practices. It is known that use of such practices increases the probability of positive outcomes for children (Buysse & Wesley, 2006). Furthermore, the increased emphasis on EBPs (e.g., Dunst & Trivette, 2009; Odom, 2009b; Wong et al., 2014) should compel school district personnel to use the best available research in combination with professional expertise. Yet there is a documented disconnect between the evidence base and practices used in EC programs (McLean, Snyder, Smith, & Sandall, 2002; Odom, 2009b). Odom (2009b) and Fixsen and Blase (2009) report that EBPs are more likely to be used when administrative systems include the following: 1) technical assistance to help state and local administrators, service systems, and practitioners learn EBPs and implementation methods that help with their adoption; 2) policies to support the use of EBPs and effective implementation practices; 3) infrastructure, including data-based decision making; and 4) ongoing professional development (PD) including coaching. High-quality preschool inclusion will hinge on identifying effective, individualized supports and adequate administrative support needed to implement these practices with fidelity, sustainability, and scalability (Fixsen, Blase, Duda, Naoom, & Van Dyke, 2010a; Snyder, Hemmeter, & McLaughlin, 2011). EC providers have a variety of backgrounds, education levels, and experiences. Designing effective administrative support and PD systems to meet the diverse needs of the EC work force is a growing challenge. Typical in-service events (e.g., one-day workshops) are insufficient to support sustained growth and implementation of EBPs for the majority of EC providers (Fixsen, Naoom, Blase, Friedman, & Wallace, 2005; Joyce & Showers, 2002). Administrative systems should include meaningful and ongoing PD, system-wide vision and leadership, recognition of staff who successfully implement inclusive practices, and foundational support (e.g., release time for PD and collaboration). Chapter 4 describes effective PD related to preschool inclusion in detail.

Ongoing Program Evaluation

High-quality inclusive programs include mechanisms for ongoing program evaluation that are sustainable, linked directly to the program philosophy, goals, and curricula, and encompass input from families and practitioners. Program evaluation might result in minor adjustments for an individual child or major program changes. Chapter 6 provides multiple tools that can be used as part of program evaluation. In addition, program evaluation should include measures of intervention and implementation fidelity to ensure that practitioners are implementing EBPs as intended and PD systems are implemented with fidelity. All adaptations to interventions, curricula, or PD systems must be informed by program data and continually monitored to ensure all children and families are successful and meeting their goals.

The following case study is woven throughout this toolbox to illustrate the use of the tools to support high-quality preschool inclusion. In this excerpt, the Maceo family and their son Raphael are introduced.

Case Study: The Maceo Family

The Maceo family currently has a third grader, Paul, enrolled in their neighborhood elementary school. They are requesting that their younger child, Raphael, who is eligible for special education services, be enrolled in the preschool program in Paul's elementary school. Raphael has been receiving early intervention services in the Maceos' home since he was 18 months old, and he was diagnosed with autism at 30 months. He uses gestures and some words to communicate and demonstrates few spontaneous social interactions. The preschool inclusion team at the school reviewed the research on inclusion to identify if there was empirical support for including children such as Raphael in general EC settings. *Does research support preschool inclusion? What research would you bring to the team?*

Then they completed the Inclusion Self-Checklist found in this section. To accurately complete the checklist, the team engaged in a number of information-gathering activities (e.g., classroom observations, informal interviews with teachers and school staff, talking with families). Following checklist completion, the team considered the scores obtained for each inclusion component of the checklist and for their overall implementation of preschool inclusion. These are important first steps in moving toward high-quality preschool inclusion. *What did your preschool inclusion team find?*

PROPOSED NEXT STEPS

- Evaluate your program according to the components of high-quality inclusive programs using the Inclusion Self-Checklist (Form 1.1) provided in this chapter. Keep in mind that this is an initial assessment of general components that can be used to monitor your progress over time. More specific assessment and evaluation tools are provided in subsequent chapters. Remember, change will not happen overnight! It is okay to have a low score when starting. Completing this evaluation means you are on the road to quality inclusion!

- Do some preschool inclusion marketing. Get the word out to stakeholders about high-quality preschool inclusion (including families and community programs).

- Determine your program's strengths and weaknesses, and start thinking about a plan of action for implementing or improving practices associated with high-quality preschool inclusion.

- Use your strengths (i.e., strong points of leverage) when planning and implementing next steps for achieving preschool inclusion (e.g., policies and procedures, PD opportunities, administrative practices).

CONCLUSION

After examining the research on inclusion, the IDEA provisions, the DEC/NAEYC joint position statement, and our framework for preschool inclusion, your views about preschool inclusion might have changed. Data establishes that not much has changed in regard to the numbers of preschool children included with their peers, despite the plethora of academic, legal, and professional support for inclusion. The following chapters will provide the tools your team needs to get started on the important and exciting path to high-quality preschool inclusion for all children.

REFLECTION QUESTIONS

1. What percentage of U.S. preschoolers with disabilities spends 80% or more of their time in regular EC programs?

2. What are the three defining features of inclusion per the DEC/NAEYC joint position statement on inclusion?

3. What are the effective components of inclusion?

4. How well does your program implement preschool inclusion? What is the current percentage of children receiving their special education and related services in regular EC programs?

5. What empirical research exists to support preschool inclusion?

6. How will you share information regarding high-quality preschool inclusion, such as the fact sheets in this book, with others?

7. Whom will you inform about your increasing understanding of the state of preschool inclusion in your program?

8. What actions do you need to take after considering the effective components of high-quality preschool inclusion?

2

Preschool Inclusion Challenges and Solutions

Barbara J. Smith, Erin E. Barton, and Alissa L. Rausch

TOOLS FROM THE TOOLBOX

- **Box 2.1** The Survey
- **Box 2.2** Policy Challenges to Preschool Inclusion
- **Figure 2.1** States and Territories Represented in the Survey
- **Figure 2.2** Attitude and Belief Challenges
- **Form 2.1** Perceptions of Attitude and Belief Challenges
- **Form 2.2** Menu of Preschool Inclusion Attitudes and Beliefs Solutions
- **Form 2.3** Perceptions of Policy and Resource Challenges
- **Form 2.4** Menu of Preschool Inclusion Policy, Procedure, and Resource Solutions
- **Table 2.1** Reported Challenges

The Introduction and Chapter 1 described the legal and scientific foundations supporting preschool inclusion as well as the limited progress that has been made nationally. This chapter of the toolbox describes the typical challenges to implementing preschool inclusion and how those challenges might be mitigated. Understanding the challenges that appear to stand in the way of preschool inclusion efforts and solutions to those challenges is key to offering the full continuum of LRE placement options for preschool children with disabilities.

IDENTIFYING THE CHALLENGES AND SOLUTIONS

There are two possible avenues for school districts to meet their responsibilities under IDEA for providing full inclusion opportunities for young children with disabilities: 1) within public school systems or 2) outside of public schools in community-based EC programs. Within public school systems, the goal is to encourage access and placement for preschool-age children with disabilities in classrooms with their typically developing peers. This can be accomplished in school-based EC programs such as state-funded prekindergarten, Title I–funded classrooms, or Head Start services provided within the school district. These programs can be offered within elementary schools or in EC centers run by the school district and can be used as inclusive placement options for children with disabilities. School districts can also provide tuition-based EC programming to young children without disabilities to join their peers with disabilities in school district preschool programs.

Inclusive opportunities outside public schools include collaborating with community-based programs such as child care centers, Head Start, and private prekindergarten, kindergarten, or preschools as placement options for children with IEPs. While many people might assume that there are significantly more challenges related to nonpublic school placements, many of the same challenges are at work when contemplating in-district inclusion. Thus, most of the challenges and solutions described in this chapter apply to both in-district and out-of-district inclusion opportunities.

As described in Chapter 1, even with the weight of research and laws supporting preschool inclusion, the practice did not increase significantly in 27 years (Smith, 2013; U.S. Department of Education, 1987, 2012). The challenges to preschool inclusion identified by administrators nationwide have also changed little since the 1980s (Barton & Smith, 2014b).

In 1989, a national survey was conducted that identified two types of common challenges or barriers to preschool inclusion: 1) policy or procedure challenges and 2) attitude and belief challenges (Smith & Rose, 1993; Smith, Salisbury, & Rose, 1992). The authors also identified strategies and solutions to the challenges from the survey results. As discussed in the Introduction to this book, Barton and Smith (2014b) conducted a follow-up survey to identify current challenges and solutions related to preschool inclusion.

The survey asked if certain categories of issues were challenges to preschool inclusion. Box 2.1 describes those issues.

Figure 2.1 lists the 32 states and one territory where respondents lived and provides a map of those states with survey participants.

BOX 2.1. The survey

Survey respondents were asked if there are challenges to preschool inclusion associated with the following:

- Ensuring program quality
- Ensuring personnel training, qualifications, and supervision
- Fiscal and contracting procedures
- Transportation
- Approval of private or nonpublic school programs as places to deliver special education and related services
- Policies between school district and nonschool district programs
- Curricula or methods between school district and nonschool district programs
- Attitudes and beliefs

Three questions were asked about each of the eight areas: 1) are there policies related to the issues that are serving as barriers to inclusion; 2) are they federal, state, or local policies; and 3) is there anyone who has "solved" the problem? If yes, describe the solution.

States and territory represented by the survey respondents (*n* = 238 respondents across 32 states and one territory)

Alabama	Kansas	Oklahoma
Arizona	Louisiana	Oregon
Arkansas	Michigan	Pennsylvania
California	Minnesota	Rhode Island
Colorado	Montana	South Carolina
Connecticut	Nebraska	Tennessee
Delaware	Nevada	Utah
Florida	New Jersey	Vermont
Guam	New Mexico	Virginia
Hawaii	North Carolina	
Idaho	North Dakota	
Illinois	Ohio	

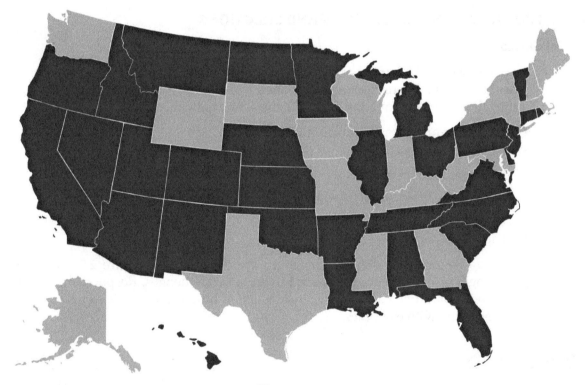

Figure 2.1. States and territory represented in the survey. (*Key:* ■, participating states. Guam not pictured.) (*Source:* Barton & Smith, 2014b.)

Three major categories of challenges to quality preschool inclusion were iden-tified by the survey respondents:

- Attitudes and beliefs challenges
- Policy and procedural challenges
- Resource challenges

A comparison of the 1989 and 2014 results indicated that typical challenges and suggested solutions have changed very little over time. However, the major change from 1989 to 2014 is that the attitude and belief challenges moved from being the second-highest-rated category of challenges to the highest-rated category of challenges. The frequencies with which issues were identified as challenges are listed in Table 2.1. Percentages are in order of frequency (most to least) and are rounded up or down to the nearest whole number. An additional change between the two surveys is the analysis of challenges and solutions associated primarily with resource issues. The previous survey did not contain a similar analysis. Smith and Rose did not distinguish resource-related challenges, whereas Barton and Smith did.

The survey respondents described challenges to preschool inclusion in their program or community and suggested solutions that they were implementing or thought would address the problem. The solutions closely resemble the solutions from the 1989 survey. The remainder of this chapter describes the challenges and solutions in detail and provides tools for the preschool inclusion team to use to identify challenges as well as possible solutions.

ATTITUDE AND BELIEF CHALLENGES AND SOLUTIONS

Challenges

As noted before, the survey asked if attitudes or beliefs present challenges to preschool inclusion. The respondents answered a resounding "yes." The survey asked if the following types of attitudes and beliefs are challenges:

- Lack of communication/collaboration
- "Someone will lose" beliefs
- Staff preparedness beliefs
- Lack of awareness/understanding
- Turf issues
- Lack of respect

The categories of attitude challenges are described in Figure 2.2 with the percentages of people who considered them to be challenges. Respondents could select more than one category. Each category of attitude and belief challenge is described next with examples.

Table 2.1. Reported challenges

Challenge	Percent
Attitudes and beliefs	30
Fiscal and contracting	19
Approval of private or nonpublic school programs for placement of a child with an individualized education program	16
Curricula or methods between school-district and non-school-district programs	15
Transportation	15
Personnel training, qualifications, and supervision	11
Policies between school district and nonschool district programs	10
Program quality	10

Source: Barton and Smith (2014b).

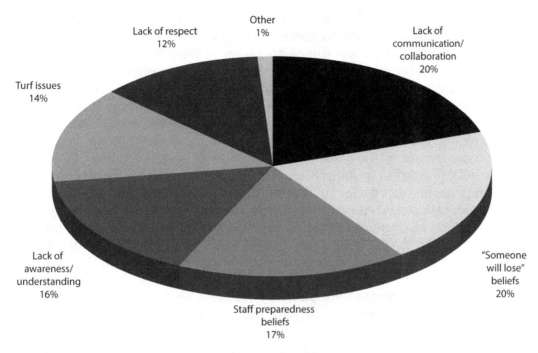

Figure 2.2. Attitude and belief challenges. (*Source:* Barton & Smith, 2014b.)

Lack of Communication/Collaboration (20%) One of the two most common challenges within the attitude and belief category is a lack of communication and collaboration among EC providers. In contrast to the DEC/NAEYC joint position statement's emphasis on collaboration, public school personnel felt that community providers were not receptive to training and technical assistance from the special education community. A lack of information sharing was reported to occur at all levels. One commenter noted, "In some communities, there is good collaboration, in other communities, not so much. Sometimes it's a comfort-zone thing, and hasn't been made a local priority." Similarly, respondents reported that information about specific programs such as Head Start or child care was not effectively being communicated.

"Someone Will Lose" Beliefs (20%) Even though the research is clear that inclusive settings are effective, survey results indicated that both EC special educators and regular EC educators believe that children with disabilities need segregated environments to meet their educational needs. Special education personnel doubted that regular EC programs have the ability to address the needs of children with a disability. Some personnel expressed concerns about the impact the child with a disability will have on other children. One commenter indicated that if a teacher's aide is not provided to the regular EC teacher for each child with a disability, the child with a disability will take teacher attention away from other children.

Staff Preparedness Beliefs (17%) Underscoring the need for PD, public school personnel reported concerns that private and community-based programs "don't always have the expertise" to serve children with disabilities. Special educators felt they had been specifically trained to deal with the learning needs of children with disabilities, and it was difficult for some of them to approve of teachers who had not had equivalent training. Survey respondents reported concerns about having children with disabilities placed in community-based preschool settings due to a lack of resources and support personnel. One respondent reported that "the private schools want to know when a student is too behaviorally disordered to be included in a general education program and if included how to handle behavior management of the student." Community providers reported that they did not feel equipped to include children with disabilities in their programs. Teacher preservice (higher education) training in both EC special education and regular early education was reportedly seen as inadequate for successful inclusion. Survey respondents also reported that the curricula of some pre-K and kindergarten programs have an academic focus and that the K–12 "push down" of academics affects whether community-based programs are seen as appropriate alternatives.

Lack of Awareness/Understanding (16%)   There were several comments about the lack of understanding on the part of principals and other administrators regarding the effectiveness and importance of preschool inclusion. "Attitudes of the gen ed [general education] director are not supportive of inclusion." Concerns were also voiced about the beliefs of the regular EC personnel: "Regular education teachers feel they shouldn't have to teach special education; there should be a preschool special education teacher for that." "Some teachers think segregation is the best way to teach children with moderate to severe disabilities." Some thought that using "pull out" services was the best way to serve children even if they were in community-based settings.

Turf Issues (14%)   Some respondents indicated that special education teachers want to keep "small classes with mostly children with disabilities." For example, one respondent commented, "School districts are reluctant to use public money to support students in private settings." Another respondent reported that they had no "control" over the methods and curricula that the community-based programs use. Several respondents also reported that community-based programs were not always receptive to outside training and technical assistance from special educators.

Lack of Respect (12%)   The majority of the comments in this category overlapped with many of the previous categories. Most of the comments related to personnel in one setting feeling as though the personnel in another setting did not respect their skill set.

Solutions

As noted before, the survey asked respondents to describe how challenges have been successfully addressed. The strategies described in this section can be used by preschool inclusion teams to "move the needle closer" to inclusion. The strategies acknowledge what communities, districts, schools, and classrooms are doing well to ensure high-quality inclusion for all young children with disabilities.

FORM 2.1.

Perceptions of Attitude and Belief Challenges

Attitude/belief challenge	Present in program?	Comments
Lack of communication/ collaboration	Yes/No	
"Someone will lose" beliefs	Yes/No	
Staff preparedness beliefs	Yes/No	
Lack of awareness/ understanding	Yes/No	
Turf issues	Yes/No	
Lack of respect	Yes/No	
Other	Yes/No	

Menu of Preschool Inclusion Attitudes and Beliefs Solutions

Challenges related to attitudes and beliefs	Is this a challenge? Yes/No	Possible solutions (from survey respondents)	For solutions tried, write progress and outcome.
Lack of understanding and trust between 1) professionals and families, 2) school district professionals and community early childhood (EC) programs, 3) early childhood special education (ECSE) personnel and regular EC personnel, or 4) school district personnel and their administrators		Establish transdisciplinary ECE/ECSE teams that consist of a psychologist, social worker, speech pathologist, and physical/occupational therapist working together to provide support and strategies for students with individualized education programs (IEPs) to keep them in the regular classroom with their typically developing peers.	
		Establish norms for collaborative problem solving among key stakeholders.	
		Break down barriers with an interagency workgroup.	
		Develop inclusive settings with Title I providers.	
		Provide joint professional development opportunities for teachers and administrators on preschool inclusion.	
		Develop relationships between school district directors and community early childhood leaders to facilitate arrangement of joint staff meetings, in-service training, and transportation.	
		Provide joint professional development focused on inclusion to preschool staff within the school district and in community programs on their roles and responsibilities to serve children with disabilities.	
		Schedule regular meetings between the school district and community programs to combine philosophies and practices around behavior management.	
		Open the lines of communication with all teaching staff in e-mails, trainings, and celebrations.	
		Provide early childhood professional development to child care and school district providers.	
		Increase the efforts of community preschools to serve children with disabilities.	
		Develop partnerships between school districts and local Head Start or Title I programs.	
		Provide adequate time for meeting/discussing/planning at all levels.	
		Establish a culture of inclusive education by establishing norms of discourse and communication.	
		Continue efforts despite challenges and actively and collaboratively work to move through challenges together.	

(continued)

Menu of Preschool Inclusion Attitudes and Beliefs Solutions

Challenges related to attitudes and beliefs	Is this a challenge? Yes/No	Possible solutions (from survey respondents)	For solutions tried, write progress and outcome.
		Provide coteaching opportunities for general education teachers to observe the unique skills and successes of students with various disabilities.	
		Sustain a joint collaborative effort between school district and community programs, and have district staff available to provide special education support to general education teachers and children in these settings.	
		Foster more coordination, planning, and communication between special education and Head Start teachers.	
		Provide training from outside groups to build a community of respect.	
		Communicate monthly with stakeholders and partners.	
Lack of awareness or support		Develop an inclusion booklet to explain the benefits of inclusion to school district and EC directors, community members, and parents.	
		Educate administrators about the importance of preschool inclusion.	
		Encourage superintendents to publicly state that children with disabilities will be served in regular classes and that support will be given to teachers and students through a special education teacher and training, to recognize the benefits for all students.	
		Encourage compliance with legal regulations.	
		Provide visual models of what high-quality inclusion looks like, feels like, and sounds like in the classroom.	
		Develop a project team to design a vision for inclusion and address attitude and belief challenges.	
		Arrange meetings of administrators and teachers with preschool inclusion teams who are successfully including students to discuss challenges and solutions.	
		Provide opportunities for the IEP team, including the parents, special education teacher, and special services director, to meet and persuade the general education teacher to accept high-quality and supported inclusion.	
		Design an ongoing committee to address belief challenges in general education and special education professionals	
		Address values and attitudes of staff members directly.	
		Discuss the laws regarding the rights of children with disabilities with the special education director and the special education providers. Change procedures as necessary.	
		Provide an accurate picture of developmentally appropriate practice and environments for young children.	
		Celebrate small successes in the movement toward inclusion.	

There was significant overlap in types of strategies used for addressing attitude and belief challenges regardless of the type of challenge. A close examination of the six attitude and belief solutions categories led to two overarching categories of solutions: collaboration strategies and building awareness/support strategies (Barton & Smith, 2014b).

Collaboration strategies address the lack of understanding and trust between 1) professionals and families, 2) school district professionals and community EC programs, 3) ECSE personnel and regular EC personnel, and 4) school district personnel and their administrators. Awareness strategies often target the audience and the activities.

Form 2.1 can be used by the preschool inclusion team to identify attitude and belief challenges as well as solutions in your program or community. Using the descriptors of each category reviewed previously, gather perceptions of challenges through focus groups, surveys, and questionnaires. Then as a group, meet and review the perceptions, decide on categories of challenges to address, and use Form 2.2 to begin to identify possible solutions.

APPLICATION QUESTION
Did these challenges surprise you? Consider which of these attitude and belief challenges are relevant for your preschool inclusion team, program, and district. Are there other attitude and belief challenges not listed here that you have seen or faced? Discuss these questions with your preschool inclusion team. Keep reading the next section for possible solutions to your challenges.

POLICY AND PROCEDURE CHALLENGES AND SOLUTIONS

Challenges

An analysis of the comments describing policy challenges revealed that most of them were actually related to attitudes or beliefs, procedures, or lack of resources and funding. For example, a respondent indicated that "private programs are not always open to having itinerate teachers coming in." This is not a policy challenge but rather a procedural or attitudinal one. Another example was, "Training alone doesn't always change practice." Again, this is not a policy challenge but a procedural or attitudinal challenge. Out of the nearly 70 comments related to "policy challenges," only 19 were likely to actually be policy challenges. These 19 represented program, community, and statewide policies that might hinder high-quality preschool inclusion. The identified challenges that are most likely to be related to actual policies are listed in Box 2.2.

The survey also asked respondents to indicate whether they thought the policy providing the challenge was a federal policy, state policy, or local policy. The majority reported that local policies presented challenges: 111 respondents identified policies as local, 93 as state, and 46 as federal (Barton & Smith, 2014b).

APPLICATION QUESTION
Which of these strategies might work for addressing your challenges? How might you implement these strategies in your community? How will you guide discussions about preschool inclusion using these solutions? Discuss these questions with your preschool inclusion team.

Resource Challenges   Many reported challenges were related to a lack of resources. For instance, several respondents said that community programs were full and there were no available slots for the school districts to buy for children

BOX 2.2. Policy challenges to preschool inclusion

Personnel Policies

- Training or services cannot be provided in community settings.
- Personnel in community settings, including Head Start, make low wages, and it is hard to recruit and retain qualified teachers.

Fiscal Policies

- Funding streams create challenges. For instance, Title I and the Individuals with Disabilities Education Act have different requirements for who is eligible to receive services under their funding.
- Contracts with church-affiliated or nonpublic programs are not allowed.
- Reimbursement from state special education funds is not available if children are in general education or if the early childhood education teacher is in a coteaching classroom.
- State legislation prohibits general funds to be used for education below kindergarten.
- State-funded preschools must meet at-risk eligibility requirements; are first-come, first-serve; require parents to apply; or are not an option for individualized education program (IEP) teams.
- Head Start placement is based on income-eligibility requirements or limited slots.

Transportation Policies

- Transportation is only provided to students with IEPs.
- No preschool-age students can use district transportation.
- Transportation is only offered to students in self-contained classes.
- Children with special needs do not arrive at the school at the same time that other children do.
- Children in rural areas live beyond bus range.
- Parents must provide transportation, regardless of economic status.
- Transportation is limited to set geographic boundaries.

Conflicting Policies Across Programs

- Quality policies conflict (e.g., among Head Start, state quality rating and improvement system, school district).
- Private and charter schools do not accept children with disabilities.
- Private preschools are not mandated to implement the core standards.
- Hours of the school or program day vary across settings.

with IEPs. Others said that there were not enough funds to provide transportation for typically developing peers, and still others cited the lack of funding to pay for special education and related personnel to provide itinerant services in the community. However, a key finding from research on the costs associated with inclusive preschool service delivery is that *inclusive service delivery models do not cost more than separate programs* (Odom et al., 2001). There are many examples around the country of funding options for preschool inclusion that have not required additional resources but rather redistributed existing resources. An example of redistributing existing fiscal resources includes braiding funding streams to create inclusive programs and classrooms such as combining funding, personnel, and children associated with Head Start, child care, and Title I. A critical component of such budgeting solutions appears to be the ability to account for all funding and ensure that it is being used for the intended purposes.

Funding and personnel shortages are no doubt a serious issue in providing high-quality services to children and families. One solution to funding shortages is to *raise the awareness of policy makers about the importance of high-quality EC experiences, including inclusion,* so that there are more high-quality programs and opportunities for all young children. Therefore, the following strategies related to changing attitudes and raising awareness are also appropriate for the resource challenges.

Tip for Success!

Think *creatively* when planning preschool inclusion! Ask for forgiveness, not permission!

With the clarification that most of the challenges and solutions for policy, procedures, and resources are interchangeable, the categories of these challenges are as follows:

- Ensuring that inclusive settings are of high quality and meet the required standards of school district EC programs
- Ensuring that personnel who provide special education and related services meet state standards as well as ensuring that all personnel have the competence to serve young children with disabilities or are able to do so with the support of specialists
- Establishing facilitative fiscal policies and procedures that support inclusion
- Providing transportation services
- Ensuring full LRE options whether within the school district or in the community
- Ensuring curricula and practices in all settings meet standards of quality

Solutions

The solutions to these challenges that were suggested by the survey respondents are listed next by the category of the challenge (Barton & Smith, 2014b).

Ensuring program quality:

- Establish preschool programs that are high quality and include students with disabilities and typical children from the community.
- Establish cooperative and blended preschool classrooms based on approved state models.
- Integrate inclusion into the state quality rating and improvement system (QRIS) or implementation system.
- Implement high-fidelity models for inclusive classrooms.

Ensuring personnel competence:

- Provide dual endorsement for educators (e.g., combined state teaching licensure for ECSE and general early childhood).
- Provide certifications with coteaching requirements for special and general education.
- Offer training to private child care programs and preschools on topics related to special education including accommodations and intervention strategies.
- Provide district-level consultation for nondistrict programs, including observation, coaching, positive behavioral recommendations, on-site therapy, and frequent meetings.

- Establish strong working relationships between community preschool teachers and public school itinerant EC special education teachers.
- Invite nondistrict providers to district trainings.
- Build training and technical assistance into the state career ladder and other venues to equip EC personnel with knowledge and skills.
- Provide state trainings for continuing education.

Applying effective fiscal strategies:

- Braid and blend funding from multiple sources as necessary.
- Allow state educational consultants to oversee local boards, and allow children with IEPs to enroll in state pre-K programs and classes.
- Support contract negotiations with community programs that provide high-quality inclusion settings for young children with special needs.
- Write commitment letters and memoranda of agreement letters between involved parties and funders.
- Use paraprofessionals in combination with certified teachers for collaborative or coteaching.
- Create tuition-based programs for students without IEPs to attend high-quality inclusive preschools.
- Provide blended preschool programs, serving 10 at-risk students with five students with IEPs per classroom. Secure funding for a general education teacher and special education teacher in same classroom.
- At the state level, pull together a stakeholder group to discuss the barriers, and work together to try come up with solutions. Allow funding to follow each child with an IEP into the general education setting.
- Coordinate meetings between state special education directors to discuss problems and solutions.

Providing transportation:

- Reimburse parents for transporting children.
- Offer paid transportation for typically developing peers.
- Design a community "kiddie cab" service.

Ensuring full LRE options within the school district or in the community:

- Make local education agencies (LEAs) aware of creative options to provide services in the LRE.
- Design school district programs that allow expertise on inclusion to be mobile and shared throughout the district.
- Develop partnerships between public and private providers.
- Provide directors and coordinators who are knowledgeable about individual programs such as Head Start to systematically share information and build relationships with other parties.
- Provide services both on and off LEA campuses.

- Understand legislation and policies that establish partnerships among pre-K, preschool, and early intervention.

  Ensuring curriculum quality:

- Align quality-rating systems and IDEA procedures related to preschool special education (Section 619) to reduce discrepancies in services and increase accountability.

- Implement core standards of high quality across all EC service systems to ensure consistency in quality.

The preschool inclusion team can use the following forms to identify challenges and solutions. Use Form 2.3 to gather perceptions of possible challenges through focus groups, interviews, and questionnaires. Then as a group, meet and review the perceptions, decide on categories of challenges to address, and use Form 2.3 to begin to identify possible solutions.

Form 2.4 includes the solutions and strategies provided by the survey respondents for solving challenges related to policies, procedures, and resources. Once your preschool inclusion team has identified likely challenges, the team can then select which solutions or strategies to use to address them.

The following is a continuation of the Maceo family case study. This excerpt describes the challenges and solutions the preschool inclusion team faced while considering an inclusive placement.

Case Study: The Maceo Family

As described in Chapter 1, the Maceo family currently has a third grader, Paul, enrolled in their neighborhood elementary school. They are requesting that their younger child, Raphael, who has autism, be enrolled in the preschool classroom in his brother's elementary school. The preschool inclusion team at the school reviewed the research on inclusion to identify if there was empirical support for including children such as Raphael in regular EC settings. Then they completed the Inclusion Self-Checklist from Chapter 1. Following the completion and review of the Inclusion Self-Checklist, the preschool inclusion team committed to exploring possible inclusion placements for Raphael. They invited the family to participate, and as a group they reviewed and used the following tools found in this chapter:

- Perceptions of Attitude and Belief Challenges (Form 2.1)
- Perceptions of Policy and Resource Challenges (Form 2.3)
- Menu of Preschool Inclusion Attitudes and Beliefs Solutions (Form 2.2)
- Menu of Preschool Inclusion Policy, Procedure, and Resource Solutions (Form 2.4)

The team made plans to gather perceptions of challenges through focus groups of school district teaching personnel and administrators as well as community-based program administrators and teaching staff and a focus group of families. They decided to send questionnaires to the same groups. The team set a date in 3 weeks to reconvene, review the information, identify key challenges, and begin to discuss possible solutions from the menu and others they might generate on their own.

FORM 2.3.

Perceptions of Policy and Resource Challenges

Policy and resource challenge	Present in program?	Comments
Personnel policies	Yes/No	
Fiscal policies	Yes/No	
Transportation policies	Yes/No	
Conflicting policies across programs	Yes/No	
Resource challenges	Yes/No	
Other	Yes/No	

Menu of Preschool Inclusion Policy, Procedure, and Resource Solutions

Challenges related to procedures and policies	Is this a challenge? Yes/No	Possible solutions (from survey respondents)	For solutions tried, write progress and outcome.
Ensuring program quality		Establish preschool programs that are high quality and include students with disabilities and typical children from the community.	
		Establish cooperative and blended preschool classrooms based on approved state models.	
		Integrate inclusion into the state quality rating and improvement system or implementation system.	
		Implement high-fidelity models for inclusive classrooms.	
Ensuring personnel competence		Provide dual endorsement for educators (combined state teaching licensure for early childhood special education and general early childhood).	
		Provide certifications with coteaching requirements for special education and general education.	
		Offer training to private child care programs and preschools on topics related to special education, including accommodations and intervention strategies.	
		Provide district-level consultation for nondistrict programs, including observation, coaching, positive behavioral recommendations, on-site therapy, and frequent meetings.	
		Establish strong working relationships between community preschool teachers and public school itinerant early childhood special education teachers.	
		Invite nondistrict providers to district trainings.	
		Build training and technical assistance into the state career ladder and other venues to equip early childhood personnel with knowledge and skills.	
		Provide state trainings for continuous education.	

(continued)

Menu of Preschool Inclusion Policy, Procedure, and Resource Solutions

Challenges related to procedures and policies	Is this a challenge? Yes/No	Possible solutions (from survey respondents)	For solutions tried, write progress and outcome.
Applying effective fiscal strategies		Allow state educational consultants to oversee local boards, and allow children with individualized education programs (IEPs) to enroll in state pre-K programs and classes.	
		Braid and blend funding from multiple sources as necessary for mutually beneficial relationships (e.g., Individuals with Disabilities Education Act, pre-K, Title I).	
		Support contract negotiations with community programs that provide high-quality inclusion settings for young children with special needs.	
		Write commitment letters and memoranda of agreement letters between involved parties and funders.	
		Use paraprofessionals in combination with certified teachers for collaborative or coteaching.	
		Create tuition-based programs for students without IEPs to attend high-quality preschools.	
		Provide blended preschool programs, serving 10 at-risk students with five students with IEPs per session. Secure funding that pays for a general education teacher and special education teacher in the same classroom.	
		At the state level, pull together a stakeholder group to discuss the barriers, and work together to try come up with solutions. Allow funding to follow each child with an IEP into the general education setting.	

CONCLUSION

This chapter provides a picture of the landscape of EC inclusion for administrators and leaders. Based on the results of a survey study by Smith and Rose (1993) and a subsequent follow-up survey by Barton and Smith (2014b), the three major areas of challenges to high-quality preschool inclusion nationally are 1) attitudes and beliefs, 2) policies and procedures, and 3) resources. The challenges surrounding attitudes and beliefs are the most frequently reported. Educational leaders are charged with gaining the knowledge to alter attitudes and beliefs around inclusion. Using the information and activities presented in this chapter, preschool inclusion teams can begin to evaluate where their program stands in terms of attitudes and beliefs, policies and procedures, and resources related to high-quality preschool inclusion. The forms provided will help identify possible solutions to these challenges.

Educational leaders can use these strategies, fact sheets, and other resources provided in this toolbox to pave the path toward inclusive practices. In the following chapters, specific step-by-step strategies are described that have been used in many states and districts for addressing challenges, changing policies and beliefs, and establishing appropriate inclusive placement options both within schools and in the community.

REFLECTION QUESTIONS

- Are there policies or procedures presenting challenges to high-quality preschool inclusion opportunities?
- Are there beliefs or attitudes presenting challenges to high-quality preschool inclusion opportunities?
- Are there challenges related to resources that are impeding progress in establishing high-quality preschool inclusion opportunities?
- Are there strategies for solving these challenges?

3

Creating Policies and Procedures that Support Preschool Inclusion

Barbara J. Smith, Elizabeth A. Steed, and Jaclyn D. Joseph

TOOLS FROM THE TOOLBOX

- **Appendix 3A** Spotlight on Discourse, Values, and Professional Ethics
- **Appendix 3B** Sample of an Issue Brief
- **Appendix 3C** Template of an Issue Brief
- **Appendix 3D** Example Inclusion Research Brief
- **Box 3.1** Determining the Level and Branch of Government
- **Box 3.2** Effective Teaming Logistics and Practices
- **Box 3.3** Collaborative Decision-Making Activities
- **Box 3.4** Strategies to Build Positive Relationships and Communicate with Parents, Educational Leaders, and Other Stakeholders
- **Box 3.5** Creating a Vision
- **Figure 3.1** Public Policy 101
- **Figure 3.2** Mapping the Source of Policy Challenges
- **Figure 3.3** Checklist of Steps to Preschool Inclusion
- **Figure 3.4** Conceptualizing Policy Issues and Recommendations Through Backward Mapping
- **Figure 3.5** Action Plan Template and Sample
- **Form 3.1** Formulating Policy and/or Procedural Options for Recommendations
- **Table 3.1** Steps to Garner Support for Preschool Inclusion

As described in Chapter 2, solutions to common challenges to high-quality preschool inclusion involve creating facilitative policies and procedures whether the challenges are related to public policy, procedure, or attitudes and beliefs. Readers will find this chapter useful in their efforts to more thoroughly understand the public policy-making process and explain it to others. This chapter provides an overview of the systems and structures for revising and designing policies and procedures to support high-quality preschool inclusion.

First, the purposes of public policy and procedures are explained, and the differences between the two are delineated. Then, sources of public policy are discussed. Last, an effective process for establishing public policies and procedures to promote high-quality preschool inclusion that has been used by states and local programs is outlined. All the strategies in this book and in this chapter particularly are predicated on the establishment of a preschool inclusion team. This preschool inclusion team should include administrators, classroom teachers, family members, and others (e.g., transportation directors, related services personnel) who will help build support for preschool inclusion, gather important information and data, and work to implement and sustain high-quality inclusive opportunities for all children.

PRESCHOOL INCLUSION POLICIES AND PROCEDURES

Preschool inclusion may be supported or hindered by public policies or program/district procedures. This tool box uses the term "public policy" to refer to public, written documents that carry government sanction such as federal or state laws, regulations and other formal government guidance. Public policies are laws, regulations, and other legal requirements put on public schools by public institutions such as the state legislature or Congress.

Procedures and program-level policies are those written guidelines and plans that do not carry the weight of law or regulation. For instance, school district procedures or policies would include guidance for delivering PD or writing memoranda of agreement with a local child care center to serve as an inclusive placement for a child with an IEP. While most challenges to quality preschool inclusion are due to procedures and attitudes, some might be the result of actual public policies.

Making or changing public policy is more difficult than changing program procedures. However, it is seldom as difficult as people think. Public policies, even laws and regulations, are fluid and dynamic; they are the product of changing needs, values, and times. To begin the process of change, someone must point out that children's needs are no longer being sufficiently met by the current public policy. If indeed actual public policies are serving as challenges or barriers to high-quality preschool inclusion, the policies that might need to be changed could be at the federal, state, local, or program level. National survey data (Barton & Smith, 2014b) indicated that most of the policies serving as challenges to preschool inclusion are at the state or local level, which tends to be more open to change than federal policy. It is important to know what the source of the public policy is. While some challenges might be from federal policy, it is likely that changes at the state, local, or program level will serve the team's purpose. Procedural changes are easier to make than public policy changes, so if that can solve the problem, it is advisable to go that route. Thus, it is critical to determine 1) whether a challenge is really a public policy issue and, 2) if it is, where the public policy comes from—that is, the level and branch of government.

Tip for Success!

Use windows of opportunity! Windows of opportunity are certain times when both politicians and the public are more open to a new public policy idea (Kingdon, 2003). When there is a window of opportunity, you should use it! One sort of public policy window opens right after an election. The new administration may be open to change because they want to define themselves differently than the previous administration. You should begin working with the key people related to a new administration before the election so that you are well poised to influence them once they take office. So pay attention to your national and local current events and watch for windows of opportunity!

The following information can be viewed as a "public policy primer." It is an outline of the U.S. public policy landscape, including levels of government, branches of government, and more. This section will be helpful to the public policy efforts of preschool inclusion teams.

PURPOSE OF EDUCATION PUBLIC POLICY

One purpose of education public policy is to provide guidance for administrators and other school personnel in the interpretation of federal, state, or district statutes. Congress purposefully writes broad laws, so education officials at the state and local levels have to fill in the details by developing rules, regulations, or public policy guidelines (Fowler, 2013). EC coordinators, principals, and other local leaders, including parents, can play a major role in the construction of school district policies and procedures that interpret and implement federal and state policies that are conducive to high-quality, inclusive opportunities for preschool-age children with disabilities. Given this role in interpreting and implementing public policy, school district administrators, ECE leaders, and family leaders should understand how policies are developed to effectively influence public policy.

Tip for Success!

Get a copy! When you request a copy of what you think is a policy challenge to preschool inclusion, you will be able to identify the source of the policy—if indeed it is a policy at all. In our work, almost 100% of the time, a written policy assumed to be a barrier to inclusion didn't actually exist.

Most of the identified challenges to preschool inclusion are due to procedures or attitudes. Therefore, the first step for the preschool inclusion team is to identify whether the challenge is in fact a public policy challenge. The best way to determine this is to request a copy of the public policy from the state department of education or the district superintendent. If the challenge is a public policy, the team must determine whether the challenge can be remediated by a change in interpretation of the public policy or the public policy itself has to be changed. If the public policy must be changed, which is the most unlikely case, the team will need to identity the level and branch of government that it came from (Smith & Rous, 2008). Figure 3.1 is an example of a handout to use to refresh the knowledge base of the preschool inclusion team and educate other stakeholders.

State and local public policies are usually more specific about the direct services being provided to children and families. Specificity varies not only by level of government but also by the branch of government. Generally, laws (which come from the legislative branch) are less specific than regulations, standards, or guidelines (which come from the executive branch). State and local standards or guidelines are easier to change than federal laws. If a challenge or barrier is not public policy but merely the result of the *interpretation* of public policy, then the team often just needs to focus on helping people interpret the public policy more favorably.

Box 3.1 provides some common questions to ask when determining the level and branch of government for a public policy.

Many challenges that are initially assumed to be public policy challenges are, upon further analysis, found to be procedures that do not carry the weight of public policy and can be changed with very little effort. For instance, transportation policies are often set locally; with guidance, personnel in charge of transportation policy can be persuaded to change problematic procedures. In other cases, a challenging

Levels and Branches of Public Policy Making

*U.S. public policies are created at three different **levels** and **branches** of government:*

- **Levels** of government
  - **Federal**
  - **State**
  - **Local**

- **Branches** of government
  - **Legislative** (Congress, state legislatures)
  - **Executive** (president, governors, state agencies)
  - **Judicial** (courts)

Each level and branch of government writes particular types of policies.

- **Federal and State:** The *legislative* branch, Congress and the state legislatures, passes **laws** (statutes). The Individuals with Disabilities Education Act (IDEA) is the law that most relates to making preschool special education placement and service decisions. Federal laws typically are broad and need interpretation from other federal, state, and local governmental bodies. States have their own laws regarding special education, including preschool special education and education funding laws. These state laws help interpret the federal law as well as create their own requirements. The *executive* branch, through its various agencies (the U.S. Department of Education, the state departments of education, and the state boards of education), issues **regulations, standards, guidelines, clarifications, and administrative and fiscal procedures**. There are regulations and other guidelines issued by Office of Special Education Programs pertaining to IDEA at http://idea.ed.gov. State policies further interpret and explain state and federal laws as well as administrative procedures pertaining to special education and funding. The *judicial* branch issues **court rulings**, which also help interpret policies.

- **Local:** Depending on local governmental structure, there could be pertinent policies passed by city and county bodies, particularly local education agencies and school boards, as well as other school district policies pertaining to preschool special education, inclusion, and funding. These local policies can have an effect on funding, contracting, staffing, transportation, and curricular procedures that might affect preschool inclusion.

- **Program:** School district and community-based early childhood program policies and procedures are likely to be the most specific. These policies and procedures can further define the contracting, staffing, funding, transportation, collaboration, and curricular guidelines that either promote or hinder preschool inclusion.

Figure 3.1. Public policy 101.

"policy" may not exist at all! Many supposed public policies are in fact just beliefs or "myths" handed down from one school administrator to another. For example, we were once told that school districts in a particular state couldn't use public state education funds to contract with private preschools. When we requested a copy of that policy, the state department of education's legal office informed us that it did not exist. A chart such as the one in Figure 3.2 can be used to describe and identify the nature of the challenge.

BOX 3.1. Determining the level and branch of government

To determine the level and branch of government of a public policy issue, select which of the following is the source of the challenge:

- A federal law (statute) such as Individuals with Disabilities Education Act (federal legislative branch)
- A regulation or explanation of a federal law by the U.S. Department of Education (federal executive branch)
- Fiscal and/or administrative guidelines such as those administered by Office of Special Education Programs (federal executive branch)
- A state law (statute) regarding special education and/or preschool inclusion (state legislative branch)
- A regulation or guideline from the state department of education or the state school board (state executive branch)
- A local policy or procedure from the school district or a community-based early childhood program (local/program)

AN EFFECTIVE PROCESS FOR CREATING SUPPORTIVE POLICIES AND PROCEDURES

In our work with states and school districts, a set of common strategies has emerged as an effective process for creating or changing policies and procedures to promote preschool inclusion. A checklist such as the one in Figure 3.3 can be used to monitor progress toward implementation of this process. Consider placing this checklist in a prominent location and highlighting each step as they are completed to stay motivated and on track.

Write down three challenges you recognize in your program. Identify the type of challenge and the source of the challenge.

Challenge	Is it a procedure, public policy, myth, or attitude/belief?	If it is a public policy, what is its source (level and branch)?
Can't get reimbursed from state special education funds if children are in "general education" or for an EC teacher in a coteaching classroom	Public policy	State department of education

Figure 3.2. Mapping the source of policy challenges.

Steps	Check when completed
1. Form a preschool inclusion team.	
2. Write a vision statement.	
3. Develop an action plan.	
4. Create materials and opportunities to persuade and raise awareness.	
5. Propose the new policy or procedure.	
6. Develop support.	
7. Monitor the policy-making process.	
8. Follow up with policy makers.	
9. Monitor the implementation.	
10. Evaluate the team's efforts.	

Figure 3.3.   Checklist of steps to preschool inclusion.

1. Form a Preschool Inclusion Team

The first step is to identify others who want to create more high-quality preschool inclusion opportunities. It is highly unlikely that a change in public policy, procedure, or service delivery will be successful without showing that the change is recognized by a group of people representing the major stakeholders, including school district leaders, EC leaders within the school district and from the community, teachers, related services personnel, and, of course, parents. Even if the initiator or champion is a program or public policy leader, he or she will need the help of others not only to change the public policy but also to implement it. It is important not to have too many people, however. Select representatives of key groups, keeping the number of team members to no more than about 15. Team membership of no more than 15 people is critical to ensure that 1) only the key people (or representatives) are there, 2) decision making is efficient, and 3) the group is small enough to build trust and relationships.

The initial work of the preschool inclusion team is to do the following:

- *Make collaborative decisions.* This is paramount! Invite others to help create a new way of doing things by sharing ideas, reaching consensus, and working together as equals. This is the first key to success, as it builds the initial political will and buy-in to drive the initiative. It will also result in better ideas. Remember, two heads are better than one.

- *Gather information.*
  - What is the current rate of inclusive placement decisions in the district?
  - What is the nature of the challenge? Is it a public policy or procedure, or does it come from attitudes or beliefs?
  - Are there easy-to-read materials that promote inclusion, or does the team need to create materials?

- *Establish relationships.* The team must communicate with the people who will be involved in making the policy change and implementing it.

The work of the preschool inclusion team is hard and might need to be sustained over a long period of time. There are well-established teaming strategies that make teamwork effective and enjoyable. These tried-and-true strategies are described in more detail in Box 3.2. When explaining to the team why these practices are important, ask them, "Have you ever been involved in an ongoing team that had meetings that you felt were a waste of your time? Why were they not a good use of your time?" Team members will undoubtedly list things that the following strategies address (e.g., no progress made at meetings, no clear purpose, people did not feel that their voices were heard). This a good exercise to engage in at the first meeting of the preschool inclusion team (adapted from Smith, 2011).

Truly collaborative teams 1) are efficient (i.e., do not waste time), 2) ensure all voices are heard (some people may initially be uncomfortable expressing opinions in large groups), and 3) make decisions that represent the best ideas that emerge from the whole group. Box 3.3 describes a couple of collaborative decision-making activities.

One of the preschool inclusion team's most important activities is building positive relationships and communicating with other stakeholders, including

BOX 3.2. Effective teaming logistics and practices

- *Team membership:* The team should be a maximum of 15 people representing key stakeholders (e.g., administration, teachers, parents, related services, community programs). A small team produces efficient decision making, trust, and relationships. If needed, more input can be acquired through focus groups, work groups, surveys, and so forth.
- *Commitments:* The team must be committed to preschool inclusion, a multiyear process, and being positive and collaborative.
- *No substitutes at meetings:* To ensure consistency and build relationships and trust, members must attend in person, not send representatives.
- *Decisions:* Decisions should be made by consensus if possible, and members must support decisions made in their absence.
- *Shared meeting responsibilities:* Each meeting should have a volunteer timekeeper to ensure the agenda is adhered to or changes are made if time is running short, as well as a volunteer notetaker (if not provided as administrative support), a volunteer facilitator, and someone to bring snacks.
- *Standard meeting time:* Meet for 2 hours once a month, at least, and set the time and date of each meeting 6 months in advance. Provide reimbursement for parent-participation expenses, provide refreshments, and start and end on time!
- *Administrative support:* Meeting agendas should be prepared with input from team members and shared ahead of time. Brief summaries of main topics, decisions, and next steps should be distributed afterward, and meetings should be evaluated. The action plan should be updated to guide each meeting agenda.
- *Meeting facilitation:* Productive meetings must be facilitated objectively; the facilitator should not participate in decisions but ensure all voices are heard and decisions are shared. The facilitator may be a member of the team, and this assignment can rotate among members.
- *Communication rules:* Language must remain respectful, and each person should have the opportunity to talk before another speaks twice.
- *Celebrate small and big accomplishments!*

BOX 3.3. Collaborative decision-making activities

- *Sticky-wall brainstorming:* Materials: a plastic picnic tablecloth from a party store, spray mount adhesive from an office supply store, and small pieces of paper. Activity: People write their ideas on the little pieces of paper (one idea per piece) and put them on the sticky wall. Then the group discusses the similarities and differences between ideas and assigns them to clusters or categories. This is especially useful for efficient brainstorming that captures *everyone's* ideas. (Never brainstorm as a verbal "free for all"!) Tip: Spray the sticky wall ahead of time in a well-ventilated place.
- *Round robin:* Materials: flipchart paper and markers of different colors. Activity: First, small groups (or pairs) write their ideas on a topic—for example, one group addresses policy challenges, another belief and attitude challenges, and so forth. Then the groups switch flipcharts and add to what other groups have written. Finally, the team as a whole reviews all the ideas and decides what challenges to address.
- *Policy/procedure options:* Use the pros and cons chart in this chapter (Form 3.1) to list possible solutions. Then for each one, describe the pros and cons (based on data, not just opinion). Decide which solutions to pursue and in what order (short term, long term, etc.). The other activities can be used with this activity (e.g., use sticky wall to generate pros and cons).

all the district, state education, and community EC leaders that the team wants to educate (e.g., the superintendent, the school board, child care leaders). Leaders will be more likely to support new public policy and procedures if the preschool inclusion team has already established positive relationships with them.

Some ideas for building positive relationships with stakeholders and education officials are the following:

- Include them on the school or program's newsletter or listserv list.
- Tell them about the school or program in an introductory e-mail or letter.
- Invite them to attend some of the school or program's activities. (Fowler, 2013)

Make sure parents and other EC groups understand why change is needed, how it might affect them, and what the specific benefits will be. Invite them to join the preschool inclusion team's change efforts. Team members should be available to listen to what education leaders, parents, and other stakeholders have to say, because communication is a two-way street. For example, the preschool inclusion team might ask education officials about their perspective on inclusion and offer to give them information about the benefits of inclusion. Box 3.4 provides additional examples of ways to build positive relationships and communicate with leaders and stakeholders.

APPLICATION QUESTION

Who are the key stakeholders in your community? Make a list of the key stakeholders you can think of off the top of your head and then review the list with your preschool inclusion team. Who is missing? Are there new people in key positions? Keep this list updated.

2. Write a Vision Statement

The second step is to write the team's vision, values, and beliefs about the topic. This shared belief statement will clarify and drive efforts regarding current

BOX 3.4. Strategies to build positive relationships and communicate with parents, educational leaders, and other stakeholders

- Send home simple, visually appealing fact sheets.
- Briefly discuss your public policy or procedure issue during parent–teacher conferences, and explain why the issue matters to families.
- Involve early childhood groups and practitioners in the process as much as possible to encourage buy-in from the beginning.
- Host a question-and-answer session. (Tip: people are more likely to come if they are promised food and beverages. Also, consider holding two sessions at different times to ensure everyone who wants to can attend.)
- Outline the issue on classroom and/or school web sites or blogs (provide information documents and links to web sites with additional information).
- Extend invitations to community programs for opportunities to gain information, or include them in your awareness efforts.

Tip for Success!

When engaged in backward mapping, you and your team create a written scenario that describes what high-quality preschool inclusion will look like when fully implemented. This might be your vision statement. This activity helps the team reach consensus about what the clear vision is as well as what policies or procedures may need to be changed and what resources will be needed in order to realize the vision.

policies. This is an important step in turning the problem into an issue that can be addressed and that the public can get behind. The vision statement should answer the question "What do we want the future to look like?" A vision statement should be brief, clearly stated, and easy to understand. For example, "All children will experience their early childhood education together, including receiving their special education and other supports in the setting with their same-age peers."

The vision statement and other written materials will help establish terms and inclusive language that everyone will use. Language is important. For instance, IDEA was originally titled the Education of the Handicapped Act. It was later changed to the Individuals with Disabilities Education Act. This new title uses "person-first" language—that is, "Individuals with Disabilities." Similarly, at about the same time, Congress passed ADA, which also uses person-first language. This small but powerful language change makes it clear that people may have disabilities, but they are not defined by them. The fact sheet in Appendix 3A on discourse, values, and professional ethics can be used by the preschool inclusion team to help describe the importance of the language they use. While developing the vision statement, the team should agree on terms and definitions. See Box 3.5 on creating a vision.

Once the team has agreed on a written vision statement, they will answer the following question: "Why aren't we there yet?" This activity will identify the public policies, attitudes and beliefs, or program-level policies or procedures that are serving as challenges to preschool inclusion. An activity that can aid in this activity is "backward mapping" (Elmore, 1979). Figure 3.4 provides a template for backward mapping, and it can be used by the team to identify what the challenges are, their type, and their source.

BOX 3.5. Creating a vision

- A vision should describe the picture of the desired future (e.g., all children will be served in typical settings).
- A focus question that is answered by each preschool inclusion team member in three to five sentences will help guide the team toward understanding its vision. The focus question might be, "What do we want our team to achieve and/or create in 3–5 years? What achievable objectives do we want to be accomplished in this time frame? How will what we are doing help preschool inclusion?"
- The vision should attempt to incorporate as many views as possible into a cohesive, overall vision for the team in order to make it meaningful for team members and to encourage buy-in.
- Create a vision statement, but do not spend a significant amount of time worrying about its exact language and grammar. It is more important that the vision statement communicates the team's direction for moving forward and the purpose of the next steps in terms of action planning.
- As a team, frequently review the vision (e.g., start every meeting by reviewing the vision), and make the vision as visible as possible. Refine it when needed to ensure its relevance. *It is not written in stone!* It can change if the team so chooses.
- Create the vision statement in one or two meetings.
  Source: Hayden, Frederick, and Smith (2003).

3. Develop an Action Plan

Once challenges are identified, the team writes an action plan to address the challenges. This action plan then informs the agendas for team meetings. At each meeting, the team will identify what on the action plan has been accomplished and what still needs to be done. The action steps should be both long term and short term. As action steps are accomplished, the team should celebrate! An action plan should include the vision statement, objective, action steps, who will take the lead on the actions, resources needed to succeed, a time line for achieving the steps, and a method of evaluation. A sample action plan follows in Figure 3.5.

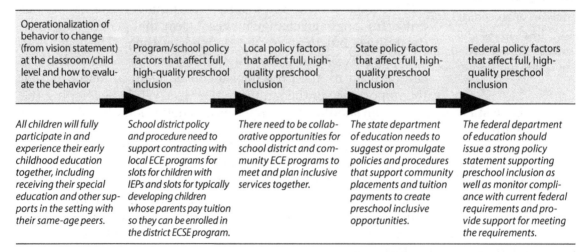

Figure 3.4. Conceptualizing policy issues and recommendations through backward mapping. (*Key:* ECE, early childhood education; IEPs, individualized education programs; ECSE, early childhood special education.)

Vision:				
Objective:				
Action steps (short and long term)	Who is responsible	Time line	Resources needed	Evaluation

Vision: *All preschool children with disabilities in our school district will be afforded high-quality inclusive opportunities for special education and related services.*

Objective: *Address the challenges related to a lack of awareness by state administrators of the importance of preschool inclusion.*

Action steps (short and long term)	Who is responsible	Time line	Resources needed	Evaluation
Form a preschool inclusion team	*Preschool coordinator, special education director*	*By August 1*	*E-mail, room, refreshments*	*August 1, team met and developed an action plan*
Team will set up meetings with state leaders; use fact sheets on research support, IDEA support, local and state data on preschool inclusion	*Special education director, family rep.*	*By September 1*	*E-mail, mileage to capitol*	*September 1, meetings held; materials distributed and reviewed; next steps defined*

Figure 3.5. Action plan template and sample.

4. Create Materials and Opportunities to Persuade and Raise Awareness

Once the preschool inclusion team has crafted its vision and identified the challenges, the team will need to prepare short, easy-to-read materials and documentation about 1) why the current public policy or procedure is a problem and 2) how it needs to be changed. Depending on the circumstance, this documentation might only need to be a letter to an administrator or policy maker, or it might need to be a series of documents written for many constituencies (e.g., parents, legislators, special education administrators). The material might vary from a simple rationale to summaries of research data. In *all* cases, keep it concise, data based, and related to the vision. The fact sheets and handouts in this toolbox are examples of effective ways of presenting information.

As part of this process, the preschool inclusion team should compile 1) evidence used to frame the problem, including dramatic anecdotes, stories, and statistics; 2) a realistic solution to the problem that will have broad appeal; and 3) powerful, values-based language that will be consistently used to describe the problem and its solution (Fowler, 2013). Issue briefs that summarize research, laws, and personal stories using compelling language in only one or two pages are very effective formats for conveying information to busy people such as administrators and policy makers. Appendixes 3B and 3C include a sample issue brief on preschool inclusion as well as a template for writing issue briefs, respectively. There also should be contact information on all materials, including issue briefs. Furthermore, the preschool inclusion team should make sure that their interpretations of policies supporting or challenging preschool inclusion are accurate. For instance, many misinterpretations of IDEA are used to challenge preschool inclusion. The fact sheet in the Introduction on the provisions of IDEA that support inclusion (see Appendix IB) lists the provisions verbatim so the language is not subject to interpretation. The policy letter from OSEP in that fact sheet is a copy of the original letter text, not an interpretation of what the letter says. Always use the actual language, not an interpretation!

School district administrators have several resources at their disposal to influence change. One of the most advantageous resources that all administrators have is a repository of data on child and program outcomes. Moral and ethical arguments can be made regarding the importance of inclusion. However, arguments that are supported by data (i.e., numbers) are especially powerful, and this is often readily available! National data are available from research journals and online resources (e.g., http://ectacenter.org/topics/inclusion; http://npdci.fpg .unc.edu; http://idea.ed.gov; https://www2.ed.gov/about/reports/annual/osep/index .html?exp=1). Administrators have access to their own district and program data related to preschool inclusion. In addition, summaries of child placement data both national and local can be developed from the annual IDEA data collected and submitted to OSEP. Use the inclusion fact sheets provided in the Introduction (Appendixes IA, IB, and IC) when the team needs to provide empirical support for inclusion.

Legislators and other key policy makers appreciate summaries of data that are easy to understand (e.g., short bullet points) and compelling (e.g., family stories and quotes). It might be best to utilize local resources (e.g., university researchers) to understand and analyze administrative data. University researchers might also help design or redesign the data collection system to collect meaningful data on placement decisions and child and program outcomes that can be used to influence policy. A powerful format to use for presenting data and arguments for supporting preschool inclusion is an "issue brief." An issue brief summarizes key data, key points, scenarios, stories, and reference information in one or two pages. A sample of an issue brief is at the end of this chapter, as well as a template for creating one (see Appendixes 3B and 3C).

5. Propose the New Policy or Procedure

The preschool inclusion team should propose the actual policy or procedural option. First, determine the type of policy or procedure change that is needed (i.e., legislation, an amendment to a regulation, a change in local procedure, or simply a clarification of an existing policy or procedure). Next, brainstorm ways to achieve the vision, list the options, and analyze the pros and cons of each option (e.g., cost, time, values alignment, feasibility). A template for formulating policy recommendations is in Form 3.1. If you are unsure of the "type" of the policy or the mechanism to be used, consult an attorney or other people who have expertise and are familiar with the policy. Finally, to save time and energy, try to take *the path of least resistance* (or least controversy and effort) to meet goals and objectives. Majchrzak (1984) notes that policy recommendations are more likely to be accepted when they are tied to existing policies.

Before proposing the new policy or procedure, the team will want to become acquainted with funding issues and identify whether the change will save money or increase costs. If needed, identify possible sources of funding. If the change will require more state funding, the team will need to understand the budget process. The budget process usually plays out at the same time as the policy proposal process (Fowler, 2013). The team will need to influence people to adopt the language of the new policy at the same time that you are trying to influence people to fund the policy. State budget processes vary (e.g., top-down or bottom-up), and district budget processes vary widely (Rubin, 2006). It is important to learn how the state or local budget process works to propose and secure funding for policy change. Unfunded mandates are not popular! Policy change needs to have its resources identified to support implementation of preschool inclusion.

An important funding approach to inclusive preschool services is the notion of "braided funding." For instance, different funding streams or sources can be used to fund an inclusive classroom: Title I, special education, state pre-K, and so forth. The term *braided* is used to indicate that the accounting procedures used can identify all funding streams and how they are allocated to meet the funding requirements. However, the end result is a classroom that is adequately and inclusively funded to meet the needs of all children.

6. Develop Support

Garner both grass roots and political support. Depending on the nature of the change, more or less support will be needed. If all that is needed is a new contracting procedure with community programs, which can be accomplished with a bookkeeper or accountant, little to no outside support is needed. However, if a new state law or regulation is needed, the preschool inclusion team might need the support of parents, professionals, legislators, state agency personnel, and the governor.

Support can be developed through public awareness materials and activities as described previously as well as through coalition building. Compelling and effective public awareness materials and activities focused on inclusive programs can mean the difference between success and failure. Some ideas for attracting attention to public policy issues are to 1) invite an expert to give a talk at a parent

Formulating Policy and/or Procedural Options for Recommendations

There is rarely one right way to do something. The following template will help you and your team consider the pros and cons of potential policy recommendations.

Note: Multiple forms may need to be used in order to consider a majority of the possible policy options.

	Pros	Cons
Policy/Procedural Option:		
Policy/Procedural Option:		
Policy/Procedural Option:		
Policy/Procedural Option:		

Things to consider:

- When developing pros and cons lists, you may want to include long-term and short-term costs and benefits; research findings and data; child, family, and personnel outcomes; and professional development implications.
- Identifying any "minefields" and their results is an important part of the recommendation development process. Policy and decision makers will want to know that you have considered this information ahead of time and that you have also considered potential solutions and/or outcomes.
- Obtain as much input from stakeholders as possible. You want to be able to say that your recommendations have broad-based support.
- Start with a small group of people when considering policy and procedural options to find out if there are aspects of the policy and/or procedural considerations that will be less negotiable than others in regard to your policy recommendations.

night; 2) sponsor a workshop on the topic for teachers; 3) write an op-ed piece to the local newspaper explaining how the issue affects the school, program, or community; 4) ask the PTA to put the topic on their meeting agenda for discussion; and 5) send information about all these efforts to legislators (Fowler, 2013).

Building coalitions of groups with the same interest can promote support for preschool inclusion efforts. EC coalitions often comprise general educators, special educators, child care and Head Start personnel, related professional groups, parents, and other advocates. It is important to include the community programs. For state or federal public policy changes, the support of other school districts may be needed. Through coalitions, decisions can be made that take into account the concerns of various groups. Typical coalition members for EC initiatives include school districts, child care programs, Head Start, family groups, and others depending on the community and the particular issue. Coalition members' individual concerns need to be part of the process for deciding what the public policy option is. Perhaps the most important group for support is parents. They have the most at stake. Parents need to understand the efficacy and legal foundations of preschool inclusion and help shape the inclusion agenda. It is critical to reach agreement on major issues and present a united front. Most public policy makers will respond to a united group who has done their homework and presents them with actual public policy language. Table 3.1 offers some guidance for garnering support.

7. Monitor the Policy-Making Process

By establishing public support and the united force of a coalition, you have the impetus and backing needed for translating goals into a public policy. In addition to these awareness and educational strategies, the preschool inclusion team should find a policy maker to serve as a sponsor for the proposed policy, preferably a policy maker who commands respect. This sponsor will be the "shepherd" for the

Table 3.1.   Steps to garner support for preschool inclusion

Who to go to for support	How to garner support
Grass roots • Parents • Community-based early childhood programs • Professional organizations • Social media participants • Professional advocacy groups • Other professionals in agreement with your effort *Political* • Government agencies • Legislators • State agency personnel • Governor	• Develop or acquire and distribute research syntheses and issue briefs. • Participate in social media. For example, start a hashtag for your effort and encourage others to use it (e.g., #inclusionow) when posting to social media. Keep in mind hashtags should be as few characters as possible. • Host a "Lunch and Learn" (bring lunch to legislators and policy makers and discuss your effort while they are eating). • Schedule formal meetings with stakeholders. • During the legislative session, send a business card to your legislator from the anteroom, and provide a 90-second speech about your effort.

proposed policy. However, the team will need to monitor the process and be available for assistance, such as providing information or support.

It is important to identify and stay connected to the professionals in the team's coalition while monitoring the policy-making process. This might mean that the team joins with professional organizations that share ideals and that will provide support during this process. For example, the team might host informal lunches with other administrators in nearby areas, or they might wish to develop a formal council, roundtable, or task force in the area that is focused specifically on preschool inclusion and other related issues (e.g., PD, quality in ECE; Fowler, 2013). These strategies can keep the team connected to the issue, build support, and work collectively toward change.

Tip for Success!

The success of this effort also will be improved with the support of the state education agency (SEA). The SEA can help set the vision, values, discourse, personnel development, and policies that facilitate providing special education and related services to children 3–5 years old with disabilities in regular early childhood programs. A partnership between the SEA and school districts is critical for the expansion and sustainability of preschool inclusion.

8. Follow Up with Policy Makers

Positive reinforcement is as vital in the public policy arena as in any educational setting. Regardless of the outcome of the team's efforts, it is critical to thank policy makers and other stakeholders who supported the team. A campaign of thanks and recognition is as important as the original public awareness campaign. If efforts failed the first time, consider possible ways to strengthen or improve the efforts. An effective, cultivated follow-up effort can help the policy agenda succeed the second time. By asking those who did not support the policy change their reasons for not doing so, the team will be better prepared next time. Also, by thanking supporters, the preschool inclusion team can help ensure their support the next time around. Be persistent! Moving an idea from a proposal to public policy can take years. There might be many roadblocks to overcome. Persistence is needed to stay with it, deal with disappointments, and see the public policy change come to fruition.

9. Monitor the Implementation

When the public policy gets adopted, the team must monitor the next steps. The implementation process can enhance or detract from the original goals of the public policy. Implementation usually requires allocation of resources, personnel awareness and training, and data collection to ensure that desired outcomes are achieved—in this case, successful, high-quality inclusion for preschool children with disabilities and positive outcomes for children, families, and professionals. Research suggests that new policies either are not implemented at all or are modified significantly during implementation (Fowler, 2013). To be successful, consider the timing of the implementation. Implementing a new public policy or procedure at the beginning of a new school year or semester is better than mid-year. Other key components are resources (e.g., time, space, personnel), staff support, and in-depth training through mentors and coaches rather than brief trainings or explanations during an all staff meeting (Fowler, 2013).

10. Evaluate the Team's Efforts

It is critically important to evaluate the preschool inclusion team's efforts. We have encouraged teams to conduct short-term and long-term evaluation as well as product or outcome evaluation. The key tool to use in the evaluation is the action plan. The action plan should have the vision, the short-term and long-term goals, and the specific challenges to be addressed. The evaluation questions, therefore, should include the following: Did we meet our short-term objectives? Did we achieve our long-term goals? Have we come closer to our vision? And of course, have we increased preschool inclusion? The evaluation of the team's work should lead to the next steps.

The following continuation of the case example of the Maceo family describes how the preschool inclusion team moved forward in their efforts to provide preschool inclusion opportunities using the tools in this section.

Case Study: The Maceo Family

As described in previous chapters, the Maceo family currently has a third grader, Paul, enrolled in their neighborhood elementary school. They are requesting that their younger child, Raphael, who has autism, also be enrolled in the preschool classroom in his brother's elementary school. Following the completion and review of the Preschool Inclusion Self-Checklist (Form 1.1), the school district preschool inclusion team committed to exploring possible inclusion placements for Raphael. The team made plans to gather perceptions of challenges through focus groups and surveys and then reviewed the information gathered to identify key challenges and solutions. They developed a vision statement and agreed on team logistics and ground rules. At the next meeting, the team identified the key challenges, both short term and long term. The team began to develop an action plan, and in doing so, they began to identify some solutions and actions to be taken. The team developed three work groups: 1) an awareness work group to prepare a packet of materials on research, IDEA, data, issue briefs, and so forth and to begin to garner support; 2) a solutions work group to draft policies and procedures to facilitate inclusion; and 3) a PD work group. The action plan is based on the goal of increasing inclusion opportunities by the coming school year.

The following case study provides an additional illustration of how a preschool inclusion team is formed, establishes a shared vision, and creates an action plan.

Case Study: Garfield School

The Garfield School District preschool coordinator, John Davis, and the special education director, Sue Johnson, have been having conversations about increasing the numbers of preschoolers with IEPs who receive their special education and related services in regular EC programs. They decided to gather information, and they formed a stakeholder team of the assistant district superintendent, two community-based EC program directors, the Title I director, the pre-K coordinator, a special education teacher, a speech therapist, a pre-K teacher, two parents of children with disabilities, and two parents of typically developing children.

The newly formed preschool inclusion team stated their vision as follows: "Within 3 years, all preschool students in Garfield School District will attend early childhood programs together and receive their special education, related services, and all other supports in those settings."

The team agreed on terms and inclusive-language guidelines. They created work groups to develop awareness materials: one group was charged with finding research fact sheets and summaries about preschool inclusion and another with analyzing national, state, and local data related to how many children are served in regular EC programs for their special education and related services. The team began holding discussion groups with community-based EC program directors and teachers, parent groups, and other education leaders. The team presented the facts about the importance of preschool inclusion, as well as the current data from their district, and gathered concerns. They then began to address the concerns by doing the following:

- Holding shared awareness meetings among school district regular EC teachers, community EC personnel, district special education and related services personnel, and parents

- Compiling data on concerns of regular EC personnel, special education personnel, administrators, and parents

- Compiling data on numbers of children with disabilities currently in (and not in) inclusive settings, as well as their demographics

- Meeting with education leaders, including the school board, and raising their awareness about the importance of preschool inclusion and how policies, procedures, and finances can be adjusted to support the new model

- Writing draft policies and procedures

- Establishing monthly collaborative meetings with community-based EC leaders to address ongoing needs and progress

- Establishing budgets and procedures for training and coaching and delivering special education and related services in community settings

- Developing a written action plan to implement and evaluate all the plans

With an action plan in place that implements these strategies, the school district will be able to increase inclusion opportunities both within their preschool programs and in community programs.

CONCLUSION

This chapter outlined strategies for developing supportive policies and procedures for preschool inclusion. The strategies outlined in this section are predicated on the establishment of a preschool inclusion team of key stakeholders that work with administration to expand the availability and quality of preschool inclusion opportunities for young children with disabilities. A key activity of the preschool inclusion team is to use tools and resources such as those found in this book to increase the awareness and knowledge of decision makers, families, and professionals of the efficacy of preschool inclusion. One of the most often cited reasons for the lack of progress in serving young children with disabilities in regular EC programs is that stakeholders do not understand the importance of preschool inclusion and do not know the legal, scientific, and ethical foundations of preschool inclusion. If people do not understand that high-quality inclusion is critical to children's learning and development, they will not be motivated to do the hard work of creating those opportunities. The preschool inclusion team represents many different stakeholder groups that can spread that information to many audiences.

REFLECTION QUESTIONS

1. What is the source of policies and procedures?
2. What policies or procedures present challenges to inclusion in your context?
3. Which individuals will you invite to be members of your preschool inclusion team?
4. What is your vision for preschool inclusion?
5. How will you garner support for your efforts?

Spotlight on Discourse, Values, and Professional Ethics

Alissa Rausch

Even with legal imperatives . . . segregation and isolation continue. So, it seems that until we go beyond the law and make inclusion a moral imperative, the status quo will continue.

—Snow (2007)

As noted throughout this chapter, research suggests that attitudes and beliefs are the greatest barrier to preschool inclusion. These realities also drive the segregation of young children with special needs. Specifically, the language or discourse used in describing young children with special needs is reflective of the values about children with special needs.

Why Does Language Matter?

The language, or discourse, used in describing young children with special needs is reflective of the collective (present and future) values about children with special needs. A good example of this is "person-first language." When children are described as disability first (i.e., "autistic child" versus "child with autism"), they are immediately labeled by their disability. This language pattern can cause devastating long-term effects on children when their families, teachers, and peers recognize their limitations before acknowledging their individuality as young children. The labeling done with language creates ongoing negative attitudes that persist for young children with special needs and follow them throughout their lives.

One critical aspect of preschool inclusion is opening a dialogue about including young children with special needs. A compilation of research regarding civil discourse reveals four tenets of inclusive civil discourse. These are pictured in the following graphic.

The implementation of preschool inclusion at the local, state, and national levels can be a challenging process. The complexity of preschool inclusion requires an ongoing evaluation of existing power structures, discourse, and culture (Fowler, 2013; Heck, 2004). Professionals, policy makers, and educators in ECE must fundamentally change the way in which they examine processes and values to effectively develop, adopt, and implement meaningful and effective inclusive education practices (Heck, 2004; Smith & Rous, 2008). EC educators and administrators who understand the benefits of preschool inclusion must be willing to accept the economic and ideological implications of inclusion.

83

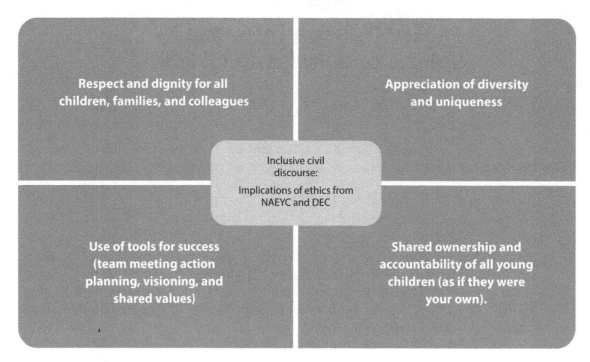

The four tenets of inclusive civil discourse.

Suggested Rules for Engaging in Inclusive Civil Discourse

- Establish ground rules or norms.
- Establish team vision and values.
- Be willing to engage in constant reflection.
- Honor silence and incompleteness.
- Understand the importance of both speaking and listening.
- Know how important a model you are to children for discourse.
- Use the ARE of dialogue:
  - *Assertion* is the main point of the argument.
  - *Reasoning* is the "because" of the argument.
  - *Evidence* is used to support reasoning.

Source: Teaching Tolerance (2011).

To effectively implement preschool inclusion, use language that ultimately shifts the attitudes and beliefs of the professionals who work with young children. This begins with the development of a team "pledge for inclusive language." The pledge process can be a formal acknowledgement of the team's values and norms of behavior about preschool inclusion. It can include a statement about the use of people-first and strengths-based language. It can also include an agreement that professionals will support one another in using language that is consistent with a high value on inclusive education. The pledge can also identify the like-minded values of professionals who work with young children with special needs. Encourage your teams at school to "take a pledge" to uphold the language rules suggested on this handout. Share this information with parents, other programs, policy makers, and community members. Encourage them to take the pledge as well. Hang the pledge in a prominent place in the school or classroom so that anyone who enters can read it.

Record your team pledge here:

_____

_____

_____

_____

Record your team mission statement here:

_____

_____

_____

_____

Record three goals for your team for this school year here:

1. _____

_____

_____

2. _____

_____

_____

3. _____

_____

_____

As your team establishes their team mission, norms, and goals, consider the important aspects of professional ethics as well. The codes of ethics from both NAEYC as well as DEC are an extension of the personal values that individual educators bring with them to the profession. Both NAEYC and DEC offer expectations about inclusive discourse and high-quality preschool inclusion.

Use the following grid to evaluate how the mission, norms, and goals that your team developed align with the professional codes of ethics from the DEC and NAEYC.

One example of how this grid is used comes from an EC center in Denver. Prior to using this table, the team developed the following mission statement: "Develop strong citizens and world-class learners." After group discussions about the DEC and NAEYC professional codes of ethics, the team altered their mission statement: "Develop a community of children and adults who care about one another, their learning, and their interactions with others around them."

Tenet of Inclusive Civil Discourse	NAEYC	DEC	DEC/NAEYC Joint Position Statement
Respect and dignity for children, family, and colleagues	To recognize and respect the unique qualities, abilities, and potential of each child To develop relationships of mutual trust and create partnerships with the families we serve	We shall demonstrate our respect and appreciation for all families' beliefs, values, customs, languages, and culture relative to their nurturance and support of their children toward achieving meaningful and relevant priorities and outcomes families' desire for themselves and their children. We shall recognize and respect the dignity, diversity, and autonomy of the families and children we serve	Develop a program philosophy on inclusion
Appreciation of diversity and uniqueness	To support the right of each child to play and learn in an inclusive environment that meets the needs of children with and without disabilities	We shall include the diverse perspectives and experiences of children and families in the conduct of research and intervention	Create high expectations for every child to reach his or her full potential
Use of tools for success	To share information about each child's education and development with families and to help them understand and appreciate the current knowledge base of the early childhood profession To share resources with coworkers, collaborating to ensure that the best possible early childhood care and education program is provided	We shall rely upon evidence-based research and interventions to inform our practice with children and families in our care. We shall use every resource, including referral when appropriate, to ensure high-quality services are accessible and are provided to children and families	Establish a system of services and supports. Revise program and professional standards
Shared ownership and accountability of young children	To support the right of each child to play and learn in an inclusive environment that meets the needs of children with and without disabilities To promote knowledge and understanding of young children and their needs To work toward greater societal acknowledgment of children's rights and greater social acceptance of responsibility for the well-being of all children	We shall recognize our responsibility to improve the developmental outcomes of children and to provide services and supports in a fair and equitable manner to all families and children. We shall utilize collaborative and interdisciplinary research for strengthening linkages between the research and practice communities, as well as for improving the quality of life of children with disabilities and their families	Achieve an inclusive professional development system

Sources: Division for Early Childhood (2009); Division for Early Childhood/National Association for the Education of Young Children (2009); National Association for the Education of Young Children (2011).

REFERENCES

DEC/NAEYC. (2009). *Early childhood inclusion: A joint position statement of the Division for Early Childhood (DEC) and the National Association for the Education of Young Children (NAEYC)*. Chapel Hill: The University of North Carolina, FPG Child Development Institute. Retrieved from http://npdci .fpg.unc.edu/sites/npdci.fpg.unc.edu/files/resources/EarlyChildhoodInclusion_0.pdf

Division for Early Childhood. (2009). *DEC code of ethics*. Retrieved from http://www.dec-sped.org/papers

Fisher, A. (2007). Creating a discourse of difference. *Education, Citizenship, and Social Justice, 2*, 159–192.

Fowler, F.C. (2013). Policy implementation: Getting people to carry out a policy. In F.C. Fowler, *Policy studies for educational leaders: An introduction* (pp. 241–277). Boston, MA: Pearson.

Heck, R.H. (2004). An introduction to policymaking and its study. In R.H. Heck, *Studying educational and social policy: Theoretical concepts and research methods* (pp. 3–34). Mahwah, NJ: Erlbaum.

National Association for the Education of Young Children. (2011). *NAEYC code of ethical conduct and statement of commitment: A position statement from the National Association for the Education of Young Children*. Retrieved from http://www.macte.org/images/Code_of_Ethical_Conduct.pdf

Smith, B.J., & Rous, B. (2008). Policy in early childhood education and early intervention: What every early childhood educator needs to know. In P. Winton, J. McCollum, & C. Catlett (Eds.), *Practical approaches to early childhood professional development: Evidence, strategies and resources* (pp. 247–262). Washington, DC: ZERO TO THREE.

Snow, K. (2007). *Revolutionary common sense: Great expectations*. Retrieved April 30, 2014, from http:// www.disabilityisnatural.com/~k061480m/images/PDF/grtexpect.pdf

Teaching Tolerance. (2011). *Building blocks for civil discourse*. Retrieved from http://www.tolerance.org /publications/chapter-2-building-blocks-civil-discourse

Quality Preschool Inclusion

What Is Preschool Inclusion?

Early childhood inclusion embodies the values, policies, and practices that support the right of every infant and young child and his or her family, regardless of ability, to participate in a broad range of activities and contexts as full members of families, communities, and society. The desired results of inclusive experiences for children with and without disabilities and their families include a sense of belonging and membership, positive social relationships and friendships, and development and learning to reach their full potential. The defining features of inclusion that can be used to identify high quality early childhood programs and services are access, participation, and supports (DEC/NAEYC, 2009, p. 2).[27]

In 27 years, preschool inclusion has increased only 5.7%, and many young children with disabilities continue to be educated in separate settings. And yet, research, law, and professional standards document the importance of inclusion for young children's optimal development.[1,2]

What Do the Facts Tell Us About Preschool Inclusion?

- Inclusion benefits all children.[3,4,5,6,7,8,9]

- Children with disabilities can be effectively educated in inclusive programs using specialized instruction.[10,11,12,13]

- Parents and teachers influence children's values regarding disabilities.[14,15,16]

- Individualized embedded instruction can be used to teach a variety of skills, including those related to early learning standards, and promote participation in inclusive preschool programs to children with and without disabilities.[17,18,19,20,21]

- Families of children with and without disabilities generally have positive views of inclusion.[22,23]

- Inclusion is not more expensive than having separate programs for children with disabilities.[24,25]

- Successful inclusion requires intentional and effective collaboration and teaming.[26]

- The individual outcomes of preschool inclusion should include access, membership, participation, friendships, and support.[27]

- Children with disabilities do not need to be "ready" to be included. Programs need to be "ready" to support all children.[28]

ENDNOTES

1. U.S. Department of Education. (2014). *2012 IDEA part B child count and educational environment.* Retrieved from https://explore.data.gov/Education/2012-IDEA-Part-B-Child-Count-and-Educational--Envir/5t72-4535

2. U.S. Department of Education. (1987). *Annual report to congress on the implementation of the Education of the Handicapped Act.* U.S. Department of Education, Washington, DC.

3. Buysse, V., Goldman, B.D., & Skinner, M.L. (2002). Setting effects on friendship formation among young children with and without disabilities. *Exceptional Children, 68,* 503–517.

4. Cross, A.F., Traub, E.K., Hutter-Pishgahi, L., & Shelton, G. (2004). Elements for successful inclusion for children with significant disabilities. *Topics in Early Childhood Special Education, 24,* 169–183.

5. Holahan, A., & Costenbader, V. (2000). A comparison of developmental gains for preschool children with disabilities in inclusive and self-contained classrooms. *Topics in Early Childhood Special Education, 20,* 224–235.

6. Odom, S.L., Zercher, C., Li, S., Marquart, J., Sandall, S., & Brown, W. (2006). Social acceptance and social rejection of young children with disabilities in inclusive classes. *Journal of Educational Psychology, 98,* 807–823.

7. Strain, P., & Hoyson, M. (2000). The need for longitudinal, intensive social skill intervention: LEAP follow-up outcomes for children with autism. *Topics in Early Childhood Special Education, 20,* 116–122.

8. Buysse, V., Wesley, P.W., Bryant, D., & Gardner, D. (1999). Quality of early childhood programs in inclusive and noninclusive settings. *Exceptional Children, 65,* 301–314.

9. Soukakou, E.P. (2012). Measuring the quality of inclusive preschool classrooms: Development and validation of the Inclusive Classroom Profile. *Early Childhood Research Quarterly, 27,* 478–488.

10. Division for Early Childhood. (2014). *DEC recommended practices in early intervention/early childhood special education.* Retrieved from http://www.dec-sped.org/recommendedpractices

11. Odom, S.L., DeKlyen, M., & Jenkins, J.R. (1984). Integrating handicapped and nonhandicapped preschool children: Developmental impact on the nonhandicapped children. *Exceptional Children, 51,* 41–48.

12. Rafferty, Y., Piscitelli, V., & Boettcher, C. (2003). The impact of inclusion on language development and social competence among preschoolers with disabilities. *Exceptional Children, 69,* 467–479.

13. Strain, P., & Bovey, E. (2011). Randomized, controlled trials of the LEAP model of early intervention for young children with Autism Spectrum Disorders. *Topics in Early Childhood Special Education, 31,* 133–154.

14. Diamond, K.E., & Huang, H. (2005). Preschoolers' ideas about disabilities. *Infants and Young Children, 18,* 37–46.

15. Innes, F., & Diamond, K.E. (1999). Typically developing children's interactions with peers with disabilities: Relationships between mothers' comments and children's ideas about disabilities. *Topics in Early Childhood Special Education, 19,* 103–111.

16. Okagaki, L., Diamond, K., Kontos, S., & Hestenes, L. (1998). Correlates of young children's interactions with classmates with disabilities. *Early Childhood Research Quarterly, 13,* 67–86.

17. Daugherty, S., Grisham-Brown, J., & Hemmeter, M.L. (2001). The effects of embedded skill instruction on the acquisition of target and nontarget skills in preschoolers with developmental delays. *Topics in Early Childhood Special Education, 21,* 213–221.

18. Grisham-Brown, J., Schuster, J.W., Hemmeter, M.L., & Collins, B.C. (2000). Using an embedding strategy to teach preschoolers with significant disabilities. *Journal of Behavioral Education, 10,* 139–162.

19. Grisham-Brown, J.L., Pretti-Frontczak, K., Hawkins, S., & Winchell, B. (2009). Addressing early learning standards for all children within blended preschool classrooms. *Topics in Early Childhood Special Education, 29,* 131–142.

20. Robertson, J., Green, K., Alper, S., Schloss, P.J., & Kohler, F. (2003). Using peer-mediated intervention to facilitate children's participation in inclusive child care activities. *Education & Treatment of Children, 26,* 182–197.

21. Venn, M.L., Wolery, M., Werts, M.G., Morris, A., DeCesare, L.D., & Cuffs, M.S. (1993). Embedding instruction in art activities to teach preschoolers with disabilities to imitate their peers. *Early Childhood Research Quarterly, 8,* 277–294.

22. Kasari, C., Freeman, S.F.N., Bauminger, N., & Alkin, M.C. (1999). Parental perspectives on inclusion: Effects of autism and down syndrome. *Journal of Autism and Developmental Disorders, 29,* 297–305.

23. Rafferty, Y., & Griffin, K.W. (2005). Benefits and risks of reverse inclusion for preschoolers with and without disabilities: Perspectives of parents and providers. *Journal of Early Intervention, 27,* 173–192.

24. Odom, S.L., Hanson, M.J., Lieber, J., Marquart, J., Sandall, S., Wolery, R., . . . Chambers, J. (2001). The costs of preschool inclusion. *Topics in Early Childhood Special Education, 21,* 46–55.

25. Odom, S.L., Parrish, T., & Hikido, C. (2001). The costs of inclusion and noninclusive special education preschool programs. *Journal of Special Education Leadership, 14,* 33–41.

26. Division for Early Childhood. (2014). *DEC recommended practices in early intervention/early childhood special education.* Retrieved from http://www.dec-sped.org/recommendedpractices

27. DEC/NAEYC. (2009). *Early childhood inclusion: A joint position statement of the Division for Early Childhood (DEC) and the National Association for the Education of Young Children (NAEYC).* Chapel Hill: University of North Carolina, FPG Child Development Institute.

28. Individuals with Disabilities Education Improvement Act (IDEA) of 2004, PL 108-446, 20 U.S.C. §§ 1400 *et seq.*

Template of an Issue Brief

ADD A CREATIVE TITLE

Use a font that is easy to read (e.g., Calibri, Times New Roman). Also, bright colors catch the reader's eye. Use complimentary bold colors throughout when possible.

Provide a brief paragraph here regarding the policy and why it is a problem.

Data and statistics that strongly emphasize the policy issue can be used here to catch a reader's attention and make him or her want to continue reading to learn more about your policy issue.

Use bulleted information in this section to create short yet significant points.

- Data on child outcomes
- Data on program outcomes
- Data on economic benefits of proposed change
- Dramatic anecdotes, stories, and/or quotes
- Pictures of children from the population you serve or of your school/program

Pull out powerful information, place it in a separate text box, and use font styles to make the information more noticeable compared with the rest of the text (e.g., larger font, different color, bold, italics).

Recommendation(s)

Include your proposal for the actual policy or procedural option in this section (e.g., "The law needs to be changed to say . . . ," "Potential funding sources for this change might include . . ."").

Depending on your audience, the recommendations section can also include a "Call to Action" portion that clearly outlines next steps for readers to take given the information you include in this document.

For More Information Please Contact:

Provide contact information in this section. Include any planned meetings or in-person opportunities to learn more about the policy issue as well. Remind readers that you want to be a resource for them in the policy-formulation process and that you are available to help in any way possible.

Example Inclusion Research Brief
Brief Summary

FACT SHEET OF RESEARCH ON PRESCHOOL INCLUSION

1. In 27 years, the practice of providing special education and related services in regular early childhood settings to preschoolers with disabilities has increased only 5.7% and many young children with disabilities continue to be educated in separate settings.[1,2]

2. Inclusion benefits children with and without disabilities.[3,4,5,6,7]

3. The quality of preschool programs including at least one student with a disability were as good as or better than preschool programs without children with disabilities. However, traditional measures of early childhood program quality might not be sufficient for assessing quality of programs that include children with disabilities.[8,9]

4. Children with disabilities can be effectively educated in inclusive programs using specialized instruction.[10,11,12,13]

5. Parents and teachers influence children's values regarding disabilities.[14,15,16]

6. Individualized embedded instruction can be used to teach a variety of skills, including those related to early learning standards, and promote participation in inclusive preschool programs to children with and without disabilities.[17,18,19,20,21]

7. Families of children with and without disabilities generally have positive views of inclusion.[22,23]

8. Inclusion is not more expensive than having separate programs for children with disabilities.[24,25]

9. Successful inclusion requires intentional and effective collaboration and teaming.[26*]

10. The individual outcomes of preschool inclusion should include access, membership, participation, friendships, and support.[27*]

11. Children with disabilities do not need to be "ready" to be included. Programs need to be "ready" to support all children.[27*]

Note: A sample of empirical citations are provided for each "fact." Thus, this fact sheet does not provide a comprehensive list of the references for each "fact." The citations were intentionally identified to include recent references, representation across disabilities when possible, and studies using rigorous methods.

ENDNOTES

1. U.S. Department of Education. (2014). *2012 IDEA part B child count and educational environment.* Retrieved from https://explore.data.gov/Education/2012-IDEA-Part-B-Child-Count-and-Educational-Envir/5t72-4535

---

* These facts are based on principles guiding the field of early childhood special education, recommended practices, and our collective knowledge and experiences.

From Barton, E.E., and Smith, B.J. (2014). *Fact sheet of research on preschool inclusion.* Denver, CO: Pyramid Plus: The Colorado Center for Social Emotional Competence and Inclusion. Retrieved from http://www.pyramidplus.org/sites/default/files/images/Inclusion%20Fact%20Sheet%202014.pdf

2. U.S. Department of Education. (1987). Annual report to congress on the implementation of the Education of theHandicapped Act.US Department of Education, Washington, D.C.

3. Buysse, V., Goldman, B.D., & Skinner, M.L. (2002). Setting effects on friendship formation among young children with and without disabilities. *Exceptional Children, 68,* 503–517.

4. Cross, A.F., Traub, E.K., Hutter-Pishgahi, L., & Shelton, G. (2004). Elements for successful inclusion for children with significant disabilities. *Topics in Early Childhood Special Education, 24,* 169–183.

5. Holahan, A., & Costenbader, V. (2000). A comparison of developmental gains for preschool children with disabilities in inclusive and self-contained classrooms. *Topics in Early Childhood Special Education, 20,* 224-235.

6. Odom, S.L., Zercher, C., Li, S., Marquart, J., Sandall, S., & Brown, W. (2006). Social acceptance and social rejection of young children with disabilities in inclusive classes. *Journal of Educational Psychology, 98,* 807–823.

7. Strain, P., & Hoyson, M. (2000). The need for longitudinal, intensive social skill intervention: LEAP follow-up outcomes for children with autism. *Topics in Early Childhood Special Education, 20,* 116–122.

8. Buysse, V., Wesley, P.W., Bryant, D., & Gardner, D. (1999). Quality of early childhood programs in inclusive and noninclusive settings. *Exceptional Children, 65,* 301–314.

9. Soukakou, E.P. (2012). Measuring the quality of inclusive preschool classrooms: Development and validation of the Inclusive Classroom Profile. *Early Childhood Research Quarterly, 27,* 478–488.

10. Division for Early Childhood. (2014). *DEC Recommended Practices in early intervention/ early childhood special education.* Retrieved from http://www.dec-sped.org/recommended practices

11. Odom, S.L., DeKlyen, M., & Jenkins, J.R. (1984). Integrating handicapped and nonhandicapped preschool children: Developmental impact on the nonhandicapped children. *Exceptional Children, 51,* 41–48.

12. Rafferty, Y., Piscitelli, V., & Boettcher, C. (2003). The impact of inclusion on language development and social competence among preschoolers with disabilities. *Exceptional Children, 69,* 467–479.

13. Strain, P., & Bovey, E. (2011). Randomized, controlled trials of the LEAP model of early intervention for young children with Autism Spectrum Disorders. *Topics in Early Childhood Special Education, 31,* 133–154.

14. Diamond, K.E., & Huang, H. (2005). Preschoolers ideas about disabilities. *Infants and Young Children, 18,* 37–46.

15. Innes, F., & Diamond, K.E. (1999). Typically developing children's interactions with peers with disabilities: Relationships between mothers' comments and children's ideas about disabilities. *Topics in Early Childhood Special Education, 19,* 103–111.

16. Okagaki, L., Diamond, K., Kontos, S., & Hestenes, L. (1998). Correlates of young children's interactions with classmates with disabilities. *Early Childhood Research Quarterly, 13,* 67–86.

17. Daugherty, S., Grisham-Brown, J., & Hemmeter, M. L. (2001). The effects of embedded skill instruction on the acquisition of target and nontarget skills in preschoolers with developmental delays. *Topics in Early Childhood Special Education, 21,* 213–221.

18. Grisham-Brown, J., Schuster, J.W., Hemmeter, M.L, & Collins, B.C. (2000). Using an embedding strategy to teach preschoolers with significant disabilities. *Journal of Behavioral Education, 10,* 139–162.

19. Grisham-Brown, J.L., Pretti-Frontczak, K., Hawkins, S., & Winchell, B. (2009). Addressing early learning standards for all children within blended preschool classrooms. *Topics in Early Childhood Special Education, 29,* 131–142.

20. Robertson, J., Green, K., Alper, S., Schloss, P. J., & Kohler, F. (2003). Using peer-mediated intervention to facilitate children's participation in inclusive child care activities. *Education & Treatment of Children, 26,* 182–197.

21. Venn, M. L., Wolery, M., Werts, M.G., Morris, A., DeCesare, L.D., & Cuffs, M.S. (1993). Embedding instruction in art activities to teach preschoolers with disabilities to imitate their peers. *Early Childhood Research Quarterly, 8,* 277–294.

22. Kasari, C., Freeman, S.F.N., Bauminger, N., & Alkin, M.C. (1999). Parental perspectives on inclusion: Effects of autism and down syndrome. *Journal of Autism and Developmental Disorders, 29,* 297–305.

23. Rafferty, Y., & Griffin, K.W. (2005). Benefits and risks of reverse inclusion for preschoolers with and without disabilities: Perspectives of parents and providers. *Journal of Early Intervention, 27,* 173–192.

24. Odom, S.L., Hanson, M.J., Lieber, J., Marquart, J., Sandall, S., Wolery, R., . . . Chambers, J. (2001). The costs of preschool inclusion. *Topics in Early Childhood Special Education, 21*, 46-55.
25. Odom, S.L., Parrish, T., & Hikido, C. (2001). The costs of inclusion and noninclusive special education preschool programs. *Journal of Special Education Leadership, 14*, 33–41.
26. Division for Early Childhood. (2014). *DEC Recommended Practices in early intervention/ early childhood special education.* Retrieved from http://www.dec-sped.org/recommended practices
27. DEC/NAEYC. (2009). *Early childhood inclusion: A joint position statement of the Division for Early Childhood (DEC) and the National Association for the Education of Young Children (NAEYC).* Chapel Hill: University of North Carolina, FPG Child Development Institute.

ADDITIONAL REFERENCES

Buysse, V. (2011). Access, participation, and supports: The defining features of high-quality inclusion. *Zero to Three, 31*(4), 24–29.
Buysse, V., & Hollingsworth, H.L. (2009). Research synthesis points on early childhood inclusion: What every practitioner and all families should know. *Young Exceptional Children, 11*, 18–30.
Lieber, J., Hanson, M.J., Beckman, P. J., Odom, S.L., Sandall, S.R., Schwartz, I.S., . . . Wolery, R. (2000). Key influences on the initiation and implementation of inclusive preschool programs. *Exceptional Children, 67*, 83–98.
National Professional Development Center on Inclusion. (2009). *Research synthesis points on early childhood inclusion.* Chapel Hill, NC: University of North Carolina, FPG Child Development Institute, Author. Retrieved from http://community.fpg.unc.edu/resources/articles/NDPCI-ResearchSynthesis-9-2007.pdf/view
Odom, S.L. (2000). Preschool inclusion: What we know and where we go from here. *Topics in Early Childhood Special Education, 20*(1), 20–27.
Odom, S.L., & Bailey, D.B. (2001). Inclusive preschool programs: Classroom ecology and child outcomes. In M. Guralnick (Ed.), *Focus on change* (pp. 253–276). Baltimore, MD: Paul H. Brookes Publishing Co.
Odom, S.L., Vitztum, J., Wolery, R., Lieber, J., Sandall, S., Hanson, M.J., . . . Horn, E. (2004). Preschool inclusion in the United States: A review of research from an ecological systems perspective. *Journal of Research in Special Educational Needs, 4*, 17–49.
Odom, S.L., Buysse, V., & Soukakou, E. (2011). Inclusion for young children with disabilities: A quarter century of research perspectives. *Journal of Early Intervention, 33*, 344–357.
Purcell, M.L., Horn, E., & Palmer, S. (2007). A qualitative study of initiation and continuation of preschool inclusion. *Exceptional Children, 74*, 85–99.
Sandall, S., Hemmeter, M.L., Smith, B.J., & McLean, M.E. (Eds.). (2005). *DEC Recommended Practices: A comprehensive guide for practical application in early intervention/early childhood special education.* Missoula, MT: Division for Early Childhood.

SUGGESTED REFERENCE

Barton, E.E. & Smith, B.J. (2014). *Brief fact sheet of research on preschool inclusion.* Denver, CO: Pyramid Plus: The Colorado Center for Social Emotional Competence and Inclusion. http://www.pyramidplus.org/

ABOUT THE AUTHORS

Erin E. Barton, Ph.D., is an Assistant Professor, Department of Special Education, Vanderbilt University.

Barbara J. Smith, Ph.D., is a Research Professor, School of Education and Human Development, University of Colorado Denver.

II

Evidence-Based Practices
that Support Preschool Inclusion

4

Administrative Support

Effective Professional Development
for High-Quality Preschool Inclusion

Elizabeth A. Steed and Barbara J. Smith

TOOLS FROM THE TOOLBOX

- **Box 4.1** Professional Development Strategies to Support Comprehensive Preschool Inclusion
- **Figure 4.1** Framework for Effective Professional Development Practices for Inclusion
- **Figure 4.2** Practice-Based Coaching Framework
- **Figure 4.3** Example E-Mail
- **Figure 4.4** Example of a Fidelity Checklist for Coaching
- **Form 4.1** Coaching Performance-Based Feedback Form for Preschool Inclusion
- **Form 4.2** Coaching Performance-Based Feedback Form for Preschool Inclusion (Completed Example)
- **Table 4.1** Key Components that Support Evidence-Based Practices
- **Table 4.2** Effectiveness of Training Components on Teachers' Knowledge, Skill Level, and Use in Classroom

---

Nationally, many of the challenges to preschool inclusion and likely causes of the lack of progress involve the lack of knowledge and skills as well as confidence to serve young children with disabilities effectively. Many solutions involve administrative supports that increase the use of EBPs through PD. In this chapter, PD is discussed in the context of implementation science. Implementation science and its role in establishing high-quality inclusion programs are explained, as well as effective PD practices and tools for high-quality inclusive programs. This chapter can be used to plan PD activities to improve preschool inclusion using an implementation science framework. The PD approach described includes the following key components: workshops for the delivery of core content, opportunities to observe and practice skills, and ongoing coaching including feedback. Tools for the preschool inclusion team are provided for planning effective and sustainable PD that supports high-quality preschool inclusion.

WHAT IS IMPLEMENTATION SCIENCE?

Improving preschool inclusion requires consideration of various systems-level administrative supports that will affect how successful inclusion is. These supports include having such things as data-based methods to collect and evaluate important outcomes, adequate resources, policies to support high-quality inclusion, and a well-trained work force that can implement recommended practices (Odom, 2009b). Fixsen and colleagues (2005) argue that the variables affecting implementation are as important to consider as the intervention itself. In other words, it is important to consider how ready the system is to support children, families, and professionals before carrying out high-quality preschool inclusion or making changes to current inclusion practices.

Implementation science is the study of how scientific knowledge, principles, and practices are used (or not used) in the real world (Fixsen et al., 2005). It is a relatively new field that studies the contextual factors that affect people's ability to use recommended practices (Metz, Halle, Bartley, & Blasberg, 2013). Implementation science was developed as a result of many years of observing the gap between research and practice across a variety of fields, including medicine, mental health, and education (Metz et al., 2013). IDEA specifically calls for EBPs to be used to guide practice for all children with IEPs, including those receiving their IEP services in inclusive classrooms. EBPs are practices that have empirical support and, when implemented effectively, produce positive outcomes for children and families; the use of EBPs increases the probability of improved outcomes for children (Buysse & Wesley, 2006). Yet EBPs are not widely used in EC programs (McLean, Snyder, Smith, & Sandall, 2002; Odom, 2009b). To have policies that mandate the use of effective practices, it is important to understand what is needed for practitioners to implement those practices and achieve positive outcomes.

Implementation science research has uncovered the common factors related to successful use of EBPs. This research has found that interventions are most effective when 1) professionals receive training that includes coaching and frequent performance-based feedback; 2) organizations provide administrative support and infrastructure for ongoing coaching; 3) communities and consumers are fully involved in choosing specific programs and practices; and 4) federal and local policies, funding streams, and regulations create an environment that supports implementation (Fixsen et al., 2005). Further, research has identified several core implementation components of effective programs, including 1) selection of practitioners who have knowledge of the field and other particular competencies that allow for them to implement the program or practice; 2) preservice and in-service training to learn background information and the elements of the program or practice, practice new skills, and receive feedback; 3) consultation and coaching to refine use of the intervention and clinical judgment; 4) ongoing evaluation through the consultation and coaching process to ensure that the program or practice is being used correctly and consistently; and 5) administrative supports in the form of data for decision making, organization of staff, and financial support (Fixsen et al., 2005).

Implementation science research specific to EC has confirmed that PD systems are most effective when they include 1) technical assistance to help state officials, service systems, and practitioners learn EBPs and implementation methods;

2) policies to support the use of EBPs and effective implementation practices; and 3) infrastructure, including data-based decision making and on-site and ongoing coaching and follow-up (Odom, 2009b). Table 4.1 describes these components of implementation science and provides examples for preschool inclusion.

IMPORTANCE OF COACHING

Preschool inclusion teams building inclusive service systems will need to understand how Recommended Practices (DEC, 2014) relate to inclusion. They will also need to know how to set up effective administrative supports for professional development that increase the competence and confidence of personnel to work in inclusive settings. Effective PD includes ongoing coaching and performance-based feedback (Fixsen, Blase, Duda, Naoom, & Van Dyke, 2010b; Snyder, Hemmeter, & McLaughlin, 2011). Administrative support in the form of data, organization, and financial resources also is important to allow for ongoing consultation and coaching (Fixsen et al., 2005). Historically, EC systems of service delivery have relied on EC teachers' preservice training to teach them to use EBPs (Bruder & Stayton, 2006). However, research has shown the inadequacy of preservice training and traditional large-group training on teachers' use of recommended practices in their classrooms (Kontos, Howes, & Galinsky, 1996). Specifically, Joyce and Showers (2002) found that 0% of teachers will use a practice in their classrooms following training in the theory and discussion of the practice, with or without demonstration of the practice (see Table 4.2). If teachers practice and receive feedback related to their use of the practice, 5% of them will use the practice in their classrooms. However, 95% of teachers will use the practice in their classroom if they receive ongoing coaching based on their use of the practice (Joyce & Showers, 2002).

A recent meta-analysis on the effects of training and coaching demonstrates the importance of coaching as part of an effective system of PD (Joyce & Showers, 2002).

Table 4.1. Key components that support evidence-based practices

Component	Description	Examples in preschool inclusion
Training and technical assistance	Practitioners receive training that includes workshops *and* coaching and performance-based feedback in order to use evidence-based practices effectively in their classrooms.	Pyramid Plus (http://www.pyramidplus.org/) provides training in inclusion to practitioners in Colorado preschool classrooms with on-site coaching and performance-based feedback.
Organizational infrastructure	Administrators must put in place concrete time and resources to support on-site coaching and use of data-based decision making.	Preschool administrators provide substitute teachers to allow classroom teachers to participate in coaching sessions, add planning time in the afternoon, and invest in software and technical support for a system for tracking and monitoring data.
Choice and local control	Communities and consumers are fully involved in choosing specific programs and practices.	Preschool teachers, administrators, and the families of young children have a voice in the specific inclusion practices chosen.
Policies, funding streams, and regulations	Policies (local and otherwise), funding, and regulations support implementation.	Various local policies might support preschool inclusion efforts. For example, districts might have a policy that states that a child's neighborhood school must be considered first when deciding placement. Funding procedures need to support inclusion by combining funding streams such as Title I, special education, and pre-K funding to support inclusive classrooms.

Table 4.2. Effectiveness of training components on teachers' knowledge, skill level, and use in classroom

Training components	Knowledge (%)	Skill level (%)	Use in classroom (%)
Theory and discussion	10	5	0
w/ Demonstration in training	30	20	0
w/ Practice and feedback in training	60	60	5
w/ Coaching in classroom	95	95	95

Republished by permission of the Association for Supervision and Curriculum Development from Joyce, B.R., and Showers, B. (2002). *Student achievement through staff development* (3rd ed., p. 78). Alexandria, VA: Association for Supervision and Curriculum Development; permission conveyed through Copyright Clearance Center, Inc.

Subsequent research on practitioners' self-reports of PD has confirmed that preschool teachers learn more from on-site coaching when compared with workshop training alone (Dunst & Raab, 2010). In contrast to the workshop-only method of PD, implementation science advises that PD should include opportunities to observe effective practices and to use those new skills with feedback from a coach or supervisor.

APPLICATION QUESTION

What PD system currently exists in your program or district? How might you use this system to meet your preschool inclusion needs? How might you adapt it to better support preschool inclusion? How might you lead discussions regarding the PD system?

WHAT ARE EFFECTIVE PROFESSIONAL DEVELOPMENT PRACTICES?

Research across disciplines has found that there are several effective PD practices that are connected to practitioners' use of skills in their work (Fixsen et al., 2005). Figure 4.1 describes a framework with the key elements and timing of effective PD practices for inclusion. First, practitioners should learn content about the history, laws, beliefs, attitudes, and research about inclusion. Next, they should have opportunities to see and practice skills associated with high-quality preschool inclusion (e.g., blended instruction). Ongoing coaching with performance-based feedback should then be provided to refine skills and build and maintain the use of those skills.

Workshop Training

First, PD to support inclusion should teach practitioners about the history, theory, philosophy, and rationale for inclusion, which can be accomplished using lecture and discussion formats. This portion of the PD would include information about the history of inclusion (and exclusion) of children with disabilities, the national laws and policies that underlie inclusion (e.g., ADA, IDEA), position statements regarding inclusion (DEC/NAEYC, 2009), beliefs and attitudes about disability and inclusion, and the research that supports high-quality preschool inclusion for children with and without disabilities (Barton & Smith, 2014a; Wolery & Odom, 2000). Many of the fact sheets and handouts included in this toolbox could be used for this type of training. Additional trainings should specifically cover targeted skills (e.g., peer interventions, embedding instruction) for teachers and related services staff. Workshops might suggest that practitioners, administrators, and preschool inclusion teams attend together as a team. Some helpful resources for workshop training materials on inclusion are included in the Resources.

Workshop training with lecture and discussion about the
history, laws, beliefs and attitudes, and research about inclusion

Workshop training with live or video demonstrations and
opportunities to practice skills associated with successful inclusion

Ongoing coaching to practice and hone skills in the preschool classroom

Performance-based feedback

Figure 4.1.   Framework for effective professional development practices for inclusion.

The next important component of the workshop training involves the opportunity to see and practice skills needed to carry out the recommended practices (DEC, 2014). For program administrators, this might involve seeing examples of other preschool program policies regarding inclusion and videos of administrators talking about the processes they use to include young children and families. It should also allow for opportunities to practice visioning for the program and setting goals related to preschool inclusion at their particular site. Practitioners, on the other hand, should view examples of teaching practices associated with high-quality preschool inclusion (e.g., use of assistive technology, adaptations, embedded instruction, peer interventions), ideally through observation or videos. Opportunities to practice the strategies through role play are helpful as well as guided discussion, reflection, and planning (completing an embedding schedule) about how the practitioners will use these strategies in their classrooms.

Coaching

Following exposure to workshop training with opportunities to see targeted practices, practitioners need coaching in their programs/classrooms. This coaching should be frequent, ongoing, reflective, and emotionally supportive, and it should involve assessment and feedback (Spouse, 2001). Coaching allows practitioners to receive intensive, differentiated support to raise their instructional practices to the highest possible level of fidelity (Knight, 2007). A coach may also help problem-solve with the preschool inclusion team when challenges arise as well as deal with the reactions of children and families that will likely have questions and concerns about the change in the program (Joyce & Showers, 2002).

A coach serves several roles: teacher, emotional supporter, and problem-solver. Central to effective coaching practices is relationship-building so that the teacher will trust the coach, listen to him or her, and use him or her as a resource (Rush & Sheldon, 2011). Following initial coaching sessions that build rapport between the coach and teacher, the coach conducts observations and provides feedback that encourages reflection and focuses on positive aspects of the teacher's classroom and teaching strategies (Fox, Hemmeter, & Snyder, 2013). The coach continues to build rapport with the teacher to strengthen their relationship and provide more concrete feedback to develop the teacher's skills over time. Initial and ongoing goal setting is important to guide the focus of coaching visits. This process of developing shared goals, focused observation, and reflection and feedback through collaborative coaching partnerships is called "practice-based coaching" (Fox et al., 2013). Figure 4.2 illustrates the practice-based coaching process.

Practice-based coaching is a cyclical process for supporting practitioners' use of practices that lead to positive outcomes for children (Fox et al., 2013). The practices involved in coaching are made specific and explicit for coaches and the practitioners they work with. The individualized process begins with needs assessment, goal setting, and action planning. Focused observations are conducted of the practitioner implementing targeted skills. During the observation, the coach unobtrusively watches the practitioner and, when agreed upon, models new skills, helps problem-solve in challenging situations, or provides support (e.g., side-by-side gestural or verbal guidance) to modify or change the practitioner's approach. The coach makes notes throughout the observation. Videotaping the focused observation is recommended so that the coach or practitioner can review the session later. Following the observation, structured, individualized, reflective, supportive, and constructive feedback is provided (Fox et al., 2013).

Practice-Based Coaching

Figure 4.2. Practice-based coaching framework. From the National Center on Quality Teaching and Learning. (n.d.). *Practice-based coaching.* Washington, DC: U.S. Department of Health and Human Services, Administration for Children and Families, Office of Head Start; reprinted by permission. Retrieved from http://eclkc.ohs.acf.hhs.gov/hslc/tta-system/teaching/docs/practice-based-coaching.pdf

Performance-Based Feedback

Central to the practice-based coaching framework is the use of ongoing performance-based feedback (Fox, Hemmeter, Snyder, Binder, & Clarke, 2011). Performance-based feedback is meant to reinforce and expand on the skills that the teacher learned in training and throughout coaching so that he or she is more competent and confident implementing the new practices (Metz et al., 2013). This is done through verbal and/or written feedback provided immediately following observation of the use of a specific skill. Coaches may observe in person or use video recordings that can be rewound repeatedly or edited for precise and specific feedback. Performance-based feedback may be delivered in person, by e-mail, or via comments attached to digital videos. If using e-mail, it will be important to consider the tone of the e-mail and that each interaction is an opportunity to foster the relationship between the coach and the practitioner (Barton, Pribble, & Chen, 2013; Hemmeter et al., 2011). In fact, the research on using e-mail to deliver performance-based feedback suggests that e-mail should include specific components: 1) a positive opening greeting, 2) data- or performance-based feedback, 3) corrective feedback if needed, 4) a question that prompts a reply to increase your confidence that the practitioner read the e-mail, and 5) a positive closing statement (Hemmeter et al., 2011; see Figure 4.3 for an example of an e-mail with all five components).

Regardless of the feedback mode (in person, e-mail, or video), a feedback form is often used that outlines the skills involved in using the practice and a rating for each of these areas. Forms 4.1 and 4.2 are examples of blank and completed performance-based feedback forms that can be completed by the coach related to inclusion (adapted from Oregon Early Childhood Inclusion Collaborative, 2014).

Tip for Success!

Performance-based feedback might be the most powerful component of coaching! It can be as simple as sending an e-mail or text to the teacher describing exactly what he or she did well.

Following the coach's observation and rating, the coach and practitioner need time to go over the feedback and allow the practitioner to reflect on what went well and what he or she would do differently next time. When considering what kind of approach to use for the feedback system, the coach should consider that the form will need to be as simple as possible. Further, the system for feedback delivery and reflection will need to be timely and work within the coach's and teacher's schedules. It is important that the feedback system is easy to implement so that it is feasible and will be used long term (see Barton, Kinder, Casey, & Artman, 2011, for additional considerations when designing a performance-based feedback system). The feedback form and process should also focus on positive recognition of what the teacher is doing well so that it is an opportunity to improve performance (Metz et al., 2013).

FEASIBILITY

One critical issue with adding coaching and other evidence-based PD (e.g., performance-based feedback) approaches to preschool programs' training model is the significant time and resources required. Both workshop trainings and on-site coaching require spending money for the training itself (e.g., speaker fees, room reservation, travel, food) as well as the cost of lost instructional time (e.g., substitutes for teachers who are out of the classroom) and opening the school for in-service days.

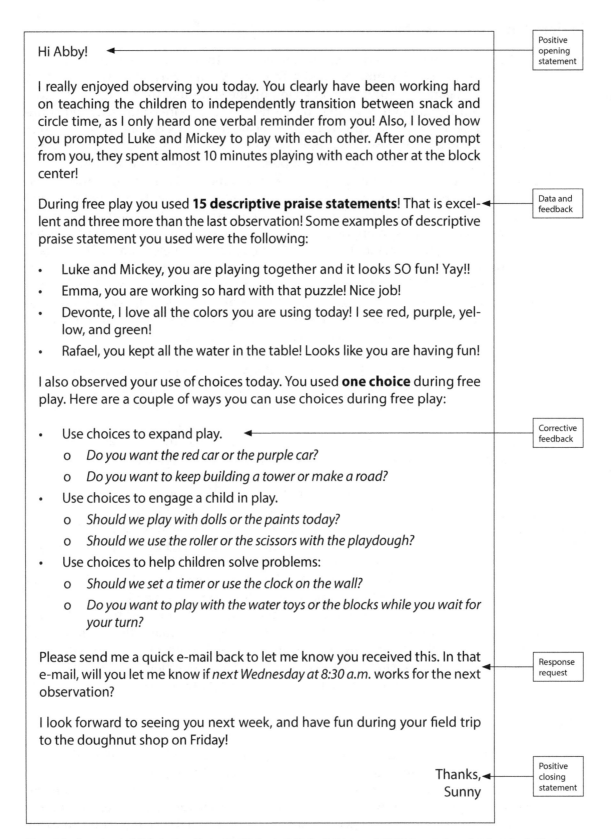

Hi Abby!   Positive opening statement

I really enjoyed observing you today. You clearly have been working hard on teaching the children to independently transition between snack and circle time, as I only heard one verbal reminder from you! Also, I loved how you prompted Luke and Mickey to play with each other. After one prompt from you, they spent almost 10 minutes playing with each other at the block center!

During free play you used **15 descriptive praise statements**! That is excel-   Data and feedback
lent and three more than the last observation! Some examples of descriptive praise statement you used were the following:

- Luke and Mickey, you are playing together and it looks SO fun! Yay!!
- Emma, you are working so hard with that puzzle! Nice job!
- Devonte, I love all the colors you are using today! I see red, purple, yellow, and green!
- Rafael, you kept all the water in the table! Looks like you are having fun!

I also observed your use of choices today. You used **one choice** during free play. Here are a couple of ways you can use choices during free play:

- Use choices to expand play.   Corrective feedback
    o *Do you want the red car or the purple car?*
    o *Do you want to keep building a tower or make a road?*
- Use choices to engage a child in play.
    o *Should we play with dolls or the paints today?*
    o *Should we use the roller or the scissors with the playdough?*
- Use choices to help children solve problems:
    o *Should we set a timer or use the clock on the wall?*
    o *Do you want to play with the water toys or the blocks while you wait for your turn?*

Please send me a quick e-mail back to let me know you received this. In that   Response request
e-mail, will you let me know if *next Wednesday at 8:30 a.m.* works for the next observation?

I look forward to seeing you next week, and have fun during your field trip to the doughnut shop on Friday!

                                                                Thanks,   Positive closing statement
                                                                Sunny

Figure 4.3.   Example e-mail. (Adapted from Hemmeter, M.L., Snyder, P., Kinder, K., & Artman, K. [2011]. Impact of e-mail performance feedback on preschool teachers' use of descriptive praise. *Early Childhood Research Quarterly, 26,* 96–109. Copyright 2011 with permission from Elsevier.)

Coaching Performance-Based Feedback Form for Preschool Inclusion

Child: _____   Date: _____

Program: _____   Time: _____ Session: _____

Coach: _____   Practitioner: _____

Goals:

Coach Observation Notes:

Coach Reflections (strengths, accomplishments since last visit):

Practitioner Reflections (strengths, accomplishments since last visit):

Specific Recommendations

Adaptations	Engagement with Peers	Embedded Instruction

Next Visit

Action	Who Is Responsible

From Oregon Early Childhood Inclusion Collaborative. (2014). *Consultation visit summary (adapted).* Monmouth: Center on Early Learning,
The Teaching Research Institute at Western Oregon University; adapted by permission. Retrieved from http://www.centeroninclusion.org/formC2.pdf
In *The Preschool Inclusion Toolbox: How to Build and Lead a High-Quality Program* by Erin E. Barton and Barbara J. Smith (2015, Paul H. Brookes Publishing Co.)

Coaching Performance-Based Feedback Form for Preschool Inclusion (Completed Example)

Child: Saanvi   Date: 10/04/14

Program: Buckhead Early Learning Center   Time: 9:30 a.m.   Session: 4

Coach: Mariana   Practitioner: Jamal

Goals: 1) Embed Saanvi's social goals across classroom routines, 2) increase peer interaction through peer training, 3) and use environmental arrangement and particular materials and activities to encourage peer interaction.

Coach Observation Notes:

Observed free play and snack. 1) Provided side-by-side verbal support to help Jamal embed Saanvi's social goal (share play materials) while at the train table with two peers. It was apparent that Jamal has provided one of the peers (AJ) with some peer training, as he was adept at providing simple verbal ("my turn") and physical cues (tap shoulder, hand out) that facilitated Saanvi sharing. She said "wow" and an approximation of "my turn," and put her hand out (instead of grabbing) for a train! 2) Observed snack. Saanvi with her snack from home at table with two peers and Karli (assistant teacher). Saanvi ate part of an apple and her rice snack quietly. The two peers (boys) at her table talked about being "warriors," then ate, made noises at each other, laughed, and threw the rest of their snack away and went to wash their hands. 3) Reviewed graphic performance feedback of Saanvi's use of social skills and language in free play from baseline and first three coaching sessions—wonderful!

Coach Reflections (strengths, accomplishments since last visit):

It's obvious that Jamal has been doing peer intervention with some peers. They are picking up the skills and using them with Saanvi with minimal prompting. Saanvi interacted and shared more than I've seen her ever do!

Practitioner Reflections (strengths, accomplishments since last visit):

Jamal was amazed at Saanvi's social skills during the train activity. It used to be an issue for her to play with the trains. She would want a specific train or want to have most of them in her hands and scream if others tried to take a train that she wanted. It's huge that she's sharing the trains now and that she also made some comments and requests directed at AJ. He has been picking up the peer intervention skills the fastest of the kids in the classroom.

Specific Recommendations

Adaptations	Engagement with Peers	Embedded Instruction
Where might Saanvi sit during snack to increase the likelihood that she'll interact with her peers? Are there particular children that she could sit next to? Can the adult sitting at her table help facilitate conversation or questions to get things started? What would be fun for the kids and Saanvi for a snack time interactive topic?	What are your plans for continuing to work with AJ on his interactions with Saanvi? Are there other children that can help make sure that AJ doesn't "burn out"? What do peers need to know how to do to help Saanvi interact at snack time?	Keep up the great work of embedding Saanvi's social goals during free play. Let's develop an activity planning matrix to ensure embedding of her social goals across all classroom routines (e.g., snack).

Next Visit

Action	Who Is Responsible
Develop activity planning matrix.	Jamal and Mariana
Choose at least one other peer to start peer intervention training.	Jamal
Talk to Karli about how you might make environmental arrangement changes (place cards at snack table) to target Saanvi sitting next to particular children at each snack and planning to do something to encourage interaction.	Jamal

(From Oregon Early Childhood Inclusion Collaborative. [2014]. *Consultation visit summary [adapted]*. Monmouth: Center on Early Learning, The Teaching Research Institute at Western Oregon University; adapted by permission. Retrieved from http://www.centeroninclusion.org/formC2.pdf)

Corcoran (1995) suggests strategies for reducing the fiscal impact of implementing a comprehensive PD approach with workshops and on-site coaching. Box 4.1 provides a list of strategies to support comprehensive preschool inclusion.

FIDELITY

Tip for Success!

The fidelity of your coaching, often referred to as implementation fidelity, is as important to consider as practitioner intervention fidelity. Thus, when evaluating child progress, consider the teacher's intervention fidelity *as well as* the coach's fidelity of effective coaching practices.

Following successful adoption of a PD approach that includes coaching, individuals must monitor the fidelity of its implementation (Fox et al., 2013). Implementation science has taught us that it is necessary to conduct ongoing evaluation throughout the consultation and coaching process to ensure that the coaching is being done correctly and resulting in targeted outcomes (Fixsen et al., 2005). The ongoing use of data collected about the coaching itself is key to making sure that the PD is being used as intended and yielding long-term positive results. One way that this can be accomplished is by completing a checklist about how coaching is being conducted. Figure 4.4 is an example of a fidelity checklist for coaching (Snyder, Hemmeter, & Fox, 2011).

In addition to making sure that coaching is being conducted well, there are checklists available to measure the fidelity of practitioners' use of skills related to preschool inclusion. Some options include the Preschool Assessment of Classroom Environment Scale–Revised (Raab & Dunst, 1997), the Inclusive Classroom Profile (Soukakou, 2010), the Preschool and Kindergarten Inclusion Readiness Checklist (Watson & McCathren, 2009), and the Quality Program Indicators (Strain & Bovey, 2011). These are described in more detail in Chapter 6.

Other administrative supports that should be considered for the long-term success of a PD approach on preschool inclusion include the following:

- A process for collecting data related to PD on preschool inclusion (these data could include fidelity checklists of the coaching process and teachers' use of targeted skills, the number of coaching goals met, and/or practitioner satisfaction with the PD they have received)

 BOX 4.1. Professional development strategies to support comprehensive preschool inclusion (*Source:* Corcoran, 1995.)

- Eliminate costly one-shot workshops that do not result in changes in classroom teaching practices.
- Use permanent substitutes or retirees for times when the primary teachers need to attend workshops or coaching sessions that occur outside of the classroom.
- Make better use of teacher, administrator, and support staff time and abilities.
- Purchase teacher time for participation in workshop training and coaching sessions by giving compensation on the weekends or during the summer.
- Use block scheduling to plan small-group workshop training and coaching during common planning times.
- Alter teachers' or administrators' responsibilities, the teaching schedule, or the school calendar to allow the professional development approach to become an integral part of the program's operations.

1. Opening the Meeting			
1.1. The coach opened the debriefing meeting with a positive social greeting.	Y	N	
1.2. The coach followed up with the teacher about priorities or issues from the previous debriefing session. *(N/A is possible if no priorities/issues were identified.)*	Y	N	N/A
1.3. The coach checked in with the teacher about progress during the previous week related to implementation of embedded instruction goals as specified in the Action Plan.	Y	N	
1.4. The coach checked in with the teacher about progress during the previous week related to his or her personal development goal(s) as specified in the Action Plan.	Y	N	
1.5. The coach reviewed implementation data the teacher collected during the week or the coach collected during observation.	Y	N	
2. Summarizing the Observation and Encouraging Teacher Reflection			
2.1. The coach reviewed his/her observations with the teacher about the teacher's implementation of embedded instruction.	Y	N	
2.2. The coach reviewed his/her observations with the teacher about the teacher's personal development goal(s).	Y	N	
2.3. The coach encouraged the teacher to reflect on his/her implementation of embedded instruction.	Y	N	
3. Supportive Feedback			
3.1. The coach's feedback emphasized positive aspects of teacher's implementation of embedded instruction.	Y	N	
3.2. The coach provided verbal or graphic feedback on the teacher's implementation of embedded instruction learning trials (i.e., CLTs).	Y	N	
3.3. The coach provided feedback about other components of embedded instruction beyond complete learning trials. *(N/A possible.)*	Y	N	N/A
3.4. The coach provided positive feedback on the teacher's progress related to his or her personal development goal(s).	Y	N	
4. Corrective Feedback			
4.1. The coach demonstrated or discussed how to deliver complete and accurate learning trials.	Y	N	
4.2. The coach provided corrective feedback about implementation of embedded instruction.	Y	N	
4.3. The coach provided corrective feedback on personal development goals.	Y	N	
5. Targeted Support			
5.1. The coach helped the teacher update the portion of the Action Plan focused on the implementation of embedded instruction. *(N/A possible if progress is not made, or goals are not achieved.)*	Y	N	N/A
5.2. The coach helped the teacher update the portion of the Action Plan focused on personal development goal(s). *(N/A possible if progress is not made, or goals are not achieved.)*	Y	N	N/A
5.3. If progress on the Action Plan was not made, the coach helped the teacher identify changes needed. *(N/A possible if progress is made or goals achieved.)*	Y	N	N/A
5.4. The coach checked in with the teacher about the target child(ren).	Y	N	
5.5. The coach provided suggestions on individualization of instruction for one or more target children. *(N/A possible due to debriefing process.)*	Y	N	N/A

Figure 4.4. Example of a fidelity checklist for coaching. (*Key:* Communicative Language Teachings.) (From Snyder, P., Hemmeter, M.L., & Fox, L. [2011]. *Coaching to support fidelity of implementation of evidence-based practices in inclusive early childhood settings.* Presentation at the 2011 International Society on Early Intervention Conference, New York, NY; reprinted by permission. Retrieved from http://challengingbehavior.fmhi.usf. edu/do/pyramid_model/research/slides/snyder_coach.pdf)

- A system for inputting, reviewing, and sharing the data related to PD on preschool inclusion with all individuals in the program and a plan for how to use the data to refine the PD approach

- A way to identify and choose priorities for topics to cover in PD for preschool inclusion that address child, family, and practitioner interests and needs and build skills according to the program's long-term vision and goals

- A plan for how PD will be worked into the program calendar and each workday

- A line item in the budget to fund effective PD that includes workshops and coaching as well as a budget item related to incentives for practitioner participation and use of targeted skills

- Additional supports and training for practitioners who are new to the program

- Connections with other programs in the area with similar PD goals to share resources (e.g., space, training materials)

Following, the story of the Maceo family and the school district preschool inclusion team is continued with a focus on how PD is used to foster preschool inclusion.

Case Study: The Maceo Family

Ms. Humphrey is the preschool teacher in the elementary school that Raphael's brother attends. She had indicated to the principal that she would be interested in having preschoolers with disabilities in her classroom if she had the supports she feels she needs to serve them appropriately and support the implementation of their IEPs. She wanted Raphael to be able to come to their school and be in an inclusive classroom, but she had never been trained on how to talk about disability or how to make accommodations, and she wanted to know more about how to support him and his family. The principal invited Ms. Humphey to join the preschool inclusion team. He also arranged for her to attend a weekend-long workshop on including preschoolers with disabilities, which was open to school district and community EC programs provided by the state. The training included activities that helped Ms. Humphrey acknowledge her biases toward individuals with disabilities (e.g., the belief that they are not capable of the same things as other individuals). The workshop provided factual information about inclusion that countered a lot of Ms. Humphrey's unvoiced concerns. She worried that her attention to Raphael might take away from her ability to give the other children what they need. She learned that there was no research to support this concern and that there was much research that showed that Raphael *and his peers* would benefit significantly by being in the same classroom.

Ms. Humphrey also learned strategies to change the way her classroom was arranged and how she structured the day as well as peer intervention strategies that would minimize the impact of Raphael's needs on her time. She learned about the strategies through a PowerPoint presentation, small-group activities, example videos, and case studies. Ms. Humphrey found the mix of ways that the trainer presented information helpful. She learned the content, discussed it with the others at her table, and completed individual and small-group activities that helped her focus specifically on Raphael. She found the real-life video examples very helpful for illustrating content. She was relieved to learn that if her environment was arranged sufficiently, she would not have to provide constant individualized support to Raphael. She planned to incorporate predictable, individualized schedules and routines depending on what he needed and to teach the other children some simple ways to help and play with him. Finally, Ms. Humphrey learned about the DEC's (2014) recommended practices. She focused on one specific recommendation: "Practitioners consider Universal Design for Learning principles to create accessible environments." She left the workshop excited about this new way of looking at how she could implement inclusion in her class.

Prior to school starting, Ms. Humphrey met with Mr. and Ms. Maceo. She learned about all the things Raphael could do, the things he liked and disliked, and the goals they had for him. She also continued as an active member of the school's preschool inclusion team and voiced the supports she felt she would need for this to be a successful year for Raphael, the other children, and herself. These supports included access to a coach that would help her with specific practices related to implementing Raphael's IEP goals as well as support from the related services therapists involved in his IEP. She said that she would like to have those services delivered in her classroom as part of the typical schedule and routines. The preschool inclusion team and the Maceo family agreed to implement these plans with regular monitoring of progress and to revisit them if necessary.

CONCLUSION

This chapter describes EBPs for providing administrative supports to address the frequently cited challenge of a lack of competence and confidence on the part of teachers, administrators, and families to have young children with disabilities placed in regular EC programs for their special education and related services. The PD practices in this chapter reflect what is known in the literature as implementation science—that is, the effective process of ensuring evidence-based education practices are implemented with fidelity. This process involves learning content (e.g., through trainings and workshops), seeing real-life examples and opportunities for practice, and then receiving ongoing coaching and performance-based feedback. Key administrative leadership decisions include how to fund these comprehensive and effective PD opportunities, how to pay for substitutes, and how to institutionalize the policies and procedures to ensure the practices are sustained and supported over time. Finally, effective PD systems use data to determine the content of the coaching, who needs to be coached, and whether the PD events are effective. Preschool inclusion teams could address all these issues and challenges in their action planning to support effective, high-quality preschool inclusion opportunities for all children in the district. A second common solution to address preschool inclusion challenges is for school districts and their preschool inclusion teams to engage in these effective PD activities with their community EC partners, such as child care and Head Start, to ensure that wherever children with disabilities are served, they are receiving evidence-based services (Barton & Smith, 2014b). The PD tools in this chapter can be used to improve the competence and confidence of teachers, related services personnel, administrators, and families to facilitate effective high-quality preschool inclusion.

REFLECTION QUESTIONS

1. How does implementation science relate to preschool inclusion?
2. How might you modify administrative supports to ensure that practitioners receive training in the relevant inclusion content, opportunities to practice, ongoing coaching, and performance-based feedback?

3. How will you prioritize the topics that you will cover in PD related to preschool inclusion? How will you determine these priorities?

4. How will PD be worked into the program calendar and each workday? How will it be funded? What additional supports will be provided for new practitioners? How will your PD be inclusive of everyone working in the program? What incentives will you use for participation? How will practitioners be recognized for participation and use of targeted skills?

5. How might you collaborate with other programs in your area to achieve your PD goals?

6. How will you use data to inform your PD efforts? How often will it be collected, and what will you use for data collection? How will the results be shared with practitioners and families?

7. What web sites, videos, or books related to preschool inclusion will you use in your PD efforts?

5

Evidence-Based Practices for Successful Inclusion

Erin E. Barton, Lois M. Pribble, and Jaclyn D. Joseph

TOOLS FROM THE TOOLBOX

- **Box 5.1** Examples of the Use of Blended Instructional Approaches in Inclusive Settings
- **Figure 5.1** Basic Response to Intervention Model for Early Childhood Education
- **Table 5.1** Examples of the Use of the DEC Recommended Practices in Inclusive Settings
- **Table 5.2** Examples of Modifications and Adaptations
- **Table 5.3** Levels of Assistive Technology
- **Table 5.4** Ways to Differentiate Instruction
- **Table 5.5** Examples of the Use of the Pyramid Model in Inclusive Settings

National surveys have revealed that families, teachers, and administrators are concerned that regular EC programs cannot meet the needs of children with disabilities (Barton & Smith, 2014b; Smith & Rose, 1993). However, research on effective instructional practices for inclusive EC services has resulted in a wealth of EBPs. The national surveys have also provided many solutions to such concerns, mainly centered on effective PD, including training and coaching on EBPs (Barton & Smith, 2014b; Smith & Rose, 1993). As described in Chapter 4, preschool inclusion teams should plan PD services, including training and follow-up coaching, on these effective practices for both general EC staff and their specialized counterparts (e.g., ECSE teachers, related services personnel).

The purpose of this chapter is to provide an overview of effective instructional practices that should be 1) implemented with high fidelity after children are placed in high-quality inclusive environments and 2) used when designing PD opportunities. The framework for the chapter focuses on increasing access, participation, and support for children with disabilities (DEC/NAEYC, 2009). This chapter does not describe all practices in detail but provides a comprehensive overview of evidence-based instructional practices and directs preschool inclusion teams to additional sources of information. Examples of selected practices are provided.

DIVISION FOR EARLY CHILDHOOD RECOMMENDED PRACTICES IN EARLY INTERVENTION/EARLY CHILDHOOD SPECIAL EDUCATION

Throughout the years, EBPs have been developed, researched, and adapted for preschool inclusion. These practices should be used to inform classroom instruction. EBPs in EI/ECSE involve empirical evidence—used as a starting point—clinical expertise, family values, and ongoing data collection. EBPs should be used and adapted as necessary with individual children and families. Adaptations should be informed by ongoing data collection. DEC (2014) recently updated their Recommended Practices in EI/ECSE to provide guidance to practitioners about effective ways to promote the development of young children with or at risk for disabilities. These Recommended Practices were designed, using research (i.e., empirical evidence) as well as the wisdom, knowledge, and experiences of people in the field, to be used by individuals working in a variety of EC settings. They were developed to help translate research into practice and to ensure that children with or at risk for developmental delays or disabilities, their families, and the personnel who support them have access to practices that result in better outcomes. Furthermore, the DEC Recommended Practices were designed to be used along with DAP for all children (Copple & Bredekamp, 2009). The DEC Recommended Practices are divided into eight topic areas:

1. Leadership
2. Assessment
3. Environment
4. Family
5. Instruction
6. Interaction
7. Teaming and collaboration
8. Transition

The DEC Recommended Practices (DEC, 2014) are particularly feasible and useful for those working in inclusive preschool settings, for the following reasons (see specific examples in Table 5.1):

- They represent the most effective and efficient practices related to socially valid outcomes for young children.
- They were designed to be used within a DAP framework and should build on (not be redundant with) NAEYC DAP.
- They are not disability specific and are relevant for all children with disabilities.
- They were developed to be used along with discipline-specific professional standards and codes of ethics. Thus, all practitioners in inclusive preschool settings should use them.
- Their topic areas include practices that are content specific (e.g., assessment, instruction, interaction) and practices that can be used to guide implementation (e.g., leadership, teaming and collaboration, working with families).

Table 5.1. Examples of the use of the Division for Early Childhood (DEC) Recommended Practices in inclusive settings

Topic area	Examples
1. Leadership	• Develop a mission and goals that support inclusion. • Develop policies and procedures that promote collaboration among stakeholders (including families). • Join professional association(s) that support and advocate for inclusion. • Ensure that practitioners know and implement inclusive practices (as outlined by legal, ethical, research, and programmatic support). • Coordinate service delivery for children and their families.
2. Assessment	• Use age-appropriate assessment materials and strategies. • Gather assessment information from as many sources as possible (including other professionals and families). • Engage in ongoing assessment, and revise instruction and/or behavior plans as necessitated by assessment results and child progress in the inclusive environment. • Share assessment results with families.
3. Environment	• Adapt environments to promote access and participation. • Use assistive technology.
4. Family	• Become aware of child and family cultural, linguistic, and socioeconomic diversity, and engage in interactions that are respectful and responsive to such diversity (i.e., learn key phrases and words in the family's home language, and encourage families to invite the individuals they would like to be included in meetings to participate as team members). • Provide information and materials to families about the research and legal foundations of preschool inclusion. • Include families in goal setting and in the development of individualized plans. • Inform families of their rights regarding inclusion in accessible formats, and provide support so that they understand them. • Teach families skills to improve their ability to support their children at home.
5. Instruction	• Use peer-mediated intervention. • Use embedded instruction by planning for and embedding a sufficient number of learning opportunities across a child's day. • In addition to teaching a dual language learner English, provide opportunities that encourage and develop use of his or her home language and that encourage the other children in the classroom to understand and use the child's home language as well.
6. Interaction	• Encourage child interaction with other children by planning and embedding social interactions into routines and activities. • Join in child's play and provide support to expand the play in ways that promote cognitive development (e.g., provide additional play suggestions, encourage varied use of toys). • Plan ways to promote the development of communication skills by promoting the child's ability to label and request naturally occurring needs and preferences.
7. Teaming and collaboration	• Have all professionals working with a child and family plan and implement services together, including general early childhood teachers, early childhood special education teachers, related services personnel, and so forth. • Identify, with families, one team member who will act as the liaison between the family and team and who will regularly communicate with the family to promote their participation as team members. • Meet and communicate (telephone, e-mail, Skype) regularly as a team to ensure that all team members are able to take part in the planning and evaluation of inclusive practices. • Use teaming practices to promote team effectiveness (e.g., development of action plans, use of meeting agenda). • Consider team-member convenience when scheduling meetings, and meet at times and in places that support the participation of all team members.
8. Transition	• Engage in information sharing at all times during the child's transition (before, during, after). • Share information that will promote successful transition to inclusive settings (e.g., recently completed reinforcer assessments, behavior intervention plans). • Provide previously developed supports that have proven to be effective in the current environment and that promote inclusion (e.g., visual supports).

BLENDED INSTRUCTIONAL APPROACHES

Just as the DEC Recommended Practices blend with the NAEYC DAP, specific specialized instructional practices can be blended with intentional teaching for typically developing children. Blended instruction is an approach in which the preschool curriculum is purposefully blended across ability levels to set the stage for teaching all children in inclusive classrooms (Grisham-Brown, Pretti-Frontczak, Hawkins, & Winchell, 2009; Grisham-Brown, Hemmeter, & Pretti-Frontczak, 2005; Pretti-Frontczak, Grisham-Brown, & Sullivan, 2014). Blended approaches ensure that practitioners in inclusive classrooms identify what to teach and how to teach to ensure that all children have access to and participate in the daily routines and activities. Blended approaches involve intentional teaching, which is an integral component of DAP (Copple & Bredekamp, 2009), and embedded instruction, which is an approach to providing planned and systematic instruction during contextually relevant, ongoing activities and routines to support child engagement and learning (Snyder, Hemmeter, McLean, Sandall, & McLaughlin, 2013). Intentional teaching asserts that effective teachers must recognize and respond to all opportunities to engage children's learning as well as purposefully organize the learning environment to create learning opportunities for children (Epstein, 2007, 2014). Embedded instruction is a practice (Wolery, 2005) in which teachers plan for and embed a sufficient number of learning opportunities across the day for those children who need additional and often individualized instructional support (Barton, Bishop, & Snyder, 2014).

Blending these two approaches includes setting the occasion for children's learning (i.e., organizing the learning environment to provide learning opportunities) and ensuring sufficient opportunities to respond. Using a blended instruction approach, the teacher in an inclusive preschool classroom organizes the learning environment and uses systematic prompting and feedback. This systematic prompting and feedback can be organized into complete learning trials (CLTs). A CLT is a three-term contingency that 1) includes a naturally occurring or planned antecedent that 2) occasions a child behavior and 3) is followed by naturally occurring or planned feedback or consequences (VanDerHeyden, Snyder, Smith, Sevin, & Longwell, 2005). CLTs are effective when teachers intentionally plan prompts and feedback in relation to an individual's or a group of individuals' learning targets, history, and context. In blended instruction, it is essential for teachers to embed a sufficient number of meaningful and effective CLTs (Barton et al., 2014). Although capitalizing on teachable moments or child-initiated learning opportunities is important, young children with disabilities might not create a sufficient number of teachable moments to ensure learning (Carta, Schwartz, Atwater, & McConnell, 1991).

Thus, effective teachers in inclusive classrooms use blended instruction to systematically and intentionally provide multiple, meaningful instructional opportunities for each child. As with all EBPs, data-based decision making is an integral aspect of blended instruction. Practitioners should collect ongoing data regarding the learning targets and the implementation of blended instruction. (For additional articles, see Barton et al., 2014.) Box 5.1 offers some examples of the use of blended instructional approaches in inclusive settings.

Tip for Success!

Keep it simple! Create a data collection system that is simple and easy to use. Data collection systems that are complicated are unlikely to be used over time. Data need to be easy to quickly summarize to provide meaningful information regarding child progress. See the Resources for support in designing and using data collection systems.

BOX 5.1. Examples of the use of blended instructional approaches in inclusive settings

- Structure small- and large-group activities to promote independence by developing visual supports for play and/or activity sequences.
- Develop routines within routines that regularly occur throughout the day and during which instructional opportunities are provided.
- Train peers as peer mediators to increase the number of learning opportunities provided to children throughout the day.
- Set up dramatic play areas with themes that promote particular roles and scripts that children can be taught and then practice over time to improve their skill repertoires. (Instructional support will most likely be needed when a new theme is introduced; however, it can be reduced as the child demonstrates more independent success with increased practice.)
- Use activities that would naturally occur to practice new skills, such as requesting a snack during snack time or greeting peers during morning routine.
- Use supports to preplan learning opportunities (e.g., activity matrix), and collect data on both progress and the implementation of blended instruction in order to make decisions to promote a child's independent participation and learning.
- Plan for and regularly use specific, effective teaching strategies (e.g., prompting, modeling, reinforcement) to teach learning objectives.
- Teach skills multiple times during a number of activities completed throughout the day.
- Consider child preferences, and plan learning opportunities around items and activities that are preferred by the child.

ACCOMMODATIONS AND MODIFICATIONS

Another important way to ensure high-quality inclusive learning environments is to provide accommodations and modifications to the typical activities and curriculum. Accommodations and modifications are simple adjustments teachers make to the classroom environment and materials to facilitate preschool inclusion and ensure all children are engaged and participating in inclusive placements (Hunt, Soto, Maier, Liboiron, & Bae, 2004; Sandall, 2003). Teachers can create appropriate accommodations and modifications by first getting to know children, finding out their strengths and interests, and observing their interactions in the classroom. Observations allow teachers to figure out where barriers to access exist and create appropriate accommodations and modifications to reduce those barriers.

Example of Accommodations and Modifications in an Inclusive Classroom

David is a new student who is going to start in Elena's classroom. Through meeting and talking with his parents, Elena finds out David has some receptive and expressive language delays and does best when provided with visual cues and short instructions. Before David begins to attend her classroom, Elena meets with the preschool inclusion team to discuss ways she can support him. She already has visuals to label different parts of the classroom and uses a large visual schedule with the children. When David starts attending the class, the school district provides a coach to help Elena to plan and implement embedded instruction with David and his peers. One of the strategies they decide on is to have Elena seat him close to her during circle time and snack time so she can monitor his understanding. She makes sure to give him short instructions during activities and provide him with a longer time to respond to questions. Elena notices that David often has a difficult time initiating interactions with peers. She decides to include "peer buddy" activities during center times so he gets more opportunities to interact with peers one to one. In peer buddy systems, the teacher intentionally pairs up children who have more advanced social skills with children with disabilities who are learning social skills. The pairs are specifically created based on each child's individual strengths and interests, thus fostering friendships over time. Peers are carefully and systematically taught to have positive and extended social interactions in both teacher-directed and child-initiated activities through daily routines. Elena also joins pretend play activities during free play and invites David and George, his peer buddy, over to play, modeling how to join in and expand on play with peers. Elena's coach works with her to collect data on these strategies to monitor effectiveness and progress.

The use of accommodations and modifications is a way for inclusive classrooms to provide a continuum of support for children. Some types of support may lead to long-term changes in the classroom (e.g., making classroom walkways wider so children who use walkers or wheelchairs have access to all areas), whereas other types of support can be faded over time. For example, a child who has a difficult time participating in circle time may benefit from an individual visual schedule of circle time activities. An adult sitting next to the child can prompt him or her to look at the schedule to see what comes next (e.g., "Now it's time to sing the welcome song"). Once the child has gotten to know the circle time routine and has started to successfully participate, the visual schedule can be faded until the child is able to participate independently.

Sandall and Schwartz (2008) identify eight different types of modifications and adaptations that can be used to ensure all children have the appropriate support needed to fully participate in inclusive preschools. Table 5.2 defines each adaptation/modification and provides examples of how they can be used within EC settings.

Assistive Technology

Assistive technology is another effective way to support preschool inclusion. Assistive technology refers to the use of technology tools to help children gain access to, and function more independently within, classroom activities and routines. Assistive technology tools can be used to help young children perform adaptive skills, maneuver the classroom, and communicate and socialize with their peers (Ostensjo, Carlberg, & Vollestad, 2005; Ragonesi, Chen, Agrawal, & Galloway, 2010; Trembath, Balandin, Togher, & Stancliffe, 2009). Assistive technologies include a range of materials that vary in complexity and expense, from simple teacher-made tools such as communication boards to high-tech augmentative communication tablets (Campbell, Milbourne, Dugan, & Wilcox, 2006).

Table 5.2. Examples of modifications and adaptations

Type	Examples
Environmental support Changes made to the physical, social, or temporal environments in a classroom	*Physical* • Cover toy shelves with fabric to signal the area is closed. • Use carpet squares for children to sit on during circle time. • Widen walkways so a child with a wheelchair or walker can move around. • Tape pictures onto shelves/bins so children know where to obtain and return toys and materials. *Social* • Create partner activities so that children are encouraged to work together. • During free play and outside time, set out materials that require peer participation (e.g., riding wagon). *Temporal* • Balance the class schedule with quiet and active times. • Provide a picture schedule so children learn the class routine. • Use a first/then board to help a child understand classroom expectations.
Materials adaptation Alteration of classroom materials (e.g., writing supplies) so that a child is able to use them more independently	• Adapt toys so they can be activated by switches. • Use a tabletop easel (instead of standing easel) for a child who needs seated support. • Provide larger, brighter, or high-contrast materials for children with visual impairments. • Use Velcro or nonslip material (e.g., Dycem) to stabilize toys so children with motor limitations can obtain them more easily.
Activity simplification Breaking an activity down into smaller parts or reducing the number of steps so it is easier for a child to complete	• Post visual process charts for multiple-step routines (e.g., hand washing, toileting). • Provide pieces of a puzzle or art project one by one. • Provide assistance for first steps in a project, and then encourage the child to complete the final steps independently.
Special equipment Specialized furniture or supplies (e.g., wheelchair, computer touchscreen) that help children gain access to and participate in classroom activities	• Use specialized chairs or standers. • Use mobility devices (e.g., wheelchair, walker). • Provide modified play equipment (e.g., modified tricycle). • Investigate the possibility of using augmentative communication device. • Use specialized feeding equipment (e.g., bowls with suction cups on bottom, utensils with special grip). • Provide pencil grips or looped scissors for art activities.
Peer support Peers actively involved in including a child with special needs within classroom activities	• A peer models the activity for the student. • The teacher pairs peers together for activities (peer buddies). • A peer physically assists child in completing a task (e.g., putting on art apron). • The teacher assists peers in learning specific strategies to engage a child with special needs in activities.
Adult support Adult support for child participation in classroom activities	• An adult models the activity for the student. • An adult provides physical assistance in completing a task.
Child preferences Incorporation of children's interests in order to encourage their participation	• Begin circle time with a child's preferred activity (e.g., blowing bubbles, favorite story) to encourage him or her to join. • Allow a child to make transitions with a favorite toy.
Invisible support Arranging classroom schedule or events to support specific children	• The classroom schedule is a balance of teacher-directed and child-chosen activities. • Special seating arrangements are used (e.g., seating a child next to a supportive peer or close to the teacher).

Example of Assistive Technology in an Inclusive Classroom

Elena places picture icons of different centers onto a laminated strip of tagboard with Velcro on it in her classroom. She presents this communication board to Sadie, a child with a communication delay, at the end of circle time. Sadie is able to communicate which center she wants to go to by pointing to, or pulling off, the icon that represents her preference. Elena models the center name ("Playdough"), and Sadie makes a verbal approximation of the name. Another child, Nico, has a difficult time communicating verbally and also has limited use of his hands. His parents and the IEP team have worked with the assistive technology support services in their community to find an assistive communication device that will help him be more independent in his communication. He uses an iPad with voice output to communicate. The assistive technology team trains both his family and teachers on how to use it with him.

Understanding the range of assistive technology tools and supports available can help teachers in inclusive preschool programs identify the type of support that will best meet a child's needs. Sadao and Robinson (2010) define three levels of assistive technology: 1) low, 2) mid, and 3) high. Table 5.3 provides a definition of and examples for each level of assistive technology.

When deciding what type of assistive technology to use with a child, it is important to consider the child's developmental level, needs, and available resources. The purpose of using assistive technology in inclusive classrooms is to increase a child's access and independence. Therefore, care and consideration need to be given to deciding which assistive technology tools most easily meet the child's needs and can be successfully implemented in the classroom. A basic rule to follow is to provide the simplest tool that will successfully meet the child's

Table 5.3.   Levels of assistive technology

Level	Examples
Low tech Inexpensive options that require no training and can be easily created and implemented by teachers	Communication icons (photos, simple pictures) Communication boards or books Visual schedules Adapted utensils, bowls, and cups Slantboard Lap tray Use of Velcro to stabilize materials Adapted books (e.g., audiobooks, e-book mobile applications) Pencil grips Triangular crayons Adapted scissors Knobbed puzzles
Mid tech Materials that require minimal training and cost less than $500	Computer adaptations (e.g., touchscreen, alternative keyboard, alternative mouse) Switches Switch-adapted battery-operated toys One-step voice output devices (e.g., Small Talk Communicator, BIGmack) Voice output devices with levels (e.g., GoTalk Communicator) Seating and mobility devices (e.g., floor sitter, walker)
High tech More expensive options (more than $500) that may require specialized training	Higher-level augmentative and alternative communication (AAC) systems (e.g., DynaVox) Seating and mobility devices (e.g., Rifton Activity Chair) High-powered wheelchair iPad

needs. Inclusive preschool programs should research the assistive technology support available in their community. Often communities and school districts have assistive technology specialists and lending libraries to help practitioners find appropriate materials for students. Preschool inclusion teams should identify all assistive technology resources, including equipment, financial resources, lending services, and PD opportunities. This information should be readily available to IEP teams, families, and inclusive programs. Free or inexpensive picture icon programs and instructions for making other low-tech options are available. For example, the Tots 'n Tech Research Institute (http://tnt.asu.edu) provides information on how to make simple adaptations to classroom toys and games as well as instructions for easy-to-make communication boards and adapted books. The Head Start Center for Inclusion also provides multiple resources for creating visual supports (http://depts.washington.edu/hscenter/teacher-tools#visual).

Tip for Success!

Use the simplest assistive technology tool available to support the child's access and participation.

Differentiated Instruction

Differentiated instruction is based on the idea that all classrooms will have a diversity of learners. Difference is seen as the norm, and students are viewed as individuals who come to the classroom with a wide range of backgrounds, interests, experiences, and skills (Tomlinson et al., 2003). Teachers identify the learning needs and styles of students through observation and assessment and use that information to create relevant and engaging curricula. Different approaches and materials are incorporated to ensure all children are supported in their learning. Teachers continually monitor student progress and modify their lessons and approaches to meet student needs.

Table 5.4. Ways to differentiate instruction

Content	Examples
Content refers to what children learn and how the teacher provides access to the information.	• Target different levels of concepts within the same unit to address a variety of skill levels (e.g., during an ocean theme unit, a teacher works with one child on learning the names of different sea animals; with another child, the teacher focuses on helping him or her identify which sea animals are mammals). • Present information in multiple ways to meet the individual needs of children in the class (e.g., some children may learn well through manipulating materials on their own and others may need direct instruction). • Provide large-group, small-group, and one-to-one activities based on how students will best learn the information. • Provide information in different formats (e.g., provide instructions verbally as well as through pictures). • Adapt the pace of instruction (e.g., allow more time for a child to process information or respond to a question).
Process	*Examples*
Process includes the different types of activities children participate in to learn the information.	• Provide choices for skill practice through a wide range of fun and engaging activities. • Use a variety of materials that incorporate students' interests and learning styles (e.g., create a class unit based on a subject matter in which students have shown an interest, use manipulatives and other hands-on learning materials). • Provide a balance between teacher-directed and student-selected activities. • Allow students differing lengths of time to complete tasks or projects.
Product	*Examples*
Product refers to how children demonstrate or express what they have learned.	• Provide various ways for students to demonstrate their learning of the same concept (e.g., one child draws a picture to demonstrate the concept of 10, another uses manipulatives). • Allow students to work with peers to complete projects.

Differentiated instruction takes purposeful planning to be effective (see the next section). This approach to teaching has been shown to have the most impact when teachers use a high-quality curriculum as the foundation, utilize children's interests, and make learning interactive and engaging (Purcell & Rosemary, 2008; Tomlinson et al., 2003). Tomlinson (2001) details ways to differentiate instruction to reach all learners in terms of content, process, and product. Table 5.4 provides a definition and examples of each of these concepts.

Steps for Implementing Differentiated Instruction   The following steps can be used as a guide for planning and implementing differentiated instruction.

1. Establish clear curriculum goals.
    Create specific goals for the curriculum unit. Goals are often linked to EC learning standards.

Mary is going to start a curriculum unit on the ocean in her preschool classroom. She has several unit goals that address different skills and concepts. One of her unit goals is for the children to recognize that numbers represent quantities and have an order to them (linked to the mathematics domain from the Head Start Child Development and Early Learning Framework).

---

2. Assess children's skills.
    Before the unit begins, assess students' current understanding of unit concepts in order to plan appropriate instruction. Assessments can range from general developmental, such as Assessment, Evaluation, and Programming System (AEPS®) for Infants and Young Children, Second Edition (Bricker, 2002), to teacher-made assessments linked to unit goals.

Mary has recently completed the Teaching Strategies GOLD assessment with all the children in her classroom (Heroman, Burts, Berke, & Bickart, 2010). Based on the assessment results, she knows her students have a range of understanding regarding numbers and operations. Some children in her class are just starting to verbally count up to five, but not always in the correct order, whereas others can already count past 20 in the correct order and are beginning to group numbers in sets to equal amounts up to 20.

---

3. Plan activities based on children's skill levels.
    Use assessment information to create activities that address the different skill levels of children in the class. Careful and intentional planning needs to be done to incorporate student interests and create engaging activities that target unit goals. Activities should be differentiated by content, process, and product (see Table 5.4).

Mary comes up with multiple ways to work with children on counting and number representation. The activities vary in their skill level, amount of adult-guided direction, number of children, and use of hands-on materials. Examples include the following:

- *Sensory table:* Mary sets up two sensory tables outside, one filled with sand and the other with water. In the sand table, she adds shells of different shapes and sizes, as well as shovels and buckets. In the water table, she adds different types and quantities of plastic sea creatures, scuba divers, and boats. Children can explore, sort, count, and make sets of the materials on their own. Teachers in the classroom can offer various levels of support by joining the children in play, modeling counting, grouping shells or sea creatures, and asking questions (e.g., "How many shells do you have?" "Are there more dolphins or sharks?").

- *Tabletop game:* Mary creates an ocean path game in which children use dice to count the number of spots the children will move. The laminated board has a short path on one side and a long path on the other, allowing children to choose the level at which they want to play. Children who play the short path game use only one die; those who play the long path game use both dice. The game is set up on a small group table. Children can choose to participate independently or in a small group. Teachers can join the children to provide support as they learn the rules of the game.

- *Book activity:* Mary creates a book activity she can do either one to one or in a small group with children in her class who are just beginning to count and understand number representation. She creates a storyboard to go along with the book *Five Little Fishes.* As she reads it with a child, she will prompt the child to add a laminated fish picture to the storyboard each time a fish is added in the story. Throughout the storybook reading, Mary can help the child count the number of fish.

4. Implement activities and monitor progress.
   Implement the unit activities and monitor for child engagement and progress toward unit goals. Progress can be monitored through observation and anecdotal notes, review of student work, and unit assessments.

Throughout the unit, Mary and her teaching assistants monitor how the children are doing with the activities. They take notes during their observations in order to track child progress. At the end of the day, Mary and her assistants review the notes and discuss how individual children are doing.

5. Make modifications.
   Use information from observations and progress monitoring to modify activities and teaching strategies as needed to increase student engagement and meet student needs.

After observing in the classroom and meeting with her team to discuss child progress, Mary notes that Evan appears to float from activity to activity rather than staying with anything for an extended period. Mary knows that Evan loves sharks. She decides to incorporate sharks in more of the activities. She also talks to her assistants about monitoring which activity he chooses, following his lead by joining him in the activity, and providing him with support to stay engaged (e.g., expanding on his play, modeling what to do). Mary and her team will meet the following week to see if their modifications have helped Evan successfully engage in the curriculum unit.

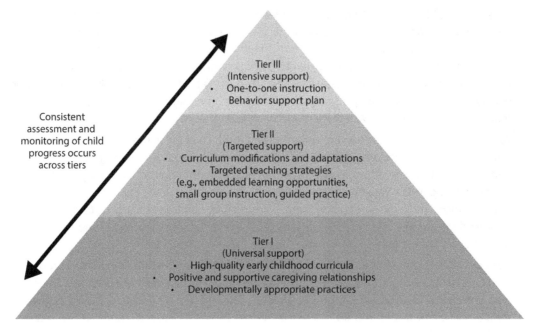

Figure 5.1. Basic response to intervention model for early childhood education.

RESPONSE TO INTERVENTION IN EARLY CHILDHOOD

Response to intervention (RTI) is a differentiated support model that focuses on providing varying levels of assistance to students based on their needs. This intervention model can be used in inclusive preschool programs to assess children's skill development and provide the appropriate level of support to ensure their success. There are four key features of the RTI model for ECE: 1) multitiered system of practices, 2) high-quality curriculum, 3) ongoing assessment and progress monitoring, and 4) collaborative problem solving (DEC, NAEYC, & National Head Start Association [NHSA], 2013). Figure 5.1 provides an example of a basic RTI pyramid model for ECE. RTI models have also been developed to target specific domains, such as the Pyramid Model for Supporting Social Emotional Competence in Infants and Young Children (Fox, Carta, Strain, Dunlap, & Hemmeter, 2009).

The multitiered system of RTI is made up of three levels: 1) Tier I (universal support), 2) Tier II (targeted support), and 3) Tier III (intensive support). Tier I forms the foundation of the RTI pyramid. Supports at this level are intended for *all children* within ECE programs. Central to this tier are the development of nurturing and responsive relationships with children and the use of a high-quality early childhood curriculum (DEC, NAEYC, & NHSA, 2013; Fox et al., 2009). A high-quality EC curriculum can be defined as one that is developmentally and culturally appropriate, uses evidence-based teaching strategies, and is intentionally designed to meet the needs of students. Tier I supports focused on general development include greeting and interacting with children positively, providing a good balance of child-directed and teacher-directed activities, posting a classroom schedule so students know what to expect, and joining in on children's play. Tier I supports focused on social-emotional development and behavior support include creating, posting, and teaching positive behavioral expectations; providing whole-group transition warnings; and using positive descriptive feedback (Fox et al., 2009). Tier I builds the foundation for a successful program. The majority of children within an ECE program may only need support at the Tier I level. However, some will need additional support in order to be successful.

Tier II is focused on providing targeted intervention for children who need extra support to gain access to the classroom curriculum. Supports include modifications and adaptations as well as specialized instruction. Examples of specialized instruction include methods such as guided practice in writing letters during a tabletop activity or asking targeted questions during a storybook reading. Tier II supports focused on supporting positive behavior include individualized transition strategies (e.g., a visual first/then board that shows the child that first they have to clean up the blocks and then they can eat a snack), individual schedules (e.g., providing a child with a visual schedule strip for circle time), and focused instruction on handling anger and disappointment (Fox et al., 2009). Targeted intervention focuses on addressing the specific skill area in which a child needs assistance. Often children are successful in many classroom routines and activities but have a specific area in which they need support.

Dominic is able to respond to questions appropriately and complete classroom tasks on his own, and he understands the unit concepts the teacher is working on. However, the teacher notices that he consistently has a difficult time interacting with his peers. The universal supports she has provided in facilitating positive peer interactions have not been enough to help Dominic be successful in engaging with peers. Therefore, she contacts the preschool inclusion team and the IEP team at the school district. An ECSE coach is provided to her. They decide to give Dominic additional targeted support to help him with his peer interactions. During free play, the teacher sets up a train set that Dominic enjoys. When he comes over to play with it, she stays at the activity, models inviting peers to play, prompts Dominic's communicative exchanges with peers, and assists him in sharing the trains. She provides positive acknowledgement and feedback during Dominic's interactions with peers ("You gave Lexie a turn. That was a great way to be a friend.").

Tier III supports are intended for children who need more intensive intervention to successfully participate in inclusive preschool classrooms and gain access to the general curriculum. Tier III interventions are provided to children who, after receiving both Tier I and Tier II interventions, are not making sufficient progress on certain skills. Tier III interventions focus on direct instruction around critical skills. This type of support often includes one-to-one instruction and multiple learning trials. Methods such as discrete trial training (DTT) can be used to provide opportunities for a child to practice a skill several times in a row in order to build competency. DTT is a one-to-one approach to instruction that teaches discrete skills in a systematic manner often using direct and repeated

APPLICATION QUESTION
Does your state or district use an RTI framework to support student learning? How is the system designed? How does the system work in EC programs? Discuss these questions with your preschool inclusion team.

prompts. Tier III supports around behavior include conducting a functional behavioral assessment and creating and implementing a behavior support plan.

Ongoing assessment and progress monitoring are essential in RTI to make sure children are receiving the appropriate level of support. Programs include assessments on all children in the classroom to determine their development and identify whether or not they need additional support (e.g., AEPS®, Teaching Strategies GOLD). Once children who need extra support are identified and support strategies are implemented, teachers collect data to measure progress and determine if the teaching practices are effective for individual children. If the child is not making progress, the teacher can increase the level of support (e.g., if a child receiving Tier II supports continues to struggle, Tier III supports can be added). In addition, if the child is making good progress, the teacher can begin to fade the level of support (e.g., once a child has learned a circle time routine successfully, use of a personal circle time schedule can be decreased and eventually faded away). Collaborative problem solving is utilized throughout the RTI model to determine the best way to support individual children. Teachers work closely with family members, administrators, and other specialists who know the child to create support plans that best address the child's needs. Working collaboratively helps ensure that information is gathered from multiple sources and those who know the child best are included in the process. A key to using practices associated with Tier III interventions is providing the support to the teacher. Such support includes training, coaching, consultation with specialists, and collaboration as a team.

PYRAMID MODEL FOR SUPPORTING SOCIAL EMOTIONAL COMPETENCE IN INFANTS AND YOUNG CHILDREN

The Pyramid Model for Supporting Social Emotional Competence in Infants and Young Children is a conceptual framework of EBPs developed using a tiered public

Table 5.5.   Examples of the use of the Pyramid Model in inclusive settings

Universal promotion	Post classroom schedule that includes visual supports depicting daily activities.
	Provide classwide warnings that are understandable for all children before transitions occur.
	Greet children by name when they enter the classroom.
	Develop activities that are developmentally appropriate and that promote engagement.
	Post positively stated classroom rules with visuals on the classroom wall.
Secondary prevention	Use small- and large-group activities to directly teach social skills.
	Have problem-solving strategies and supports freely visible/accessible for children in the classroom (e.g., solution kit, solution book).
	Read books and stories that include themes related to friendship and how to be a friend.
	Post visual supports in the classroom, such as posters, that review the steps for specific techniques (e.g., social skills, "Tucker the turtle" technique for calming down).
Tertiary intervention	When possible, include peers in positive behavior support plans.
	Individualize instruction and materials when teaching social, emotional, or problem-solving skills, and plan opportunities for children who need more learning opportunities to practice the skills with peers throughout the day.
	Provide activity schedules for children who might need support understanding the beginning, middle, and end or the steps of activities.
	Include families in behavioral assessment and in the subsequent development of a positive behavior support plan.
	Incorporate child choice into activities by providing a choice chart.

health approach. The Pyramid Model (Fox et al., 2003) is a promotion, prevention, and intervention framework EC educators can use to support young children's social and emotional development and prevent or reduce challenging behaviors. The Pyramid Model uses three tiers of intervention practice: 1) universal promotion for all children (Tier I), 2) secondary preventions to address the intervention needs for children at risk of social emotional delays (Tier II), and 3) tertiary interventions needed for children with persistent challenges (Tier III) (Fox et al., 2003; Hemmeter, Ostrosky, & Fox, 2006). The Pyramid Model includes interventions needed to support children who are typically developing and who have or are at risk for developmental delays or disabilities (Hunter & Hemmeter, 2009), can be implemented in inclusive preschool classrooms, and builds on other evidence-based curricular approaches (see Table 5.5 for examples of the use of the model in inclusive settings). A randomized controlled trial of the Pyramid Model examined the effects of coaching and training on teachers' implementation of Pyramid Model practices and children's social skills and challenging behaviors (Hemmeter, Snyder, Kinder, & Artman, 2011; Hemmeter et al., 2011). The findings demonstrated that classrooms with teachers implementing the Pyramid Model with fidelity had better social and behavioral outcomes for children.

In the following excerpt from the Maceo family case study, Raphael's teachers and coach are planning instruction and considering how to ensure he achieves his IEP goals and participates in classroom activities and routines.

Case Study: The Maceo Family

The preschool inclusion team and the IEP team agreed to provide a coach to Ms. Humphrey. Ms. Martinez is an ECSE specialist in the school district who is serving as the first district coach to off-campus EC programs that are including children with IEPs. Raphael's IEP goals include using one and two words to request and comment; increasing social interactions with peers; engaging in pretend play activities; and using a variety of tools to draw, paint, and write. Ms. Humphrey and Ms. Martinez met and planned several new approaches. Ms. Humphrey revised her instructional approach to use something she learned about at the state inclusion workshop she attended. She planned to use embedded learning opportunities throughout the day and to ensure Raphael received a sufficient number of learning opportunities for each goal. This also allowed her to intentionally think about and focus on specific individual and group goals for the rest of the children. She was excited that she did not have to plan individual activities for each goal. If she planned ahead of time, she could intentionally embed learning opportunities throughout the day!

She and Ms. Martinez reviewed the DEC's Recommended Practices and the *Blending Practices to Strengthen Quality Early Learning Programs for ALL Children* monograph (Barton et al., 2014). She decided to use a blended instructional approach to ensure she promoted maximum engagement and participation across the day while maintaining sufficient amounts of instructional opportunities to ensure all children achieve their individual goals. They worked with the assistant teacher, Ms. Ebony, to create specific planning forms for each of Raphael's goals and identified multiple times each day, across activities and routines, to embed each goal. For example, during arrival, Raphael could "sign in" by writing his name each morning using a variety of tools (e.g., markers, pencils, crayons). Ms. Humphrey and Ms. Ebony will intentionally include different writing tools at the art center and incorporate different writing tools into the science center and sensory table when appropriate. Also, they will plan to use several accommodations to ensure Raphael participates fully in each routine. For example, Raphael will use his own visual schedule during more difficult routines and transitions such as washing hands and the transition from his most preferred activity (outside time). He also will use an individual visual schedule during snack time and while making the transition to naptime. Ms. Humphrey and Ms. Ebony will intentionally embed multiple opportunities for him to request using one and two words during preferred activities such as outdoor play and music time. For example, when he points or gestures to request a specific toy on the playground or instrument during music, the teachers will verbally model the word and wait for him to repeat the model. If he does not repeat right away or gestures again, they will repeat the word again and then give him the item.

Ms. Martinez will visit the classroom at least once a week, more often if necessary, to observe Ms. Humphrey and provide feedback to her. She will also help Ms. Humphrey and Ms. Ebony with observation and monitoring tools. Ms. Humphrey and Ms. Ebony will carefully monitor Raphael's progress to ensure he is consistently working toward his IEP goals and will review progress data regularly with Ms. Martinez.

CONCLUSION

This chapter provided a comprehensive overview of evidence-based instructional practices that can be implemented in inclusive preschool classrooms. The preschool inclusion team and the IEP team can use the detailed examples to plan instruction. Multiple additional resources are provided at the end of the book to help the instructional team plan, implement, and evaluate instruction. Planning instruction might also be a good time to go back and review the characteristics of high-quality inclusion in Chapter 1.

Preschool inclusion teams should plan PD using these EBPs, both training and coaching. This content combined with PD practices outlined in Chapter 4 specifically address a frequently mentioned challenged to preschool inclusion: General EC teachers do not feel competent or confident to teach children with disabilities (Barton & Smith, 2014b). Remember the goal is to ensure *all* children have the supports needed to participate fully in the classroom environment. These practices help ensure that all children are successful and that the personnel have the supports and resources they need. The intensive or Tier III practices also prevent unnecessary referrals to more restrictive environments. These practices, and particularly individualized intervention practices, will need to be accompanied by training and ongoing site-based coaching to ensure high-fidelity implementation. Fidelity data and progress monitoring should be used regularly with the coaching to ensure children are making adequate progress. Chapter 6 describes specific practices and measures for evaluating quality in inclusive preschool programs.

REFLECTION QUESTIONS

1. List examples of EBPs to increase access, participation, and supports for children with disabilities.

2. What are three specific ways your preschool inclusion team will use the DEC Recommended Practices in EI/ECSE?

3. What is blended instruction? Why is blended instruction particularly useful for inclusive classrooms?

4. What are the four key features of the RTI model for ECE and how might your preschool inclusion team use these key features?

5. What is an example of a practice at each tier of the Pyramid Model that can be used in inclusive classrooms?

6. Develop a yearlong PD plan for general EC teachers and specialized services personnel using the EBPs in this chapter, including training and coaching.

III

Making Preschool
Inclusion Happen

6

Measuring the Quality of Inclusive Classrooms

Ching-I Chen, Erin E. Barton, and Geneva J. Hallett

TOOLS FROM THE TOOLBOX

- **Table 6.1** Classroom Observation Tools
- **Table 6.2** Inclusion Checklist for Classrooms
- **Table 6.3** Checklists and Assessments that Support Inclusion for Individual Children
- **Table 6.4** Sample Page of the Ecological Congruence Assessment

The purpose of this chapter is to guide preschool inclusion teams in measuring the quality of inclusive preschool classrooms. This chapter describes the importance of using multiple measures, individual information including child progress and parent satisfaction, and ongoing monitoring to ensure that preschool inclusion opportunities for children with disabilities are high quality.

QUALITY INCLUSION

More than 25 years ago, the legal foundation of EC inclusion was established through PL 99-457, the 1986 amendments to the Education of the Handicapped Act that later became IDEA. These amendments extended the right to a FAPE in the LRE to children with disabilities 3–5 years of age (Odom, Buysse, & Soukakou, 2011). Since then, researchers, administrators, and professionals have devoted much effort to advocating and promoting a natural and least restrictive placement for young children with disabilities at the research, policy, and practice levels and ensuring that sufficient and individualized support is provided to maximize the learning opportunities for young children with disabilities (Buysse & Hollingsworth, 2009; Cate, Diefendorf, McCullough, Peters, & Whaley, 2010).

The joint statement on inclusion released by NAEYC and DEC (2009) defined three critical indicators for high-quality inclusive programs: *access, participation,* and *supports.* As described in Chapter 1, *access* refers to the provision of optimal opportunities for children with special needs to gain access to the environment and practice and acquire critical developmental skills. *Participation* indicates the accommodations and support provided in addition to the environmental arrangement to facilitate belonging, engagement, and participation of young children with and without special needs. *Supports* denote the underlying system-level infrastructure that sustains the efforts toward *access* and *participation.*

To measure the quality of an inclusive preschool program, there are least two levels of evaluation:

1. First, the quality of the foundational program for all children should be ensured through some form of measure for general EC programs such as NAEYC accreditation or a state quality rating system.

2. Second, once the foundational quality is ensured, the setting and practices need to be viewed through the lens of appropriateness for a child with a disability from both the overall classroom level and the individual child level.

We describe two types of measures for this evaluation: self-assessment and observation. The three DEC/NAEYC indicators (access, participation, and supports) should be examined along with the overall environment, specific aspects of the context (i.e., personal, instructional, structural), and target levels of support (i.e., individual, classroom, program). The results of multiple measures, including reviewing the organization of physical space, classroom materials, instructional practices, team and family collaboration, and individualized supports (e.g., child progress and parent satisfaction), should be periodically examined to fully capture the specific inclusive practices implemented and the individual experience of children with disabilities and their families (Cate et al., 2010).

The ongoing review process will serve the purpose of program evaluation and will inform programs of the changes that need to be made to achieve desirable outcomes for children and families. Typically developing children also will benefit from being in a high-quality inclusive preschool classroom that is carefully designed, equipped with competent classroom staff, and using DAP. A one-time, overall, average rating quality measure is simply not sufficient in assessing program quality and providing a comprehensive picture for evaluation (DEC/NAEYC, 2009). One-time measures are not helpful for identifying or addressing needed program improvements.

Several instruments have been developed to assess the quality of EC programs (Halle, Vick Whittaker, & Anderson, 2010). Some of them focus on the broader general EC settings and population, whereas others specifically target EC inclusive programs, at either the program or the individual child level. The following sections provide a review of quality indicators and a compilation of measures under three categories:

1. Measures to assess the foundational quality of the typical EC classroom, including state QRISs.

2. Classroom observation tools to assess the quality of the classroom with a focus on serving children with disabilities.

3. Measures to assess the experience of individual children with disabilities in inclusive preschool classrooms.

GENERAL EARLY CHILDHOOD CLASSROOM OBSERVATION TOOLS

Classroom observation tools are measures that allow users to observe and assess the quality practices in general EC programs or provide an overall rating of the environment. These tools also can be administered in inclusive settings to examine the overall learning experience of all children and create a profile of the program quality. Four frequently used classroom checklists are summarized in Table 6.1.

Assessment Profile for Early Childhood Programs

The Assessment Profile for Early Childhood Programs (APECP; Abbott-Shim & Sibley, 1987) is a formative, comprehensive measure used for program improvement. The APECP is a self-evaluation tool for assessing the administrative practices and quality of center-based EC settings that serve children age birth to 10 years. The APECP examines the safety, learning environment, scheduling, curriculum methods, interacting, and individualizing practices of an EC classroom, as well as the physical facilities, food service, program management, personnel, and program development aspects of administrative practices.

Data are collected through observation, review of program records, and interviews with stakeholders. Specific criteria are developed to help score the results and can be used to highlight the strengths of the program, identify areas for improvement, and develop plans to optimize resources and prepare for program accreditation. Adequate psychometric technical adequacy (i.e., reliability and validity) has been reported in a series of psychometric studies conducted by the authors (Abbott-Shim, Lambert, & McCarty, 2000; Abbott-Shim, Neel, & Sibley, 1992, 2001).

Classroom Assessment Scoring System

The Classroom Assessment Scoring System® (CLASS®; Hamre, La Paro, Pianta, & LoCasale-Crouch, 2014; La Paro, Hamre, & ®Pianta, 2012; Pianta, LeParo, & Hamre, 2008a, 2008b) is an observation tool developed to measure the quality of prekindergarten to third-grade classrooms. Instead of assessing environmental characteristics, the CLASS examines the child–adult interactions in the classroom. This tool can be used by administrators or practitioners and can serve the purposes of PD or program evaluation and improvement. The rating is based on a 7-point Likert scale, with 1 and 2 being considered as low scores; 3, 4, and 5 as mid; and 6 and 7 as high. Ten classroom quality indicators are assessed under three broad dimensions:

- Emotional support
    1. Positive climate
    2. Negative climate
    3. Teacher sensitivity
    4. Regard for student perspectives
- Classroom organization
    1. Behavior management
    2. Productivity
    3. Instructional learning formats

Table 6.1. Classroom observation tools

Name	Author	Year	Publisher	Purpose	Age range	Format	Administration	Technical adequacy reported?	Formal training required?
Assessment Profile for Early Childhood Programs (APECP)	Abbott-Shim and Sibley	1987	Quality Assist, Inc.	A formative, comprehensive measure used for program improvement	Birth to 10 years	1. Examines the safety, learning environment, scheduling, curriculum methods, interacting, and individualizing practices of an early childhood classroom, as well as the physical facilities, food service, program management, personnel, and program development aspects of administrative practices 2. Specific criteria are developed to help score the results.	Through observation, review of program records, and interviews with stakeholders	Yes	Yes
Classroom Assessment Scoring System® (CLASS®)	Pianta, La Paro, and Hamre. (Pre-K, K–3); La Paro, Hamre, and Pianta (Toddler); Hamre, La Paro, Pianta, and LoCasale-Crouch (Infant)	2008 (Pre-K, K–3); 2012 (Toddler); 2014 (Infant)	Paul H. Brookes Publishing Co.	Examines the child–adult interactions in the classroom to assess classroom quality	Birth to third grade	1. Ten classroom quality indicators are assessed under three dimensions: emotional support, classroom organization, and instructional support. 2. The rating is based on a 7-point Likert scale.	Through classroom observation in the context of daily routines and activities	Yes	Yes
Infant Toddler Environment Rating Scale, Revised (ITERS-R)	Harms, Cryer, and Clifford	2006	Teacher's College Press	Rates the overall quality of early childhood infant/toddler programs	Birth to 30 months	1. Seven subscales are used; space and furnishing, personal care routines, listening and talking, activities, interactions, program structure, and parents and staff. 2. A 7-point rating scale is used.	Through structured classroom observations in the context of daily routines and activities	Yes	Yes
Early Childhood Environment Rating Scale, Revised (ECERS-R)	Harms, Cryer, and Clifford	2005	Teacher's College Press	Rates the overall quality of early childhood prekindergarten programs	2½–5 years	1. Seven subscales are used; space and furnishing, personal care routines, language-reasoning, activities, interactions, program structure, and parents and staff. 2. A 7-point rating scale is used.	Through structured classroom observations in the context of daily routines and activities	Yes	Yes

- Instructional support
  1. Concept development
  2. Quality of feedback
  3. Language modeling
  4. Literacy focus (available upon request)

The CLASS manual reports that solid reliability and validity has been established for the tool based on the results of previous psychometric studies.

Infant Toddler Environment Rating Scale, Revised, and Early Childhood Environment Rating Scale, Revised

The Infant Toddler Environment Rating Scale, Revised (ITERS-R; Harms, Cryer, & Clifford, 2006), and the Early Childhood Environment Rating Scale, Revised (ECERS-R; Harms, Cryer, & Clifford, 2005), are the updated versions of the original ITERS and ECERS published in the 1980s and 1990s. Both instruments are designed to rate the overall quality of EC programs. The ITERS-R is intended to be used with center-based EC settings for children from birth to 30 months of age, whereas the ECERS-R is meant to assess programs that serve children from age 2 ½ to 5 years. A 7-point rating scale is adopted by both ITERS-R and ECERS-R, with 1 as inadequate and 7 as excellent. Based on observations, the classroom is rated on seven subscales:

1. Space and furnishing
2. Personal care routines
3. Listening and talking (ITERS-R); Language-reasoning (ECERS-R)
4. Activities
5. Interactions
6. Program structure
7. Parents and staff

In terms of psychometric properties (i.e., reliability and validity), the authors report strong technical adequacy for both ITERS-R and ECERS-R in the manuals.

State Quality Rating and Improvement Systems

A QRIS is a systems-level approach to assess, improve, and communicate measures of quality in child care and, in some states, other EC settings (see http://www.qrisnetwork.org; http://qriscompendium.org). As of February 2014, more than 40 states have developed and launched a QRIS. These systems typically are based on state child care licensing standards/requirements. QRISs are usually tiered systems with the lowest tier reflecting minimal state licensing standards and the highest tier including national program accreditation (e.g., NAEYC). Effective QRISs use a school-reform approach and develop a comprehensive, statewide EC system. QRISs are used to evaluate, recognize, and support quality across a range of public and private EC programs. QRISs typically address the following quality features (NAEYC, 2011):

- Physical environment (e.g., health, safety, adult–child ratio)
- Staff qualifications and PD
- Interactions among teachers, staff, children, and families
- Developmentally appropriate and culturally responsive curricula and instructional practices
- Ongoing program evaluation
- Access to effective mentoring and technical assistance to help programs move up tiers

Your state's QRIS will not be sufficient for addressing the quality of inclusive preschool programs. For example, a program might have a high QRIS rating but a low rating on the Inclusive Classroom Profile (Soukakou, 2010). However, the reverse is unlikely—that is, if your program has a low QRIS rating, it is unlikely that your program would have a high rating on any of the measures to assess the overall quality of inclusive preschool classrooms. Thus, programs should consider the QRIS complementary and an important tool in establishing the foundational quality for a possible inclusive preschool program.

OBSERVATION CHECKLISTS FOR QUALITY INCLUSIVE CLASSROOMS

Chapter 1 outlined the empirically supported components of inclusion:

1. Intentional, sufficient, and supported interactions between peers with and without disabilities
2. Specialized, individualized supports
3. Family involvement
4. Inclusive, interdisciplinary services and collaborative teaming
5. Focus on critical sociological outcomes
6. Effective, ongoing PD
7. Ongoing program evaluation (Odom et al., 2011; NECTAC, 2010; Salisbury, 1990)

These indicators should be used to guide you in both assessing and establishing inclusive programs along with more formal measures of quality. Measures to assess the overall quality of inclusive preschool classrooms help administrators or teachers evaluate to what extent high-quality practices are embedded in their EC inclusive setting/program. Administrators or teachers can self-assess the instructional, environmental, and structural supports that are in place and identify areas for improvement. These results can then be used to enhance the overall inclusion experience of children and families.

According to Odom and colleagues (2011), efforts related to preschool inclusion have been focused on 1) outcomes and benefits of inclusion, 2) the importance of specialized instruction, 3) collaboration, and 4) system-level support. With the advancement of research, policies, and practices related to preschool inclusion, an evolving theme that should be stressed is the *quality* of inclusive programs. NAEYC established a program accreditation system in 1985 and published EC program standards to guide and improve the quality of early care and education settings

(McDonald, 2009; NAEYC, 2008) based on a DAP framework, but these standards are not specifically developed for children with special needs. An EC program that fulfills the NAEYC standards might not be effective in addressing the needs of children with disabilities or providing the special education and related services in their IEPs. Therefore, DEC established standards for young children with disabilities and their families: the DEC Recommended Practices in Early Intervention/ Early Childhood Special Education (2014; briefly described in Chapter 5). The DEC Recommended Practices do not address the quality indicators for typical EC programs but rather describe practices that would build on that foundational quality meet the unique needs of children with disabilities:

> While developmentally appropriate practices are the foundation of quality programs for all young children and families (Copple & Bredekamp, 2009), we believe that young children who have or are at risk for developmental delays/disabilities often need more specialized practices that allow them to participate and engage meaningfully in their daily living routines and learning activities. While we acknowledge the important role of developmentally appropriate practices in the education and care of all children, we do not include those foundational practices in this document. (p. 2)

NAEYC's DAP should form the foundation of quality programs for all young children and families. The DAP framework is grounded in research on how children develop and learn and designed to promote young children's optimal learning and development (Copple & Bredekamp, 2009). Likewise, the DEC Recommended Practices are supported by research and known to have a considerable impact on the learning and development of young children with special needs. While the DAP framework should form the foundation of high-quality EC programs, the DEC Recommended Practices should also be an integral component of high-quality *inclusive* preschool classrooms. The most recent set of recommended practices was released in the summer of 2014, so current programmatic evaluations (including all those described in this chapter) will not directly reflect these practices. Thus, preschool inclusion teams should use the DEC Recommended Practices as part of their program evaluation. The eight topic areas address different components of any inclusive EC program and can be used as part of an ongoing programmatic evaluation. The DEC Recommended Practices can be found at http://www.dec-sped.org/recommendedpractices.

APPLICATION QUESTION
How will you use the DEC Recommended Practices to improve preschool inclusion in your program? Discuss the use of the DEC Recommended Practices within your preschool inclusion team.

In addition, eight commonly used checklists for evaluating inclusive preschool classrooms are summarized in Table 6.2.

Inclusive Classroom Profile

The Inclusive Classroom Profile (ICP; Soukakou, 2010), first disseminated by Soukakou in 2007, is a structured classroom observation tool for EC inclusive settings. To complement existing EC program quality measures, this checklist is designed to specifically examine a broad range of aspects in daily classroom practices that support the unique needs and learning characteristics of children age 2 ½ to 5 with disabilities. Twelve aspects are measured:

Table 6.2. Inclusion checklist for classrooms

Name	Author	Year	Publisher	Purpose	Age range	Format	Administration	Technical adequacy reported?	Formal training required?
Inclusive Classroom Profile	Soukakou	2010	Tool is not published yet, but information regarding the tool can be found at http://npdci.fpg.unc.edu/measuring-quality-inclusion-inclusive-classroom-profile	Assesses the quality of provisions and daily practices that support the developmental needs of children with disabilities in early childhood settings	2½–5 years	1. This is an 11-item, 7-point rating scale with examples provided for clarification. 2. This is designed to be used in conjunction with other early childhood environment rating scales and measures.	Through structured classroom observations in the context of daily routines and activities	Yes	Yes
Inclusion Planning Checklist: Center-Based Early Care and Education Programs	SpecialQuest Birth to Five	2008	Publicly available at http://www.specialquest.org/sqtm/inc_plan_chklist_center.pdf	Provides collaborative services when including infants, toddlers, or preschoolers with disabilities and their families in center-based early care and educational programs	Birth to 5 years	1. This includes four sections: build relationships, gather and share information and resources, develop and implement plans, and review and evaluate services. 2. These are open spaces for writing in roles and assistance needed.	Team members individually complete checklist, then discuss with other team members how to support each other	No	No
Preschool Assessment of Classroom Scale–Revised	Raab and Dunst	1997	Publicly available at http://www.puckett.org/index.php	Assesses classroom quality in inclusive programs with regard to the needs of children with disabilities	Preschool	1. This includes seven quality indicators: program foundation and philosophy, management and training, environment organization, staff patterns, instructional content, instructional techniques, and program evaluation. 2. This is a checklist.	Through classroom observation in the context of daily routines and activities and discussions among program or classroom staff	No	No
Preschool and Kindergarten Inclusion Readiness Checklist	Watson and McCathren	2009	Available from the National Association for the Education of Young Children: http://www.naeyc.org/files/yc/file/200903/BTJWatson.pdf	Helps early childhood administrators and teachers increase their awareness and confidence in providing appropriate and individualized services to children with special needs	Preschool and kindergarten	1. This includes checklists for all children and for children with different types of special needs. 2. Each section contains a set of questions for teachers and administrators to answer "yes/not yet."	Through staff discussions about the curriculum, physical space, daily schedule, and approach to discipline	No	No

Name	Author	Year	Source	Purpose	Notes	Administration		
Quality Inclusive Practices Checklist	Wills, Darragh-Ernst, and Presley	2012	Publicly available at http://www.heartland.edu/documents/heip/faculty2/CHLD201/Handouts/QualityInclusivePracticesChecklist.pdf	Help administrators or teachers reflect on their program or classroom practices and quality and make relevant modifications.	1. This is based on the three indicators (access, participation, and supports) of high-quality inclusive programs specified in the joint statement of DEC and NAEYC (2009). 2. Users answer "yes/no" and write in evidence.	Through classroom observation in the context of daily routines and activities, and discussions among program or classroom staff	No	No
Quality Program Indicators	Leveraging Educational Assistance Partnership Outreach Project Staff	2002	Strain, P.S., & Bovey, E.H. (2011). Randomized, controlled trial of the LEAP model of early intervention for young children with autism spectrum disorders. *Topics in Early Childhood Special Education, 31,* 133–154.	Using the LEAP model framework, the QPI helps classroom staff implement LEAP model practices. The LEAP is a model of education for young children with autism within inclusive public preschool settings.	Based on the LEAP model of preschool inclusion, observers rate the fidelity of implementation of 38 items across eight categories using a five-point scale, from "full implementation" (5) to "needs work" (1). Preschool	LEAP staff observe a classroom for one full day, then complete scale; data are used for program evaluation and monitoring of LEAP model implementation	Yes	No
Universal Design for Learning Checklist for Early Childhood Environments–Revised	Cunconan-Lahr and Stifel	2013	Publicly available at http://www.northampton.edu/Documents/ece/checklist%20and%20Questions.pdf	Uses sets of guiding questions to help users self-assess a universally designed learning environment and create a high-quality environment	1. This is based on the three principles of UDL: Provide multiple means of *presentation, expression,* and *engagement* in early childhood environments. 2. This can be used as a set of questions for discussion or as a checklist	Through classroom observation in the context of daily routines and activities and discussions among program or classroom staff	No	No
The SpeciaLink Early Childhood Inclusion Quality Scale	Irwin	2009	Breton Books	Can be used to augment research on children's inclusive experience for improving instructional quality, evaluate program strengths and areas of need, help develop inclusive quality standards and policy, and demonstrate accountability	1. The instrument centers on 11 practices and six principles as its assessment areas. 2. Items are scored on a 7-point rating scale.	Through classroom observation in the context of daily routines and activities	Yes	Yes

Key: DEC, Division for Early Childhood; NAEYC, National Association for the Education of Young Children; LEAP, Leveraging Educational Assistance Partnership; UDL, Universal Design for Learning.

1. Adaptations of space and materials/equipment
2. Adult involvement in peer interactions
3. Adults' guidance of children's play
4. Conflict resolution
5. Membership
6. Relationships between adults and children
7. Support for communication
8. Adaptation of group activities
9. Transitions between activities
10. Feedback
11. Family–professional partnerships
12. Monitoring children's learning

A 7-point rating scale, with 1 as the lowest degree of quality and 7 as the highest, is used to reflect the extent to which observed practices in the EC classroom promote individual adaptations, easy access, and active participation of children with specific needs (Soukakou, 2010). Soukakou, Winton, and West (2012) reported that the ICP shows adequate reliability and validity and is well perceived by the observers in terms of relevance and user friendliness.

Inclusion Planning Checklist: Center-Based Early Care and Education Programs

The Inclusion Planning Checklist: Center-Based Early Care and Education Programs (IPC; SpecialQuest Birth to Five, 2008) was developed by the SpecialQuest Birth to Five: Head Start/Hilton Foundation Training Program, an initiative funded by the Department of Health and Human Services and the Office of Head Start to support inclusive EC services. The checklist provides practical suggestions in collaborative practices for center-based early care and education programs to be responsive and effective in fully including children with disabilities and their families in daily classroom activities. The IPC measures four facets of inclusion planning: 1) building relationships, 2) gathering and sharing information and resources, 3) developing and implementing plans, and 4) reviewing and evaluating services. Each facet contains a set of related tasks that are designed to promote inclusion and open spaces for EC intervention team members to write down their roles and responsibilities. Discussions should follow to support all team members in understanding and implementing the practices. A full version of the IPC can be obtained from http://www.specialquest.org/sqtm/inc_plan_chklist_center.pdf.

Preschool Assessment of Classroom Environment–Revised

In *An Administrator's Guide to Preschool Inclusion* (Wolery & Odom, 2000), the Preschool Assessment of Classroom Environment Scale–Revised (PACE-R; Raab & Dunst, 1997) is suggested as a measure that takes into account the needs of children with disabilities when assessing the classroom quality of inclusive programs (see Table 2 on page 44 of the *Administrator's Guide*). The PACE-R includes seven quality indicators:

1. Program foundation and philosophy
2. Management and training
3. Environment organization
4. Staff patterns
5. Instructional content
6. Instructional techniques
7. Program evaluation

The characteristics of a high-quality inclusive program are described under each indicator. A checklist version of PACE-R, adapted by Cate and colleagues (2010), can be retrieved from http://ectacenter.org/~pdfs/pubs/qualityindicators inclusion.pdf.

Preschool and Kindergarten Inclusion Readiness Checklist

Watson and McCathren (2009) developed the Preschool and Kindergarten Inclusion Readiness Checklist (PKIRC) to increase administrators' and teachers' awareness and confidence in providing appropriate and individualized services to children with special needs. The PKIRC can be used to facilitate discussions among program staff on their readiness to create a high-quality inclusive environment that allows *all* children to be successful. This checklist consists of a set of questionnaires, with one that focuses on all children in the classroom or program and the rest specific to different types of disabilities. The PKIRC items are dichotomous (i.e., the answer choices are "yes" and "not yet"); are built on the concepts of universal design; and embody developmental, instructional, and environmental considerations. The more "yes" answers a classroom or a program receives from the PKIRC, the more ready it is for providing a high-quality placement for children with special needs.

Quality Inclusive Practices Checklist

The design of the Quality Inclusive Practices Checklist (QIPC; Wills, Darragh-Ernst, & Presley, 2012) is based on the three indicators (access, participation, and supports) of high-quality inclusive programs specified in the joint statement of DEC and NAEYC (2009). This framework serves as the conceptual model for the QIPC and guides the categorization of the checklist items. All items are evidence-based indicators. By answering "yes/no" and writing in the evidence, administrators or teachers will be able to reflect on their program/classroom practices and quality. Furthermore, corresponding toolboxes and resources for each indicator are attached for making relevant modifications. To see a full version, go to http://www.heartland.edu/documents/heip/faculty2/CHLD201/Handouts/QualityInclusivePracticesChecklist.pdf.

Quality Program Indicators

The Quality Program Indicators (QPI; Strain & Bovey, 2011) is a procedural rating scale used to monitor and measure implementation of the LEAP preschool model of inclusion. The LEAP model was designed to support the inclusion of young children with autism into inclusive preschool classrooms within public schools. The LEAP model promotes establishing a setting of high quality for typically developing children and promoting the full inclusion and participation of children with autism. The QPI has good short-term test-retest reliability (.88 across 3 days), it is sensitive to training effects, and implementation of all components predicts child engagement increases and rapid growth on social, cognitive, and language measures (Strain & Hoyson, 2000). Classroom staff observe a classroom for one full day and then complete the scale. The data are used to guide coaching and program evaluation. Research suggests that self-assessment using the QPI is a critical ingredient to maintaining program integrity and a high-quality inclusive classroom that supports children with autism.

Universal Design for Learning Checklist for Early Childhood Environments–Revised

The Universal Design for Learning Checklist for Early Childhood Environments–Revised (2013) was first developed by Cunconan-Lahr and Stifel in 2007, based on the three principles of UDL: providing multiple means of *presentation, expression,* and *engagement* in EC environments. This checklist contains sets of guiding questions that help administrators or teachers self-assess in three broad areas of a universally designed learning environment: 1) curriculum, 2) physical environment, and 3) relationships. Administrators or teachers can utilize the questions to provoke thoughts and initiate discussions for planning among program or classroom staff. A checklist example is also provided for doing a quick evaluation or starting short conversations. A full version of the checklist can be obtained from http://www.northampton.edu/Documents/Departments/ece/checklist%20and%20Questions.pdf.

The SpeciaLink Early Childhood Inclusion Quality Scale

The SpeciaLink Early Childhood Inclusion Quality Scale (Irwin, 2009) is a 7-point rating scale instrument that assesses the program quality of EC inclusive settings. The results can be used to summarize information on children's inclusion experiences for improving instructional quality, evaluate program strengths and areas of needs, help develop inclusive quality standards and policy, and demonstrate accountability (Cate et al., 2010). The instrument centers on 11 practices and 6 principles critical to the design of a high-quality inclusive program as its assessment areas (Irwin, 2009):

- Practices
  1. Physical environment and special needs
  2. Equipment and materials
  3. Direction and inclusion
  4. Staff support
  5. Staff training
  6. Therapies: physiotherapy, occupational therapy, speech and language, behavioral consultation

7. Individual program plans (IPPs)
8. Parents of children with special needs
9. Involvement of typical children
10. Board of directors and other similar units
11. Preparing for transition to school

- Principles
  1. Zero rejection
  2. Naturally occurring proportions
  3. Same hours of attendance available to all children
  4. Full participation
  5. Maximum feasible parent participation
  6. Proactive strategies and advocacy for high-quality inclusive child care

Inclusion Checklists for Individual Children

Inclusion checklists for individual children measure child-focused quality indicators that depict the individual inclusion experience of children with disabilities (and possibly also of their families). Generally, this type of checklist is completed for *each* child with disabilities in the inclusive classroom/program. Results can be used to evaluate the effectiveness of current practices and inform the individualized adaptations required. Four frequently used inclusion checklists are summarized in Table 6.3.

CARA's Kit: Creating Adaptations for Routines and Activities

CARA's Kit: Creating Adaptations for Routines and Activities (Milbourne & Campbell, 2007) is a checklist that bridges current research findings on utilizing adaptations as an effective intervention with EC curriculum and standards. This checklist is designed to help EC educators understand the needs of children 3–6 years old by rating their performance and engagement in daily classroom routines and activities and the use of adaptations to maximize learning and participation opportunities for all children. Program directors and supporting staff in the classroom are also encouraged to provide input when completing the checklist.

When reviewing the checklist, the teacher (or the entire staff) rates his or her level of satisfaction and expectation of a child's performance in two domains: activity and developmental area/skill. In the activity domain, a variety of classroom routines and activities (e.g., language and literacy, small-group play, arrival and departure) are measured, whereas in the developmental area/skill domain, crucial competencies (e.g., socializing, communicating, following directions) for children to succeed in an EC classroom are examined. Once the administration is concluded, the decision matrix that follows the least to most intrusive hierarchy can be used to adapt environment, daily schedule, activities/routines, materials, or instruction. There also is a similar product for younger children, CARA's Kit for Toddlers: Creating Adaptations for Routines and Activities (Campbell, Kennedy, & Milbourne, 2012), which provides practical solutions for ensuring all

Table 6.3. Checklists and assessments that support inclusion for individual children

Name	Author	Year	Publisher	Purpose	Age range	Format	Administration	Technical adequacy reported?	Formal training required?
CARA's Kit: Creating Adaptations for Routines and Activities	Milbourne and Campbell	2007	Division for Early Childhood	Helps reader understand the needs of children by rating their performance and engagement in daily classroom routines and activities and the use of adaptations to maximize learning and participation opportunities for all children	3–6 years	1. This focuses on level of satisfaction and expectation of a child's performance in two domains: activity and developmental area/skill. 2. This is a checklist.	Through classroom observation in the context of daily routines and activities and discussions among program or classroom staff	No	No
Ecological Congruence Assessment	Wolery, Brashers, and Neitzel	2002	Wolery, M., Brashers, M.S., & Neitzel, J.C. (2002). Ecological Congruence Assessment for Classroom Activities and Routines. *Topics in Early Childhood Special Education, 22,* 131–142.	Strategy for identifying goals and interventions for children with disabilities in inclusive classrooms	Not specified, but likely to be birth to 5 years	This focuses on the classroom daily routines and activities. The classroom staff records the child's participation and the level of assistance the child needs to participate in the classroom activities and routines.	Through classroom observation within the context of daily routines and activities	No	No
Member of the Class: Teachers Guide	Head Start Center for Inclusion	N/A	Publicly available at http://depts.washington.edu/hscenter/sites/default/files/teachers%20guide-MOC.pdf	Is developed as a resource to guide the classroom inclusion practices for teachers	Pre-school	This is a set of yes/no questions with open fields for writing down next steps if needed.	Self-evaluation, but from the perspective of a child with special needs	No	No
The Quality Inclusive Experiences Measure	Wolery, Pauca, Brashers, and Grant	2000[a]	Publicly available at http://nceln.fpg.unc.edu/sites/nceln.fpg.unc.edu/files/resources/Quality_of_Inclusive_Experiences_Measure.pdf	Provides a comprehensive overview of a child's inclusive experience in a classroom or program	Not specified, but likely to be birth to 5 years	1. This measures seven dimensions: program goals and purposes, staff supports and perceptions, accessibility of the physical environment, individualization, children's participation and engagement, adult–child contacts and relationships, and child–child contacts and interaction. 2. It is a combination of anecdotal notes, ratings, and event recordings.	Completed via a combination of direct observations of the target child, stakeholder interviews, as well as ratings of the program quality	No	No

[a] In 2005, the Quality Inclusive Experiences Measure–Revised was published by Milbourne and Schmidt. The revision was primarily for format and layout, and no changes were made to content or administration. Thus, instead of the revised version, the original one was introduced in this chapter.

toddlers are participating, engaged, and learning across classroom activities and routines.

Ecological Congruence Assessment

The Ecological Congruence Assessment (ECA; Wolery, Brashers, & Neitzel, 2002) is a process developed to support the inclusion of young children within child care settings. The ECA process provides child care teachers a resource to give input toward the goals and interventions of children with special needs within their care. The ECA also gives specialists information regarding each child's functioning within the daily routines and activities in the child care settings. Table 6.4 provides a sample page from the ECA.

Member of the Class: Teacher Guide

Member of the Class: Teacher Guide is a resource developed by the Head Start Center for Inclusion for teachers to increase their use of classroom inclusion practices.

Table 6.4.   Sample page of the Ecological Congruence Assessment

Teacher:	Child's name:	Date:	Classroom:
Activity	**Child's participation**	**Helping issues**	**Notes**
Arrival	Is the child doing the same thing as peers? If no, what is the child doing? What are peers doing?	Does the child require more help than peers? Yes/No If yes, what kind of help? • Getting engaged • Staying engaged • Interacting with peers • Doesn't have skills to do the activity	
Center time	Is the child doing the same thing as peers? If no, what is the child doing? What are peers doing?	Does the child require more help than peers? Yes/No If yes, what kind of help? • Getting engaged • Staying engaged • Interacting with peers • Doesn't have skills to do the activity	
Circle time	Is the child doing the same thing as peers? If no, what is the child doing? What are peers doing?	Does the child require more help than peers? Yes/No If yes, what kind of help? • Getting engaged • Staying engaged • Interacting with peers • Doesn't have skills to do the activity	
Snack	Is the child doing the same thing as peers? If no, what is the child doing? What are peers doing?	Does the child require more help than peers? Yes/No If yes, what kind of help? • Getting engaged • Staying engaged • Interacting with peers • Doesn't have skills to do the activity	

From Wolery, M., Brashers, M.S., Grant, S., and Pauca, T. (2000). *Ecological congruence assessment for classroom activities and routines in childcare.* Chapel Hill, NC: Frank Porter Graham Child Development Center. As used in Wolery, M., Brashers, M.S., and Neitzel, J.C. (2002). Ecological congruence assessment for classroom activities and routines: Identifying goals and intervention practices in childcare. *Topics in Early Childhood Special Education* 22(3), 131–142. Copyright © 2000 by SAGE Publications. Adapted by Permission of SAGE Publications.

All questions are designed to help teachers promote membership in the classroom and optimize the opportunities for children with special needs to interact with peers and engage in daily classroom routines and activities. Teachers answer the yes/no questions as if they were a child with special needs and plan the next steps when the answer is *no*. This teacher guide can be downloaded from the Head Start Center for Inclusion: http://depts.washington.edu/hscenter/sites/default/files/teachers%20guide-MOC.pdf.

The Quality Inclusive Experiences Measure

The Quality Inclusive Experiences Measure (QuIEM; Wolery, Pauca, Brashers, & Grant, 2000) provides a comprehensive overview of a child's inclusive experience in a classroom/program. The QuIEM is intended to be completed by both administrators and teachers for each child with special needs enrolled in their classroom/program, and it can be individualized to pinpoint program practices that are deemed relevant for the child's needs so that positive child outcomes can be promoted (Dugan, Milbourne, & Schmidt, 2005). Seven dimensions are measured in the QuIEM:

1. Program goals and purposes

2. Staff supports and perceptions

3. Accessibility of the physical environment

4. Individualization

5. Children's participation and engagement

6. Adult–child contacts and relationships

7. Child–child contacts and interaction

The QuIEM is completed via a combination of direct observations of a target child, stakeholder interviews, as well as ratings of program quality. For a revised version of QuIEM with updated format and layout, go to http://nceln.fpg.unc.edu/sites/nceln.fpg.unc.edu/files/resources/Quality_of_Inclusive_Experiences_Measure.pdf.

The following continuation of the case example of the Maceo family describes how Ms. Humphrey used her knowledge gained at the workshop to plan instruction for Raphael and set up her classroom environment.

Case Study: The Maceo Family

Ms. Humphrey and the school's preschool inclusion team were excited about having Raphael included in the general education setting and recognized the need to measure the quality of the preschool classrooms. In the past, Ms. Humphrey had used the ECERS-R, and in the last year, her state developed a QRIS. However, she knew these were not focused specifically on inclusion. The preschool inclusion team discussed the possibly of identifying and using a new measure to monitor the quality of the inclusive classroom as part of their action plan. While researching preschool inclusion measures of quality, Ms. Humphrey and the team also realized they might want to measure Raphael's individual experience in the inclusive classroom. They reviewed several measures and decided to use the QuIEM (Wolery, Pauca,

Brashers, & Grant, 2000) to measure Raphael's individual experience with inclusion as well as the PACE-R (Raab & Dunst, 1997) because they were freely available and both had some research to support their use. At Ms. Humphrey's suggestion, the preschool inclusion team also used the DEC Recommended Practices as an evaluation tool. They completed the PACE-R immediately, even though they knew they were still getting the classroom up and running, to establish a baseline and see where they were. They planned to complete the same measure again in 2 months.

After completing the checklist version of the PACE-R, the preschool inclusion team, Ms. Humphrey, and her coach, Ms. Martinez, identified several items they already had in place and several items to address.

"Things we are already doing well":

- Arrange for on-the-job training.

- Clearly divide open classrooms into learning areas.

- Have appropriate child-size furniture.

- Select adequate material.

- Define staff schedules and ensure they are followed.

- Ensure learning activities are developmentally appropriate.

- Ensure children do not wait for activities to begin or end.

- Make multiple activity options available to children throughout the day.

- Respond to child-initiated behaviors.

- Provide individual attention.

"Things to work on":

- Create a written program philosophy that supports inclusion.

- Intentionally communicate with parents more often.

- Monitor staff performance.

- Increase time for staff planning and meeting.

- Review all child goals for functionality.

- Keep working on embedded instruction to ensure all learning takes place during naturally occurring classroom routines and appropriate strategies are used to promote practice and learning.

- Ensure all behavior management procedures are planned and used consistently.

- Intentionally plan evaluation of overall classroom.

- Regularly review individual child data.

These outcomes were not surprising, and they provided a starting point and specific things to address for implementing quality preschool inclusion. The team also planned to complete the QuIEM and review the DEC Recommended Practices 1 month after Raphael started to get baseline measures once the classroom schedules were in place. Because this was so new to Ms. Humphrey and Ms. Ebony, they also planned to use CARA's Kit: Creating Adaptations for Routines and Activities (Milbourne & Campbell, 2007). This checklist was designed to help EC educators understand the needs of children 3–6 years of age by rating their performance and engagement in daily classroom routines and activities and the use of adaptations to maximize learning and participation opportunities for all children; this seemed perfect for helping Ms. Humphrey get the classroom up and running! Ms. Humphrey was excited to incorporate CARA's Kit into her regular practice, as it seemed practical and easy to use.

CONCLUSION

One thing is certain in regard to preschool inclusion: The positive impact accrues to children only when the inclusive experience is of sufficient quality and intensity. In other words, children need to be *educated with their peers*—not merely placed in the same environment. The measures described in this chapter can be used to assess your preschool program and should be used to make improvements to ensure all children are fully engaged and participating members of the classroom. Several common features of these measures have been summarized into the following recommendations for planning and implementing quality preschool inclusion:

1. Ensure you have administrative and professional commitment to preschool inclusion.

2. Plan and implement frequent social and educational interactions between children with and without disabilities.

3. Embed comprehensive EBPs and procedures that include intensive parent involvement, intentional instruction, repeated outcome assessment, and well-defined curricular content.

4. Identify and use a curriculum that is individualized to learner needs and abilities and is developmentally appropriate.

5. Establish a system of fully inclusive and "blended" services, staff, classrooms, and instructional practices between regular and special education.

6. Provide adequate supports for teachers and an ongoing commitment to PD in effective practices.

7. Emphasize collaborative teaming, planning, and decision making between personnel trained in special and general education.

8. Establish a system for ongoing, overall program evaluation that includes collecting and evaluating the opinions of consumers.

The tools described in this chapter can be used as your preschool inclusion team develops a plan to implement and sustain quality inclusion. Preschool inclusion teams should identify one or two tools that meet their program needs and use them along with the DEC Recommended Practices to regularly monitor program quality. These data can then be used to "show off" how well programs are doing and highlight any improvements made using the ongoing data collected. The preschool inclusion team should plan to regularly review programmatic data along with individual child data to ensure the needs of all children and families are being met and to make decisions about programmatic improvements.

REFLECTION QUESTIONS

1. Name four quality indicators of inclusion.
2. Name three measures of quality inclusion that can be used to evaluate EC inclusive programs.
3. Name three inclusion checklists that can be used for individual children.
4. Name four classroom observation tools that assess the quality of practices in general EC programs or provide an overall rating of the classroom environment.

7

Making Individualized Child Placement Decisions

Erin E. Barton, Debbie Cate, Katy McCullough, and Geneva J. Hallett

TOOLS FROM THE TOOLBOX

- **Box 7.1** State Education Agency Support for Preschool Inclusion
- **Form 7.1** Placement Options Consideration Planning Form
- **Form 7.2** Advantages and Limitations of Placement Options
- **Table 7.1** Using the DEC Recommended Practices in Early Intervention/Early Childhood Special Education to Guide the Development of Inclusive Systems

In the previous chapters of the toolbox, tools are provided for preschool inclusion teams to 1) develop a school district vision and action plan for preschool inclusion; 2) raise awareness of the importance of preschool inclusion; 3) identify and change policies, procedures, and beliefs limiting preschool inclusion; 4) create PD systems including training and coaching; and 5) provide the foundation for IEP teams to be able to provide high-quality inclusive experiences and placements for young children with disabilities.

The purpose of this chapter is to outline the principles and practices that should guide individual child placement decisions. This chapter provides sample procedures and considerations for individualized placement options and for sustaining successful, high-quality inclusive practices. Examples of preschool inclusion policies and recommendations from several states are provided as well as forms that programs/districts can use to make individualized placement decisions. As you read this chapter, also recall the definition of high-quality inclusion provided in the Introduction. Inclusion means children are given access to a range of experiences and provided the supports they need to fully participate alongside their typical peers in the general education classroom.

GUIDING PRINCIPLES FOR INDIVIDUALIZED PLACEMENT DECISIONS

In Chapters 2 and 3, we discussed the importance of the preschool inclusion team establishing a written vision statement for preschool inclusion and developing an action plan to guide preschool inclusion efforts. The following three principles should be considered while establishing the vision statement and action plan to ensure that IEP teams will have the necessary resources and procedures when making placement decisions for individual children:

1. The IEP team, including parents and professionals, must ensure that individual placement decisions are in the LRE within a full range of placement options and per IDEA with a preference for the general education setting (Musgrove, 2012).

2. All placement options should reflect *high quality* and be able to support the delivery of appropriate and effective special education and related services with supports from the school district including supplementary aids and services and training and technical assistance.

3. Placement decisions should be based on the individual needs of the child and consideration of family preferences, as agreed on in the IEP.

These three principles should be used by the preschool inclusion team to develop policies and procedures that facilitate appropriate individualized placement decisions by the IEP team.

Principle 1: Least Restrictive Environment

The IEP team, including parents and professionals, must ensure that individual placement decisions are in the least restrictive environment (LRE) within a full range of placement options and per IDEA with a preference for the general education setting (Musgrove, 2012). A full range of placement options should be available for educational and legal reasons—that is, special education and related services are not a one-size-fits-all approach. The needs and strengths of children and families vary; thus, services and supports should be tailored to meet individual child and family needs. Legally, Part B of IDEA specifies these requirements:

(a) Each public agency must ensure that a continuum of alternative placements is available to meet the needs of children with disabilities for special education and related services.

(b) The continuum required in paragraph (a) of this section must:

    (1) Include the alternative placements listed in the definition of special education under § 300.38 (instruction in regular classes, special classes, special schools, home instruction, and instruction in hospitals and institutions); and

    (2) Make provision for supplementary services (such as resource room or itinerant instruction) to be provided in conjunction with regular class placement. (§ 300.115 Continuum of alternative placements)

According to IDEA regulations (34 CFR §300) and U.S. Department of Education policy (see Appendixes IB and IC), IDEA has a "strong preference for educating students with disabilities in the regular classes with appropriate aids and supports" (Musgrove, 2012). The regulations also state, "Each public agency must ensure that a continuum of alternative placements is available to meet the needs of children with disabilities for special education and related services" (34 CFR §300.115[a]) and "is as close as possible to the child's home" (34 CFR §300.116[b][3]).

(a) General:

    (1) Except as provided in § 300.324(d)(2) (regarding children with disabilities in adult prisons), the State must have in effect policies and procedures to ensure

that public agencies in the State meet the LRE requirements of this section and §§ 300.115 through 300.120.

(2) Each public agency must ensure that:

(i) To the maximum extent appropriate, children with disabilities, including children in public or private institutions or other care facilities, are educated with children who are nondisabled; and

(ii) Special classes, separate schooling, or other removal of children with disabilities from the regular educational environment occurs only if the nature or severity of the disability is such that education in regular classes with the use of supplementary aids and services cannot be achieved satisfactorily. (§ 300.114 LRE requirements)

The IDEA LRE requirements apply to all public school systems, including those that do not operate preschool programs for children without disabilities (Musgrove, 2012; Salisbury & Smith, 1991). Alternatives for children in these systems include the following:

1. Providing opportunities for the participation (even part-time) of preschool children with disabilities in other preschool programs operated by public agencies (e.g., Head Start, child care).

2. Placing children with disabilities in private preschool programs or child care.

3. Creating inclusive preschool programs within the school. This can be done by intentionally blending classrooms of children attending programs such as state pre-K, Head Start, or Title I, depending on the programs in the district. Another way to create an inclusive environment is by enrolling children without disabilities into the public school program. Some districts might charge a fee for children without disabilities to attend the program, though this varies greatly across states and districts.

Inclusion at the pre-K level presents a unique set of challenges. Unlike K–12 education, which is available to all students through the public schools, districts might not have inclusive preschool classrooms. The first step in establishing a range of options is to take inventory of the resources and programs in your school, district, and community, including any program the child with a disability is already attending, such as a child care program. Districts that do not have inclusive preschools must explore other inclusion options, such as those described previously. These nondistrict programs need to reflect high quality and meet children's needs. They can do so with supports from the school district such as training, coaching, and technical assistance. For example, school districts can provide itinerant special education teachers or related services personnel to work with child care programs, community preschools, Head Start classrooms, or other nondistrict programs in which children with IEPs currently attend.

Principle 2: Ensure Quality, Appropriateness, and Effectiveness of Services

All placement options should reflect *high quality* and be able to support the delivery of appropriate and effective special education and related services with supports from the school district including supplementary aids and services and training and technical assistance.

APPLICATION QUESTION
Now that you have read Chapter 6, what plans or procedures does your preschool inclusion team have in place to monitor classroom quality and the quality of preschool inclusion? How often will the team be collecting and reviewing this programmatic data? Discuss these questions with your preschool inclusion team.

Each school and district needs to establish policies and procedures that support preschool inclusion *and* ensure that the special education services and classroom environment reflect quality and promote the child's learning and development. Part B of IDEA requires that all special education and related services provided to eligible children be "appropriate," "meet the standards of the state educational agency," and be "provided in conformity with an individualized education program" (34 CFR §300.4). To ensure effectiveness, IDEA stipulates that supplementary aids and services as well as training and technical assistance must be provided in the general education environment.

Supplementary aids and services means aids, services, and other supports that are provided in regular education classes, other education-related settings, and in extracurricular and nonacademic settings, to enable children with disabilities to be educated with nondisabled children to the maximum extent appropriate in accordance with §§ 300.114 through 300.116. (§ 300.42 Supplementary aids and services)

Each SEA must carry out activities to ensure that teachers and administrators in all public agencies:

(a) Are fully informed about their responsibilities for implementing § 300.114; and

(b) Are provided with technical assistance and training necessary to assist them in this effort. (§ 300.119 Technical assistance and training activities)

As described in Chapters 2 and 3, one of the most frequently reported challenges to preschool inclusion (especially nonschool based) is the concern of not being able to ensure the quality and appropriateness of services and instruction (Barton & Smith, 2014b). However, there are multiple procedures and measures for assessing quality of preschool inclusion, as described in Chapters 5 and 6. The preschool inclusion team needs to decide which measure is most appropriate for the program and how to evaluate and use the data. These measures should be used to complement the state's QRIS. The results of these measures can target the programmatic needs of a placement setting and guide technical assistance activities. Chapter 1 summarizes characteristics of high-quality, effective preschool inclusion.

Principle 3: Make Individualized Placement Decisions

Placement decisions should be based on the individual needs of the child and consideration of family preferences, as agreed on in the IEP.

According to the Education Law Center,

Pre-k children have the right to a free and appropriate public education in the least restrictive environment, or LRE. The law requires that pre-k children with disabilities receive their education together with children without disabilities to the maximum extent appropriate. Hence, the vast majority of pre-k children with disabilities should be placed in regular early education programs. An LEA may meet its obligation to provide inclusive pre-k services by placing a child in a district pre-k or in any of the other programs available in the community for the general population, such as a Head Start program, or a private, community-based pre-k program.

LEAs are required to have a wide range of pre-k placement options to meet the unique needs of each child. If placement outside of a regular early childhood classroom is necessary for a child's educational benefit, an LEA still must include the child in programs with children who do not have disabilities to the maximum extent possible. The individualized education program, or IEP, of a pre-k child provides the LRE framework. In addition to specifying the child's special education and related services, the IEP must include, among other components, a statement of how the child's disability affects his or her participation in appropriate pre-k activities. (2010, pp. 3–4)

By developing facilitative policies, the preschool inclusion team has laid the foundation for implementing high-quality preschool inclusion. The team should have also identified a range of placement options; developed a PD system that provides training, coaching, and technical assistance; and established a process for recognizing effective and appropriate programs. The next step is to make sure individual placement options are appropriate and effective for each child's learning and development.

Since first introduced into law in 1975, IDEA has clearly displayed a strong preference for children with disabilities to be educated alongside their peers without disabilities (Musgrove, 2012). IDEA not only states a preference for inclusive services but requires that supplementary aids and services accompany the child into the setting with peers without disabilities and training and technical assistance be provided to teachers and administrators.

These LRE requirements apply to preschool children with disabilities receiving services under IDEA. Placement decisions are individually determined based on each child's abilities and needs as described in their IEPs. Specifically IDEA says,

In determining the educational placement of a child with a disability, including a preschool child with a disability, each public agency must ensure that—

(a) The placement decision:
   (1) Is made by a group of persons, including the parents, and other persons knowledgeable about the child, the meaning of the evaluation data, and the placement options; and
   (2) Is made in conformity with the LRE provisions of this subpart, including §§ 300.114 through 300.118;

(b) The child's placement:
   (1) Is determined at least annually;
   (2) Is based on the child's IEP; and
   (3) Is as close as possible to the child's home;

(c) Unless the IEP of a child with a disability requires some other arrangement, the child is educated in the school that he or she would attend if nondisabled;

(d) In selecting the LRE, consideration is given to any potential harmful effect on the child or on the quality of services that he or she needs; and

(e) A child with a disability is not removed from education in age appropriate regular classrooms solely because of needed modifications in the general education curriculum. (§ 300.116 Placements)

The IEP team's discussion of placement options begins after the child's strengths, needs, and goals are considered as well as supplementary aids and services that might need to be provided in the setting. If a young child with a disability can be satisfactorily educated according to his or her IEP in a regular EC program (with needed supplementary aids and services), then a regular EC program is that child's LRE. Placing this child in a segregated class or separate program because that is the only type of EC placement or program the district has available would not be consistent with the LRE provisions in IDEA. Placement decisions based on funding streams are also inconsistent with IDEA. IDEA provides that IDEA funds can benefit children without disabilities in the general education environment if that is the most appropriate placement for a child with a disability.

> (a) *Uses.* Notwithstanding §§ 300.202, 300.203(a), and 300.162(b), funds provided to an LEA under Part B of the Act may be used for the following activities:
>
>> (1) *Services and aids that also benefit nondisabled children.* For the costs of special education and related services, and supplementary aids and services, provided in a regular class or other education-related setting to a child with a disability in accordance with the IEP of the child, even if one or more nondisabled children benefit from these services. (§ 300.208 Permissive use of funds)

Few states and school districts operate universal programs for all 3- and 4-year-old children, making it challenging to provide opportunities for inclusive environments for young children with disabilities. OSEP has provided guidance for alternative methods that may be used to meet the LRE requirements (Musgrove, 2012). Depending on the needs of the individual child being considered, public agencies can do one of the following:

- Provide opportunities for the participation of preschool children with disabilities in preschool programs operated by public agencies such as Head Start, Title I, state prekindergarten, or child care
- Enroll children with disabilities in private preschool programs for children who do not have disabilities and/or provide special education and related itinerant services on-site to children enrolled in private preschools

For data collection purposes, a regular EC program is defined by OSEP as a program that includes a majority (at least 50%) of typically developing children (i.e., children who do not have IEPs). These programs may include the following:

- Head Start
- Kindergarten
- Preschool classes offered to an eligible prekindergarten population by the public school system, such as Title I or state prekindergarten programs
- Private kindergartens or preschools
- Child development centers or child care

States can help school districts understand their educational environment data and how to use those data to set targets for improvement.

Administrative Challenges and Supports   In addition to making good LRE decisions for individual children, intentional planning and design among district and community preschool programs is necessary to ensure availability of placement options for preschool children with disabilities to participate in regular EC programs. The process of blending and integrating EC programs with different funding sources and program requirements necessitates collaboration, commitment, and planning to ensure that teachers have the skills necessary to ensure positive outcomes for all children. Such collaborative planning has the added value of reducing duplication of effort across programs (e.g., PD and instructional coaching) and maximizing resources to support all high-quality EC programs. This is an important task of the preschool inclusion team.

Administrators, at both the state and local levels, can be in a challenging position when it comes to encouraging and supporting the implementation of inclusive service delivery options for young children. State-level administrators often lack the authority to enforce inclusive service delivery options in districts, which can vary greatly not only by size and demographics but also by availability of community programs. This is particularly true if the state special education director or the local administration does not understand the importance of and embrace preschool inclusion as a departmental priority. The DEC Recommended Practices in EI/ECSE can help guide state and local administrators in embedding preschool inclusion into their policies and infrastructure for special education.

The Part B regulations of IDEA specify that the IEP must contain a "statement of the special education and related services and supplementary aids and services, *based on peer-reviewed research to the extent practicable,* to be provided to the child, or on behalf of the child, and a statement of the program modifications or supports for school personnel that will be provided" (34 CFR §300.320[a][4]). While there is no reference to EBPs, a review of the literature reveals trends in direct support of the topical areas identified in the DEC Recommended Practices of leadership, assessment, environment, family, instruction, interaction, teaming and collaboration, and transition. The DEC Recommended Practices are based on the best available evidence as well as knowledge, values, and expertise from the field.

When looking to the DEC Recommended Practices as a guide to support state and district administrators in ensuring quality and effective services in inclusive settings, it may be helpful to consider implications in accordance to the various infrastructure components of the service delivery system, such as governance, personnel, finance, quality standards, data collection, and accountability and quality improvement (http://ectacenter.org/sysframe; ECTA, 2014). Table 7.1 depicts each of the system components, their purpose, the relevant topic areas from the DEC Recommended Practices, and suggestions for administrators and preschool inclusion teams for what they can do at a systems level to ensure quality and effective services in inclusive settings.

TOOLS FOR MAKING INDIVIDUALIZED INCLUSIVE PLACEMENT DECISIONS

IDEA requires that the extent to which a child with a disability can participate in general education programs must be included on his or her IEP. Thus, each child's IEP team, including the child's family, should collaboratively identify the placement, supports and services needed, and accommodations or modifications that are necessary for the child's learning and development. The preschool inclusion team should have provided the foundation for these decisions through awareness, policies, procedures, and PD systems. The following sample procedures and forms are provided to support appropriate, individualized preschool placement decisions.

Table 7.1. Using the DEC Recommended Practices in early intervention/early childhood special education to guide the development of inclusive systems

System component	Purpose	DEC Recommended Practices topic areas	What can the preschool inclusion team do?
Governance	Provide the foundation or authority underpinning the program, including vision and structure, and leverage resources and collaboration.	Leadership	Know who your early childhood partners are based on where typically developing children (in your community) spend their time. Share information on the benefits of inclusion for all stakeholders—children, families, communities, practitioners—as well as other findings from the research. Include DEC Recommended Practices in memoranda of understanding with other early childhood partners. Draft guidance documents on service delivery models and braiding of funds with potential community partners.
Personnel	Implement a coordinated system of professional development that includes recruitment and retention, standards and competencies, and ongoing systematic professional development strategies.	Assessment Environment Family Instruction Interaction Teaming and collaboration Transition	Align professional development (PD) and technical assistance efforts with the seven DEC Recommended Practices topic areas for practitioners. Actively engage in cross-sector PD opportunities by jointly planning events, invite partners to special education–sponsored PD events, and request information on partner PD that special education and itinerant staff could participate in. Look for opportunities to systemically support coaching and mentoring for practitioners. Allow time for teaming and collaboration by service delivery team and more broadly across early childhood partners.
Finance	Use fiscal and program data to engage in a financial planning process to identify funds and resources needed to sustain the system.	Leadership	Review demographic data on IDEA-eligible children to consider what other programmatic resources and funding supports may be available for collaboration. Be on the lookout for upcoming funding opportunities with other EC partners at the local, state, and national levels. Minimize administrative burden to adhere to funding requirements from multiple funding streams.
Quality standards	Establish and support the use of child-level and program-level standards to support the implementation of high-quality practices.	Assessment Environment Family Instruction Interaction Teaming and collaboration Transition	Cross-walk various program standards and adhere to the most rigorous.
Data collection	Collect data about children, families, the work force, and/or program characteristics (e.g., program quality), as well as analyze, report, and use information associated with those data.	Leadership Assessment Instruction	Be familiar with what current data are available—fiscal, programmatic, and demographic—both within and across early childhood programs. Draft or identify brief documents to report and track data on strategies implemented, by whom, how often, and performance.
Accountability and quality improvement	Plan for accountability and improvement by collecting and analyzing performance data and using results for continuous improvement.	Leadership	Create incentives, using discretionary funds, to track performance and drive program improvement.

Key: DEC, Division for Early Childhood; PD, professional development; IDEA, Individuals with Disabilities Education Act; EC, early childhood.

SAMPLE PROCESS FOR MAKING INDIVIDUALIZED INCLUSIVE PRESCHOOL PLACEMENTS DURING INDIVIDUALIZED EDUCATION PROGRAM MEETINGS

1. After collaborating with the family to develop the child's goals and objectives, the IEP team (including the parents and regular EC teacher) should consider the appropriate environments for achieving these goals and objectives. When considering each possible placement setting, the IEP team must consider the provisions of IDEA, including what adaptations, modifications, supplementary aids and services, *and training and technical assistance* can make that setting successful for the child. Form 7.1 includes a list of examples of possible placement options.

2. If the child is currently in an inclusive setting, the IEP team should consider if it is likely that the child can achieve his or her goals and objectives in this setting with the special education and related services being provided there. This should be documented in the child's IEP.

3. If the IEP team determines that the child is unlikely to achieve his or her goals and objectives in the current setting without modifications, accommodations, supplementary aids and services, or training and technical assistance, the team should identify all that is needed.

4. Parent preferences regarding placement options should be discussed and considered.

5. The IEP team should identify the necessary characteristics of the proposed placement including the characteristics that are of particular importance to the family. This step in the process is essential for identifying and verifying the most appropriate LRE in which the child can receive special education and related services as specified on his or her IEP.

6. After completing each of the previous steps, the IEP team is ready to make a placement decision. This might involve removing the child from his or her current placement. This step should be documented on his or her IEP.

7. The IEP team should summarize the discussion regarding placement options on the IEP, including listing the other placements that were considered and why they were rejected. Any differing viewpoints also should be noted on the IEP. Form 7.2 includes space to present a summary statement.

STATE EDUCATION AGENCY SUPPORT

State education agency (SEA) support and leadership is crucial for preschool inclusion at the local level. The SEA must set a vision and direction and help develop facilitative policies, resources, PD opportunities, and funding mechanisms. Box 7.1 provides a list of ways the SEA can support preschool inclusion. Following are examples from a few of the states that have developed recommendations regarding preschool inclusion.

New Jersey

The following are excerpts from the New Jersey Department of Education Preschool Program Implementation Guidelines (2010):

Placement Options Consideration Planning Form

1. What specific strengths and needs does the child have that must be considered when considering placement options?

   List all:

2. What program or classroom characteristics are needed in an appropriate placement for this child?

   List all:

3. Where does the child currently attend school or special education and related services?

4. Is the current location of services inclusive?

   ___ Yes   ___ No

5. What are the family's preferences?

6. Is it likely that the child can achieve his or her goals and objectives in this setting with the special education and related services being provided there?

   ___ Yes   ___ No

   Rationale:

7. Are accommodations, modifications, supplementary aids and services, or training and technical assistance needed in the current placement to make that setting successful for the child?

   ___ Yes   ___ No

   What is needed?

   Accommodations:

   Modifications:

   Supplementary aids and services:

   Training and technical assistance:

8. If the individualized education program team determines that the child is unlikely to achieve his or her goals and objectives in the current setting with modifications, accommodations, supplementary aids and services, and training and technical assistance, what other placements are available?

   Consider each of the following:

   ___ Community preschools/child care

   ___ Combination of community/public school settings

   ___ Recreational programs in the community (e.g., YMCA, libraries)

   ___ Home

   ___ State preschool programs

   ___ Head Start

FORM 7.2.

Advantages and Limitations of Placement Options

Placement Option and Potential Location	Advantages	Limitations	Rank

Option Recommended:

Summary of Rationale:

As per N.J.A.C.6A: 14-4.2(a) Students with disabilities shall be educated in the least restrictive environment . . .

- To the maximum extent appropriate, a student with a disability is educated with children who are not disabled;

- Special classes, separate schooling or other removal of a student with a disability from the student's general education class occurs only when the nature or severity of the educational disability is such that education in the student's general education class with the use of appropriate supplementary aids and services cannot be achieved satisfactorily;

- A student with a disability is not removed from the age-appropriate general education classroom solely based on needed modifications to the general education curriculum;

In the event that there is disagreement, the school district has an obligation to inform parents of due process rights in referral. A parent and a preschool teacher or an administrator who is familiar with the school district's preschool programs must be present at all meetings when determining special education services and placement. Classroom teachers are involved in the planning process.

APPLICATION QUESTION

Do a search on your state's department of education web site for preschool inclusion. What resources does your state provide to support preschool inclusion? Discuss this within your preschool inclusion team.

The following describes referral for an evaluation:

When a potential disability is suspected, or if a child's screening results require it, a written referral to the school district's child study team starts the process of determining whether a child may be eligible for special education. The parent, preschool teacher, PIRT [preschool intervention and referral team] and the child study team meet to determine the need for evaluation and discuss the assessments to be completed. After completion of the evaluation and a determination of eligibility, an Individualized Education Program (IEP) is developed. In addition to special education personnel, the IEP team always includes the parent and the preschool teacher. The team determines what types of support are necessary, such as modifications to the classroom or special education services. To the maximum extent appropriate, preschoolers with disabilities should receive their preschool education with their peers.

The following are recommendations regarding inclusion:

- Administrative supports are in place that facilitate inclusion

BOX 7.1. State education agency support for preschool inclusion

Develop a state-level vision statement that clearly establishes preschool inclusion as a value and priority.

Use language that promotes the importance and value of all young children being educated together, including providing special education and related services to 3- to 5-year-olds in regular early childhood settings.

Provide training and technical assistance to school district administrators, teachers, related service personnel, and families on high-quality preschool inclusion practices and procedures.

Work with school district administrators and preschool inclusion teams to identify and change policies, procedures, and funding mechanisms that are challenges to preschool inclusion.

Provide incentives to recognize and reward school districts that explore new ways to provide high-quality preschool inclusion and increase the numbers of children in inclusive settings.

- Children with special needs are served in least restrictive environments with IEP goals addressed in the context of the curriculum and daily activities
- Children with special needs are served in general education classrooms to the maximum extent possible
- The proportion of children with and without special needs reflects that of the general population
- The IEP team includes the teacher, parent, child study team member, and special education personnel
- Push in and pull out services are not used or are used on a limited basis. [*Push in* refers to the special education teacher or related services therapist providing services *in* the regular classroom in an individual or small-group setting. *Pull out* refers to the special education teacher or related services therapist providing services *outside* of the regular classroom in an individual or small-group setting.]

The following are recommendations for districts regarding community support:

- An Early Childhood Advisory Council is in place and participates in program planning, community needs assessment, and the self-assessment
- The Early Childhood Advisory Council includes appropriate community representatives and meets at least quarterly
- Regular meetings are scheduled with private providers, including Head Start
- The needs and goals of the community, as determined by a community needs assessment, are met

California

The following excerpts are from All Children Have Individual Needs, Building an Inclusive Preschool for All Program, Principles and Considerations for Planning and Implementation (2004):

Delivery System: An inclusive preschool delivery system must integrate special education and related services into all aspects of its program to create a system that addresses the needs of preschool children, taking into account the varying forms of care children experience prior to preschool and the importance of seamless transition from early care to preschool and preschool to kindergarten. It must:

- integrate children into full-day, full-year programs as family circumstances require while maintaining the flexibility that children with disabilities and their families may need.
- ensure that all child-based state standards are written to include children with special needs.
- promote coordinated delivery of services and create a streamlined process that avoids requiring families to apply to multiple agencies to receive the services they need.
- make specialty services available in a way that is appropriate and convenient by, e.g., bringing services to children rather than transporting children to services.
- establish adult/child ratios that allow for inclusion of children of all abilities and needs.
- establish and support an oversight entity (individual or office) whose function is to help parents navigate the complex system of services for their children with disabilities.
- make special efforts to avoid disruption of services at points such as the transition from child care or early intervention programs to pre-school and pre-school to kindergarten.
- incorporate a child's IFSP, IPP, IEP, Section 504 plans and any informal individual plans within the delivery of services.
- minimize the number of transitions and settings the child experiences on a daily or weekly basis, and the number of adults with whom the child must interact, while still meeting the family's needs for child care.

- formalize agreements between agencies (e.g., California Department of Education, Resource & Referral Agencies, Family Resource Centers, Special Education Providers, Special Education Local Planning Agencies, child care, Head Start, etc.) to promote coownership of responsibility for meeting children's needs.
- integrate public and private programs at the management/administration level to foster collaboration.
- anticipate the needs of families who have the greatest difficulty in ensuring that their children's needs are met, such as homeless, foster, migrant, and mobile families.
- anticipate barriers to inclusion and address them at the policy and planning stages.
- address the particular challenges to rural programs when rural communities are included in the service area.
- throughout the child's preschool experience, involve parents in service planning, including participation in developing IEP's, IFP's, IFSP's, Section 504 plans and informal individual plans to foster a smooth transition to kindergarten. Effective education and service planning should include all appropriate family members and service providers.

Workforce Development: An inclusive preschool program must recruit, develop, and retain a workforce that understands the importance of the relationship among children, family members, and staff and possesses the capacity and qualifications to serve, relate to, and advocate for a broad range of children. The program must:

- integrate qualifications to serve children with disabilities and other special needs into the overall definition of qualifications and ensure that institutes of higher education offer classes to reach this goal.
- train education workforce in inclusion principles and practices, implementation of these principles and practices within the whole system, how to build partnerships with families, and how to work with all the child's service providers. Training must:
  - include a working knowledge of the relevant laws and regulations that applies to educating children with disabilities and other special needs.
  - include both "specialized" providers who also have knowledge of how to work in groups and general education teachers who know how to work with children with disabilities and other special needs.
  - include direct experience in inclusion settings.
  - include model parent-professional partnerships.
  - involve both parents and providers, be ongoing, and be offered in multiple settings.
  - promote seamless transitions between the early intervention/special education system and the child's preschool.
- involve service providers and educators who work with children with special needs in planning preschool programs.
- ensure inclusion and disability and behavioral health specialists in leadership and administrative positions to implement the adoption of policies to meet children's special needs.
- make ongoing support and joint training available to teachers, parents, and service providers to promote integration of all services and service providers into the preschool setting.
- provide opportunities for the workforce to develop best practices for accommodating children with different abilities, including communication at the important transition points between Early Intervention and preschool and between preschool and the K-12 system.
- ensure that the workforce has access to ongoing technical assistance and support from disability specialists, e.g., physical, occupational, and speech therapists and mental health care providers.

- help create an early care and education career ladder that includes opportunities for specialized training in inclusive preschool services that leads to an additional degree or credential (e.g. dual credentials in Early Childhood Education and Early Childhood Special Education).
- ensure that staff receive support from their supervision in their work with families, including time for Reflective Supervision.

Financing: An inclusive preschool program must have sufficient financing in place to provide necessary services. It must:

- establish a rate structure that recognizes both the real cost of high quality inclusive programs for all children and the special needs of particular children.
- blend funding streams creatively and appropriately to craft a cost-efficient system that can meet each family's needs and maximize access for all families.
- leverage existing funds and explore new sources of funds.

Pennsylvania

The following excerpts are from Early Intervention Infant, Toddler, and Family Guidelines to Support the Early Intervention Process: Inclusion (2006).
Pennsylvania's inclusion guidelines specify the following:

Inclusion is not just a school issue. It's about preparing our children to become adults who are actively participating members of their communities. It is about participation of individuals with disabilities as equal and accepted members of society. Research and anecdotal evidence shows that when we embrace children at a young age, so that they experience acceptance early on, it sets affirming expectations for their families. But if families have negative experiences early on they learn to expect failure for their child as they reach school age . . . In Pennsylvania our vision is that ALL young children will participate and succeed in the same activities and environments as their same-aged peers.

Pennsylvania guidelines propose the following as essential components to effective inclusion:

1. Program philosophy that embraces inclusion
2. Effective, strong family partnerships
3. Community partnerships that promote engagement
4. Embedded learning opportunities for all children
5. Effective collaborative consultation
6. Individualized education
7. Ongoing professional development and support
8. Universal design for all children
9. Focus on the natural environment for children younger than 3 years and LRE for preschool-age children

Pennsylvania also has the Preschool Early Intervention Performance Grant, which eligible districts (i.e., low-performing on B6) can apply to participate in. If they achieve their targets, they receive $6,000 in discretionary funds at the end of the year.

Additional Examples of State Inclusion Online Resources

- This link is for the North Carolina Learning Network, Inclusion Resources page, which includes multiple resources for communities and EC programs to expand their inclusive placement options for preschoolers: http://nceln.fpg.unc.edu/inclusionresources.

- This link is for the Florida Department of Education, Bureau of Exceptional Education and Student Services document, "Prekindergarten Children with Disabilities: Expanding Opportunities for Providing Services." The purpose of this document is to assist school districts in making decisions about inclusive EC placements for prekindergarten children with disabilities: http://www.fldoe.org/ese/pdf/PreK-disabALL.pdf.

- This link is for the Arizona Department of Education Early Childhood Inclusion Coalition web site. The coalition is a cross-agency initiative to promote inclusive options for young children with disabilities: http://www.azed.gov/early-childhood/preschool/preschool-programs/ecse/inclusion/ecic.

- This web site is for the Oregon Early Childhood Inclusion Collaborative (OECIC), which is a statewide, cross-agency initiative to enhance and expand inclusive opportunities for young children with and without disabilities in Oregon: http://www.centeroninclusion.org/OECIC.htm.

- This link is for the "Early Childhood Inclusion: For All Children in Louisiana" document: http://www.louisianabelieves.com/resources/library/early-childhood. This guidance document promotes the inclusion of children with disabilities in EC programs across the state.

- This web site is for the online preschool inclusion course offered by the Colorado Department of Education, Preschool Special Education Services: http://www.cde.state.co.us/early/presped-pd-online.

- The Illinois State Board of Education has an inclusion resource page: http://www.isbe.net/earlychi/html/ec_speced_lre.htm. Information about the state's Preschool for All program can be found at http://www.isbe.net/earlychi/preschool/default.htm, and an explicit classroom configurations guide appears at http://www.livebinders.com/play/play?id=839232#anchor.

The following is a continuation of the Maceo family case study. This excerpt summarizes the case and describes the placement decision.

Case Study: The Maceo Family

As described in Chapter 1, the Maceo family requested that their younger child, Raphael, who is eligible for special education services, be enrolled in the preschool program in his older brother's elementary school. His IEP team, including his parents, considered this option and determined that this was the most appropriate placement considering his individual strengths and needs. As described in the previous chapters, the team created an inclusive setting in the preschool classroom at the elementary school. For example, as described in Chapter 4, Ms. Humphrey, his teacher, received the coaching and support she needed to implement EBPs to support Raphael's education. Further, as described in Chapter 5, Ms. Humphrey used scientifically based practices, including the DEC Recommended Practices, to support Raphael in meeting his IEP goals. Finally, as described in Chapter 6, the preschool inclusion team used specific programmatic evaluation tools to conduct ongoing monitoring of the program to ensure the program was meeting the needs of all children and families. The Maceo

Tip for Success!

Check the Early Childhood Technical Assistance Center often for updated resources on inclusion and examples from states: http://www.ectacenter.org.

family case study illustrated how the IEP team collaborates with the family to develop the child's goals and objectives and then considers the appropriate environments for acquiring these goals and objectives. When considering each possible placement setting, the IEP team must consider the provisions of IDEA, including what adaptations, modifications, supplementary aids and services, and training and technical assistance can make that setting successful for the child. In this case, the team determined that creating an inclusive setting at Raphael's community elementary school, where his older brother attended, would be appropriate to meet his needs.

Following, another case study illustrates a different, family-centered, individualized placement decision-making process. As you read this case study, pay particular attention to the information the team gathers, the considerations of the individual needs of Charlie and his family, and the rationale for the rejected and recommended placements.

Case Study: Charlie

Charlie is almost 3 years old and will soon be making the transition from early intervention. He is an active child who attends a "mother's morning out" preschool program 2 days a week, in a class of eight children. He is very independent in all his daily routines at home and at preschool. Charlie has difficulty communicating with words and phrases, and he prefers to play alone. He has been determined to be eligible for special education and related services through the school system. The IEP team, including his mother and regular EC teacher, met and developed an IEP for Charlie, including goals to increase his communication and socialization skills. After developing Charlie's educational goals, the team considered several placement options, which included the following:

- A district-blended special education, Title I, and state prekindergarten classroom, generally comprising 12 children, with at least half the children without IEPs; options available for 3-, 4-, or 5-day placements; generally full day
- Itinerant special education and related services that would most likely occur in Charlie's "mother's morning out" program 2 hours a week
- A district speech and language playgroup of children with typically developing peers that meets twice a week for 2 hours
- Speech and language group therapy, most likely at Charlie's local elementary school

The IEP team, including Charlie's parents, decided on itinerant special education and related services in Charlie's "mother's morning out" program 2 hours a week. The team also decided for Charlie to attend a speech and language therapy group at his local school for 30 minutes once a week. The district program was discussed but thought to be too long a day for Charlie, and it had more children in the classroom. Charlie could have attended for half a day, but it didn't make sense to move Charlie from an environment where he was doing well and where his IEP goals could be met.

Now the team thought about what would need to be in place for Charlie to receive effective services in the two agreed upon placement options:

1. Itinerant special education and related services
2. Speech and language group therapy at a district school

Practitioners in early intervention, preschool special education, and the "mother's morning out" program would need to exchange information before, during, and after Charlie's transition regarding practices that are most likely to support his successful adjustment and positive outcomes. There would need to be endorsement from leadership to support the itinerant staff to travel to and provide supports and services as well as coaching at the "mother's morning out" program. The staff of the EC special education program would have to know (or learn) about the "mother's morning out" program and foster effective working relationships with staff there via teaming and collaboration. Means of ongoing and effective communication would need to be in place among the itinerant staff, the "mother's morning out" staff, and the family to exchange expertise, knowledge, and information. Strategies would need to be consistent across both placement options as well as at home. Data and other forms of feedback on what is and is not working well would have to be shared with all practitioners and caregivers supporting Charlie as he develops and grows.

The following is a summary of the rationale statement for Charlie's recommended placements:

- *Rejected Placement Option 1: District Program.* The IEP team felt the district program would be too long a day for Charlie and he might not get the individual attention he needs. Although Charlie could have attended for half a day, the team recognized he was doing fine now and a change might be too disruptive.

- *Rejected Placement Option 2: District Speech and Language Play Group.* After considering the district speech and language playgroup that meets twice a week for 2 hours, the family expressed concern that the playgroup meets in a location that is 30 minutes away by bus. The IEP team agreed and considered additional options.

- *Recommended Placement Option:* The IEP team decided itinerant special education and related services would be appropriate to meet Charlie's special education and related services needs. The first *location* for services will be in Charlie's "mother's morning out" program 2 hours a week. The second *location* will be a speech and language therapy group at his local school, which Charlie will attend for 30 minutes once a week. The family agreed that this location and these hours will work well for Charlie. The team also reported that the teachers across both locations have agreed to collaborate and to work with the team, including the family, on an ongoing basis as well as to collect the necessary data to monitor his progress.

CONCLUSION

The principles outlined in this chapter can be used to guide your preschool inclusion team's policies and procedures for supporting the IEP teams' individual child placement decisions. As mentioned throughout this chapter, placement decisions are a vital component of each child's IEP. The child's placement will influence where a child spends his or her time, where and how services are provided, and, perhaps most important, who a child interacts with and the relationships the child will develop within the school and community. The law clearly outlines that children with disabilities should receive educational services in settings that meet their educational needs alongside peers without disabilities to the maximum extent appropriate. Thus, IEP teams have a responsibility to ensure that children with disabilities have the utmost opportunities, meaningful access, and appropriate supports needed to be educated alongside their peers and thus fully participate in their communities.

REFLECTION QUESTIONS

1. What are three principles that should guide individual child placement decisions?

2. What are effective considerations for sustaining successful, high-quality inclusive practices?

3. Does your state/district have preschool inclusion policies and recommendations already in place? If so, how can you incorporate these into your program?

4. How will the IDEA provisions supporting inclusive placements be used by the IEP team?

5. How will the preschool inclusion team monitor whether their policies and procedures have a) helped IEP teams make high-quality, successful inclusive placement decisions and b) resulted in more inclusive placements?

8

Bringing It All Together

Erin E. Barton

The primary purpose of this book is to provide a useful and feasible set of "tools" for assisting school districts and their preschool inclusion teams in developing policies and procedures that promote preschool inclusion. We also hope that this book will influence the larger national agenda to support policies and practices that affect inclusion of children, students, and people with disabilities across schools, communities, and agencies. We support *inclusion for all*.

It has been almost 15 years since Guralnick (2001) published *Early Childhood Inclusion: Focus on Change*. In the first chapter of his text, he describes how the law (i.e., IDEA) and changes to the law were often the catalyst for changing and improving the education of children with disabilities and increasing their access to general education settings. Enacting the law (e.g., FAPE, LRE) often required broad-scale change across multiple, complicated facets of the educational system (e.g., administrative structures, PD, research, policies, practices). Although considerable progress has been achieved through these changes, change is hard and the reality is that access to inclusive preschool environments remains unobtainable for many children with disabilities across many communities. As described in Chapter 1 (Figure 1.1), the practice of providing special education and related services to preschool children with disabilities in regular EC settings increased by only 5.7% in 27 years.

In a chapter in Guralnick's text, Strain, McGee, and Kohler (2001) outlined the myths associated with inclusion for young children with autism. Their myths are easily applied to all children with disabilities. For example, the behavior-control myth argues that inclusive environments cannot be designed to appropriately address (or control) the challenging behaviors of children with autism. This myth is easily refuted with the empirical literature and practical realities. Multiple studies have demonstrated the effectiveness of applying function-based interventions within a positive behavior support framework in inclusive, EC classrooms to address and reduce challenging behaviors and promote the social competence of children with a variety of disabilities (Dunlap & Fox, 2011). This and the other myths they described (e.g., overstimulation, readiness) could be easily refuted with empirical research in that time and even more so today. However, the myth that was perhaps most detrimental to the promotion of preschool inclusion is that inclusion is easy. Implementing high-quality preschool inclusion is *not* easy. Our text is not a panacea for implementing preschool inclusion. Each chapter provides a specific set of tools to help administrators and preschool inclusion teams foster successful high-quality inclusion with appropriate access, needed supports, and full participation (DEC/NAEYC, 2009).

USING EACH CHAPTER

The Introduction sets the tone for the toolbox by describing our survey, providing resources, and offering a personal account of inclusion. Chapter 1 provides important background information to use during the initial phases and to address the foremost national challenge: attitudes and beliefs. The research on the current state of inclusion, research demonstrating the effectiveness of inclusion, and IDEA provisions supporting inclusion are provided to establish the *facts* about preschool inclusion versus the *myths*. Our framework for inclusion and effective components of high-quality preschool inclusion can be used to start planning implementation. The DEC/NAEYC (2009) joint position statement provided in the Introduction and described in Chapter 1 should be shared widely, as it outlines a practical, evidence-based definition of preschool inclusion.

Chapter 2 introduces data from a recent survey (Barton & Smith, 2014b) regarding the challenges and solutions to preschool inclusion. This chapter can be used to identify, anticipate, and address challenges. The framework provided should help preschool inclusion teams address typical challenges that they might encounter from both attitudes and policies. As preschool inclusion teams plan implementation, they are likely to encounter policies or procedures that need to be reinterpreted, revised, or changed. However, as described throughout this book, attitudes and beliefs are the most common challenge to preschool inclusion.

Chapter 3 outlines strategies for designing policies and procedures that will address both policy and attitude challenges. This chapter can be used to review your current policies and procedures and make appropriate changes to support high-quality preschool inclusion.

Chapter 4 addresses an important and frequently cited challenge to preschool inclusion: PD. Insufficient PD is likely one of the causes of the lack of progress nationwide regarding inclusion. An implementation science framework is used to describe an effective approach to PD that can be adopted by districts and programs to implement, sustain, and scale up high-quality preschool inclusion.

Chapter 5 provides what can become the content of the PD efforts—that is, descriptions of illustrations of EBPs for educating young children with disabilities in inclusive classrooms.

Chapter 6 describes the importance of monitoring progress at the program level. Several measures are provided to help preschool inclusion teams plan, implement, and evaluate inclusive preschool programs at the classroom and child levels.

Finally, Chapter 7 provides a framework for helping preschool inclusion teams support appropriate individual placement decisions. The chapter unpacks the law regarding placement decisions and can be used to assist a child's IEP team, including his or her family, in making appropriate placement decisions. We also provide examples of preschool inclusion policies and recommendations from several states. While writing this text, we searched for individual states with policies and procedures supporting inclusion and found numerous districts and states with evidence-based, clearly outlined guidelines, handbooks, or listed procedures supporting preschool inclusion available online. This suggests that despite the dismal increases in preschool inclusion over the past 30 years, there are preschool inclusion champions across the United States. Thus, there is good reason to be optimistic and hopeful!

CONCLUSION

Throughout this text, we argue that there is a legal, empirical, professional, and moral basis for preschool inclusion. However, a point Diane Bricker made 20 years ago is still highly relevant today: Implementing quality preschool inclusion takes more than just embracing inclusion at the conceptual level. "Considerable thought and planning are required to ensure that inclusion efforts are successful for children, parents, teachers, and the larger community" (Bricker, 1995, pp. 180–181)—that is, it takes more than holding states and districts accountable to LRE and more than just creating a preschool inclusion team. However, thanks to the preschool inclusion champions of the last several decades, today—in 2015—we have laws, research, *and* support from professional organizations. There are no excuses: *It is time to do the heavy lifting and make inclusion for all a reality.*

References

Abbott-Shim, M., Lambert, R., & McCarty, F. (2000). Structural model of Head Start classroom quality. *Early Childhood Research Quarterly, 15,* 115–134.

Abbott-Shim, M., Neel, J., & Sibley, A. (2001). *Assessment profile for early childhood programs: Research technical manual* (2nd ed.). Atlanta, GA: Quality Assist, Inc.

Abbott-Shim, M., & Sibley, A. (1987). *Assessment profile for early childhood programs.* Atlanta, GA: Quality Assist, Inc.

Abbott-Shim, M., Sibley, A., & Neel, J. (1992). *Assessment profile for early childhood programs: Research manual.* Atlanta, GA: Quality Assist, Inc.

Americans with Disabilities Act (ADA) of 1990, PL 101-336, 42 U.S.C. §§ 12101 *et seq.*

Assistance to States for the Education of Children With Disabilities and Preschool Grants for Children With Disabilities, 34 C.F.R. § 300 (2006).

Barnett, W.S., Carolan, M.E., Squires, J.H., & Clarke Brown, K. (2013). *The state of preschool 2013: State preschool yearbook.* New Brunswick, NJ: National Institute for Early Education Research.

Barton, E.E., Bishop, C., & Snyder, P. (2014). *High quality instruction through complete learning trials: Blending intentional teaching with embedded instruction.* Young Exceptional Children Monograph 16: Blending Practices to Strengthen Quality Early Learning Programs for ALL Children. Manuscript submitted for publication.

Barton, E.E., Kinder, K., Casey, A.M., & Artman, K.M. (2011). Finding your feedback fit: Strategies for designing and delivering performance feedback systems. *Young Exceptional Children, 14,* 29–46.

Barton, E.E., Pribble, L., & Chen, C. (2013). Use of email to deliver performance-based feedback to early childhood practitioners. *Journal of Early Intervention, 35,* 270–297.

Barton, E.E., & Smith, B.J. (2014a). *Fact sheet of research on preschool inclusion.* Denver, CO: Pyramid Plus: The Colorado Center for Social Emotional Competence and Inclusion. Retrieved from http://www.pyramidplus.org

Barton, E.E., & Smith, B.J. (2014b). *Preschool inclusion 20 years later: What are the challenges and solutions?* Manuscript submitted for publication.

Barton, E.E., & Smith, B.J. (2014c). *IDEA provisions supporting preschool inclusion.* Denver, CO: Pyramid Plus: The Colorado Center for Social Emotional Competence and Inclusion. Retrieved from http://www.pyramidplus.org/sites/default/files/images/IDEA%20Provisions%20Supporting%20Preschool%20Inclusion.pdf

Bricker, D. (1995). The challenge of inclusion. *Journal of Early Intervention, 19*(3), 179–194.

Bricker, D. (Ed.). (2002). *Assessment, Evaluation, and Programming System (AEPS®) for Infants and Children* (2nd ed., Vols. 1–4). Baltimore, MD: Paul H. Brookes Publishing Co.

Bricker, D.D., & Widerstrom, A.H. (1996). *Preparing personnel to work with infants and young children and their families: A team approach.* Baltimore, MD: Paul H. Brookes Publishing Co.

Brown, W.H., Odom, S.L., Li, S., & Zercher, C. (1999). Ecobehavioral assessment in early childhood programs: A portrait of preschool inclusion. *Journal of Special Education, 33,* 138–153.

Bruder, M.B., & Stayton, V. (2006). *The center to inform personnel preparation and practice in early intervention and preschool education: Study VI. Training and technical assistance survey of Part C & 619 coordinators.* Retrieved from http://www.uconnucedd.org/pdfs/projects/per_prep/presentation_studyvi_partc_and_619_training_and_ta_11_07.pdf

Buysse, V., & Hollingsworth, H.L. (2009). Program quality and early childhood inclusion: Recommendations for professional development. *Topics in Early Childhood Special Education, 29,* 119–128.

Buysse, V., & Wesley, P.W. (2006). *Evidence-based practice in the early childhood field.* Washington, DC: ZERO TO THREE.

Camilli, G., Vargas, S., Ryan, S., & Barnett, W.S. (2010). Meta-analysis of the effects of early education interventions on cognitive and social development. *Teachers College Record, 112,* 579–620.

Campbell, P.H., Kennedy, A.A., & Milbourne, S.A. (2012). *CARA's Kit for Toddlers: Creating adaptations for routines and activities.* Baltimore, MD: Paul H. Brookes Publishing Co.

Campbell, P.H., Milbourne, S., Dugan, L.M., & Wilcox, M.J. (2006). A review of evidence on practices for teaching young children to use assistive technology devices. *Topics in Early Childhood Special Education, 26,* 3–13.

Carta, J.J., Schwartz, I.S., Atwater, J.B., & McConnell, S.R. (1991). Developmentally appropriate practice: Appraising its usefulness for young children with disabilities. *Topics in Early Childhood Special Education, 11,* 1–20.

Cate, D., Diefendorf, M., McCullough, K., Peters, M.L., & Whaley, K. (Eds.). (2010). *Quality indicators of inclusive early childhood programs/practices: A compilation of selected resources.* Chapel Hill: University of North Carolina, Frank Porter Graham Child Development Center, National Early Childhood Technical Assistance Center.

Child Care Law Center. (2004). *All children have individual needs: Building an inclusive Preschool for All program, principles and considerations for planning and implementation.* San Francisco, CA: Author. Retrieved from http://www.cdrcp.com/pdf/Building%20an%20Inclusive%20Preschool.pdf

Copple, C., & Bredekamp, S. (Eds.). (2009). *Developmentally appropriate practice in early childhood programs serving children from birth through age 8* (3rd ed.). Washington, DC: National Association for the Education of Young Children.

Corcoran, T.B. (1995). *Helping teachers teach well: Transforming professional development* (No. 16). New Brunswick, NJ: Consortium for Policy Research in Education.

Cunconan-Lahr, R.L., & Stifel, S. (2013). *Universal design for learning (UDL) checklist for early childhood environments* (Rev. ed.). Bethlehem, PA: Northampton Community College and Pennsylvania Developmental Disabilities Council.

Data Accountability Center. (2011). *Number of children and students served under IDEA, Part B, by age group and state.* [Data file]. Retrieved from https://www.ideadata.org/TABLES35TH/B1-1.xls

Diamond, K.E., & Hong, S. (2010). Young children's decisions to include peers with physical disabilities in play. *Journal of Early Intervention, 32,* 163–177.

Division for Early Childhood. (2009). *DEC code of ethics.* Los Angeles, CA: Author. Retrieved from http://www.dec-sped.org/papers

Division for Early Childhood. (2014). *DEC recommended practices in early intervention/early childhood special education 2014.* Retrieved from http://www.dec-sped.org/recommendedpractices

Division for Early Childhood/National Association for the Education of Young Children. (2009). *Early childhood inclusion: A joint position statement of the Division for Early Childhood (DEC) and the National Association for the Education of Young Children (NAEYC).* Chapel Hill: The University of North Carolina, FPG Child Development Institute. http://www.naeyc.org/positionstatements/

Division for Early Childhood, National Association for the Education of Young Children, & National Head Start Association. (2013). *Framework for response to intervention in early childhood: Description and implications.* Retrieved from http://www.naeyc.org/files/naeyc/RTI%20in%20Early%20Childhood.pdf

Dugan, L., Milbourne, S.A., & Schmidt, M. (2005). *Quality of inclusive experiences measure—revised.* Chapel Hill, NC: Frank Porter Graham Child Development Center, University of North Carolina at Chapel Hill.

Dunlap, G., & Fox, L. (2011). Function based interventions for children with challenging behavior. *Journal of Early Intervention, 33,* 333–343.

Dunst, C.J., & Raab, M. (2010). Practitioners' self-evaluations of contrasting types of professional development. *Journal of Early Intervention, 32,* 239–254.

Dunst, C.J., & Trivette, C.M. (2009). Using research evidence to inform and evaluate early childhood intervention practices. *Topics in Early Childhood Special Education, 29,* 40–52.

Education Law Center. (2010). *Including children with disabilities in state pre-K programs.* Pre-K Policy Brief Series. Newark, NJ: Author. Retrieved from http://www.edlawcenter.org/assets/files/pdfs/publications/PreKPolicyBrief_InclusionChildrenWithDisabilities.pdf

Elmore, R.F. (1979). Backward mapping: Implementation research and policy decisions. *Political Science Quarterly, 94*(4), 601–616.

Epstein, A.S. (2007). *The intentional teacher: Choosing the best strategies for young children's learning.* Washington, DC: National Association for the Education of Young Children.

Epstein, A.S. (2014). *The intentional teacher: Choosing the best strategies for young children's learning* (2nd ed.). Washington, DC: National Association for the Education of Young Children.

Espinosa, L.M. (2002, November). High quality preschool: Why we need it and what it looks like. *Preschool Policy Matters, 1.* Retrieved from http://nieer.org/resources/policybriefs/1.pdf

Fixsen, D.L., & Blase, K.A. (2009). Technical assistance in special education: Past, present, and future. *Topics in Early Childhood Special Education, 29,* 62–64.

Fixsen, D.L., Blase, K.A., Duda, M.A., Naoom, S.F., & Van Dyke, M. (2010a). Implementation of evidence-based treatments for children and adolescents: Research findings and their implications for the future. In J. Weisz & A. Kazdin (Eds.), *Evidence-based psychotherapies for children and adolescents* (2nd ed., pp. 435–450). New York, NY: Guilford Press.

Fixsen, D.L., Blase, K.A., Duda, M., Naoom, S.F., & Van Dyke, M. (2010b). Sustainability of evidence-based programs in education. *Journal of Evidence-Based Practices for Schools, 11*(1), 30–46.

Fixsen, D.L., Naoom, S.F., Blase, K.A., Friedman, R.M., & Wallace, F. (2005). *Implementation research: A synthesis of the literature* (FMHI Publication #231). Tampa, FL: University of South Florida, Louis de la Parte Florida Mental Health Institute, National Implementation Research Network.

Fowler, F.C. (2013). *Policy studies for educational leaders: An introduction* (3rd ed.). Alexandria, VA: Prentice Hall.

Fox, L., Carta, J., Strain, P., Dunlap, G., & Hemmeter, M.L. (2009). *Response to intervention and the pyramid model*. Tampa, FL: University of South Florida, Technical Assistance Center on Social Emotional Intervention for Young Children.

Fox, L., Dunlap, G., Hemmeter, M.L., Joseph, G., & Strain, P. (2003). The Teaching Pyramid: A model for supporting social emotional competence and preventing challenging behavior in young children. *Young Children, 58*(4), 48–52.

Fox, L., Hemmeter, M.L., & Snyder, P. (2013, October). *Unpacking coaching: Using practice-based coaching to ensure fidelity of implementation*. Presentation at the annual meeting of the Division for Early Childhood, San Francisco, CA.

Fox, L., Hemmeter, M.L., Snyder, P., Binder, D.P., & Clarke, S. (2011). Coaching early childhood special educators to implement a comprehensive model for promoting young children's social competence. *Topics in Early Childhood Special Education, 31*, 178–192.

Grisham-Brown, J.L., Hemmeter, M.L., & Pretti-Frontczak, K.L. (2005). *Blended practices in early childhood and early childhood special education*. Baltimore, MD: Paul H. Brookes Publishing Co.

Grisham-Brown, J.L., Pretti-Frontczak, K., Hawkins, S., & Winchell, B. (2009). An examination of how to address early learning standards for all children within blended preschool classrooms. *Topics in Early Childhood Special Education, 29*(3), 131–142.

Guralnick, M.J. (Ed.). (2001). *Early childhood inclusion: Focus on change*. Baltimore, MD: Paul H. Brookes Publishing Co.

Guralnick, M.J., Neville, B., Hammond, M.A., & Connor, R.T. (2007a). The friendships of young children with developmental delays: A longitudinal analysis. *Journal of Applied Developmental Psychology, 28*, 64–79.

Guralnick, M.J., Neville, B., Hammond, M.A., & Connor, R.T. (2007b). Linkages between delayed children's social interactions with mothers and peers. *Child Development, 78*(2), 459–473.

Halle, T., Vick Whittaker, J.E., & Anderson, R. (2010). *Quality in early childhood care and education settings: A compendium of measures* (2nd ed.). Washington, DC: Child Trends. Prepared by Child Trends for the Office of Planning, Research and Evaluation, Administration for Children and Families, U.S. Department of Health and Human Services.

Hamre, B.K., La Paro, K.M., Pianta, R.C., & LoCasale-Crouch, J. (2014). *Classroom Assessment Scoring System® (CLASS®) manual, infant*. Baltimore, MD: Paul H. Brookes Publishing Co.

Harbin, G.L., McWilliam, R.A., & Gallagher, J.J. (2000). Services for young children with disabilities and their families. In J.P. Shonkoff & S.J. Meisels (Eds.), *Handbook of early childhood intervention* (2nd ed., pp. 387–415). Cambridge, UK: Cambridge University Press.

Harbin, G., Rous, B., & McLean, M. (2005). Issues in designing state accountability systems. *Journal of Early Intervention, 27*, 137–164.

Harms, T., Cryer, D., & Clifford, R.M. (2005). *Early Childhood Environment Rating Scale* (Rev. ed.). New York, NY: Teachers College Press.

Harms, T., Cryer, D., & Clifford, R.M. (2006). *Infant/Toddler Environment Rating Scale* (Rev. ed.). New York, NY: Teachers College Press.

Hayden, P., Frederick, L., & Smith, B.J., & Special Education Programs (U.S.). (2003). *A road map for facilitating collaborative teams*. Longmont, CO: Sopris West.

Head Start Center for Inclusion. (n.d.). *Member of the class: Teachers guide*. Washington, DC: U.S. Department of Health and Human Services, Office of Head Start.

Hebbeler, K., Spiker, D., & Kahn, L. (2012). Individuals with Disabilities Education Act's early childhood programs: Powerful vision and pesky details. *Topics in Early Childhood Special Education, 31*, 199–207.

Hemmeter, M.L., Ostrosky, M.M., & Fox, L. (2006). Social and emotional foundations for early learning: A conceptual model for intervention. *School Psychology Review, 35*, 583–601.

Hemmeter, M.L., Snyder, P., Fox, L., & Algina, J. (2011). *Efficacy of a classroom wide model for promoting social-emotional development and preventing challenging behavior*. Paper presented at the annual meeting of the American Educational Research Association, New Orleans, LA.

Hemmeter, M.L., Snyder, P., Kinder, K., & Artman, K. (2011). Impact of e-mail performance feedback on preschool teachers' use of descriptive praise. *Early Childhood Research Quarterly, 26*, 96–109.

Henry, G.T., & Rickman, D.K. (2007). Do peers influence children's skill development in preschool? *Economics of Education Review, 26,* 100–112.

Heroman, C., Burts, D.C., Berke, K., & Bickart, T. (2010). *Teaching strategies GOLD objectives for development & learning: Birth through kindergarten.* Washington, DC: Teaching Strategies, Inc.

Hopgood, S. (2011). *Five little fishes.* Suffolk, UK: Top That Publishing.

Hunt, P., Soto, G., Maier, J., Liboiron, N., & Bae, S. (2004). Collaborative teaming to support preschoolers with severe disabilities who are placed in general education early childhood programs. *Topics in Early Childhood Special Education, 24,* 123–142.

Hunter, A., & Hemmeter, M.L. (2009). The Center on the Social and Emotional Foundations for Early Learning: Addressing challenging behavior in infants and toddlers. *Zero to Three, 29*(3), 5–12.

Individuals with Disabilities Education Improvement Act (IDEA) of 2004, PL 108-446, 20 U.S.C. §§ 1400 *et seq.*

Irwin, S.H. (2009). *SpecialLink child care inclusion practices profile and principles scale.* Winnipeg, Canada: SpecialLink—The National Centre for Child Care Inclusion. Retrieved from http://www.specialinkcanada.org/home_en.html

Joyce, B., & Showers, B. (2002). *Student achievement through staff development* (3rd ed.). Alexandria, VA: Association for Supervision and Curriculum Development.

Justice, L.M., Logan, J.R., Tzu-Jung, L., & Kaderavek, J.N. (2014). Peer effects in early childhood education: Testing the assumptions of special education inclusion. *Psychological Science, 25,* 1722–1729.

Kingdon, J.W. (2003). *Agendas, alternatives, and public policies* (2nd ed.). New York, NY: Longman.

Knight, J. (2007). *Instructional coaching: A partnership approach to improving instruction.* Thousand Oaks, CA: Sage.

Kontos, S., Howes, C., & Galinsky, E. (1996). Does training make a difference to quality in family child care? *Early Childhood Research Quarterly, 11,* 427–445.

La Paro, K.M., Hamre, B.K., & Pianta, R.C. (2012). *Classroom Assessment Scoring System® (CLASS®) manual, toddler.* Baltimore, MD: Paul H. Brookes Publishing Co.

Lieber, J., Beckman, P.J., Hanson, M.J., Janko, S., Marquart, J.M., Horn, E.M., & Odom, S.L. (1997). The impact of changing roles on relationships between professionals in inclusive programs for young children. *Early Education and Development, 8,* 67–83.

Majchrzak, A. (1984). *Methods for policy research.* Newbury Park, CA: Sage.

Mashburn, A.J., Justice, L.M., Downer, J.T., & Pianta, R.C. (2009). Peer effects on children's language achievement during pre-kindergarten. *Child Development, 80,* 686–702.

McConnell, S.R. (2002). Interventions to facilitate social interaction for young children with autism: Review of available research and recommendations for educational intervention and future research. *Journal of Autism and Developmental Disorders, 32,* 351–372.

McDonald, D. (2009). *Elevating the field: Using NAEYC early childhood program accreditation to support and reach higher quality in early childhood programs.* Washington, DC: National Association for the Education of Young Children.

McLean, M.E., Snyder, P., Smith, B.J., & Sandall, S.R. (2002). The DEC recommended practices in early intervention/early childhood special education: Social validation. *Journal of Early Intervention, 25,* 120–128.

Merriam-Webster's Collegiate Dictionary (11th ed.). (2005). Springfield, MA: Merriam-Webster.

Metz, A., Halle, T., Bartley, L., & Blasberg, A. (2013). The key components of successful implementation. In T. Halle, A. Metz, & I. Martinez-Beck (Eds.), *Applying implementation science in early childhood programs and systems* (pp. 269–294). Baltimore, MD: Paul H. Brookes Publishing Co.

Milbourne, D.L., & Schmidt, M. (2005). Quality of Inclusive Experiences Measure–Revised (QuIEM-R). Retrieved from http://nceln.fpg.unc.edu/sites/nceln.fpg.unc.edu/files/resources/Quality_of_Inclusive_Experiences_Measure.pdf

Milbourne, S.A., & Campbell, P.H. (2007). *CARA's Kit: Creating adaptations for routines and activities.* Philadelphia, PA: Child and Family Studies Research Programs, Thomas Jefferson University.

Musgrove, M. (2012, February 29). *OSEP dear colleague letter on preschool (LRE).* Retrieved from http://www2.ed.gov/policy/speced/guid/idea/memosdcltrs/preschoollre22912.pdf

National Association for the Education of Young Children. (2008). *Overview of the NAEYC early childhood program standards.* Retrieved from http://www.naeyc.org/files/academy/file/OverviewStandards.pdf

National Association for the Education of Young Children. (2011). *NAEYC code of ethical conduct and statement of commitment: A position statement from the National Association for the Education of Young Children.* Washington, DC: Author. Retrieved from http://www.macte.org/images/Code of Ethical Conduct.pdf

National Association for the Education of Young Children. (2011). *NAEYC position on quality rating and improvement systems.* Retrieved from http://www.naeyc.org/files/naeyc/2011_QRIS_Statement_0.pdf

National Center on Quality Teaching and Learning. (n.d.). *Practice-based coaching.* Washington, DC: U.S. Department of Health and Human Services, Administration for Children and Families, Office of Head Start. Retrieved from http://eclkc.ohs.acf.hhs.gov/hslc/tta-system/teaching/docs/practice -based-coaching.pdf

National Early Childhood Technical Assistance Center. (2010). *Expanding opportunities: An interagency inclusion initiative.* Retrieved from http://ectacenter.org/~pdfs/pubs/nectac_eval_expopps.pdf

National Professional Development Center on Inclusion. (2011). *Research synthesis points on practices that support inclusion.* Chapel Hill: University of North Carolina, Frank Porter Graham Child Development Center, Author. Retrieved from http://npdci.fpg.unc.edu

New Jersey Department of Education. (2010). *Preschool program implementation guidelines.* Retrieved from http://www.nj.gov/education/ece/guide/impguidelines.pdf

Odom, S.L. (2009a). *Handbook of developmental disabilities.* New York, NY: Guilford Press.

Odom, S.L. (2009b). The tie that binds: Evidence-based practice, implementation science, and outcomes for children. *Topics in Early Childhood Special Education, 29,* 53–61.

Odom, S.L., Buysse, V., & Soukakou, E. (2011). Inclusion for young children with disabilities: A quarter century of research perspectives. *Journal of Early Intervention, 33,* 344–356.

Odom, S.L., Hanson, M.J., Lieber, J., Marquart, J., Sandall, S., Wolery, R., . . . Chambers, J. (2001). The costs of preschool inclusion. *Topics in Early Childhood Special Education, 21,* 46–55.

Oregon Early Childhood Inclusion Collaborative. (2014). *Consultation visit summary* (adapted). Retrieved from http://www.centeroninclusion.org/OECICforms.htm

Ostensjo, S., Carlberg, E., & Vollestad, N. (2005). The use and impact of assistive devices and other environmental modifications on everyday activities and care in young children with cerebral palsy. *Disability and Rehabilitation, 27,* 849–861.

Pennsylvania Departments of Public Welfare and Education, Office of Child Development and Early Learning. (2006). *Early intervention infant, toddler, and family guidelines to support the early intervention process: Inclusion.* Retrieved from http://www.ectacenter.org/~pdfs/topics/inclusion/inclusion _guidelines.pdf

Pianta, R.C., Barnett, W.S., Burchinal, M., & Thornburg, K.R. (2009). The effects of preschool education: What we know, how public policy is or is not aligned with the evidence base, and what we need to know. *Psychological Science in the Public Interest, 10,* 49–88.

Pianta, R.C., La Paro, K.M., & Hamre, B.K. (2008a). *Classroom Assessment Scoring System® (CLASS®) manual, K–3.* Baltimore, MD: Paul H. Brookes Publishing Co.

Pianta, R.C., La Paro, K.M., & Hamre, B.K. (2008b). *Classroom Assessment Scoring System® (CLASS®) manual, pre-K.* Baltimore, MD: Paul H. Brookes Publishing Co.

Pretti-Frontczak, K., Grisham-Brown, J., & Sullivan, L. (2014). *Blending practices for all children.* Young Exceptional Children Monograph Series, Monograph 16. Los Angeles, CA: Division for Early Childhood.

Purcell, T., & Rosemary, C.A. (2008). Differentiating instruction in the preschool classroom: Bridging emergent literacy instruction and developmentally appropriate practice. In L.M. Justice & C. Vukelich (Eds.), *Achieving excellence in preschool literacy instruction* (pp. 221–241). New York, NY: Guilford Press.

Raab, M.M., & Dunst, C.J. (1997). *Preschool Assessment of the Classroom Environment–Revised (PACE-R).* Asheville, NC: Orelena Hawks Puckett Institute. Retrieved from http://www.puckett .org/index.php

Ragonesi, C., Chen, X., Agrawal, S., & Galloway, J. (2010). Power mobility and socialization in preschool: A case study of a child with cerebral palsy. *Pediatric Physical Therapy, 22,* 322–329.

Rogers, S.J. (2000). Interventions that facilitate socialization in children with autism. *Journal of Autism and Developmental Disorders, 30,* 399–409.

Rose, D.F., & Smith, B.J. (1993). Preschool mainstreaming: Attitude barriers and strategies for addressing them. *Young Children, 48*(4), 59–62. Reprinted in Paciorek, K.M., & Munro, J.H. (Eds.). (1994 & 1995). *Early Childhood Education: Annual Editions.* Guilford, CT: Dushkin.

Rose, D.F., & Smith, B.J. (1994). Providing public education services to preschoolers with disabilities in community-based programs: Who's responsible for what? *Young Children, 49*(6), 64–68. Reprinted in the *American Speech, Language, Hearing Associations (ASHA) Interdisciplinary Preschool Project Resource Manual.*

Rubin, I.S. (2006). *The politics of public budgeting* (5th ed.). Washington, DC: CQ Press.

Rush, D.D., & Sheldon, M.L. (2011). *The early childhood coaching handbook.* Baltimore, MD: Paul H. Brookes Publishing Co.

Sadao, K.C., & Robinson, N.B. (2010). *Assistive technology for young children: Creating inclusive learning environments.* Baltimore, MD: Paul H. Brookes Publishing Co.

Salisbury, C.L. (1990). *Providing effective early intervention services: Why and how?* Pittsburgh, PA: Allegheny-Singer Research Institute.

Salisbury, C.L., & Smith, B.J. (1991, September). The least restrictive environment: Understanding the options. *Principal,* 24–27.

Sandall, S. (2003). Play modifications for children with disabilities. *Young Children, 58*(3), 54–55.

Sandall, S.R., Hemmeter, M.L., Smith, B., & McLean, M. (Eds.). (2005). *DEC recommended practices: A comprehensive guide for practical application in early intervention/early childhood special education.* Missoula, MT: Division for Early Childhood.

Sandall, S.R., & Schwartz, I.S. (2008). *Building blocks for teaching preschoolers with special needs* (2nd ed.). Baltimore, MD: Paul H. Brookes Publishing Co.

Smith, B.J. (2013, October). *Ask not what your country can do for you . . .* Keynote speech, DEC annual conference, San Francisco, CA.

Smith, B., & Rose, D. (1991). *Identifying policy options for preschool mainstreaming.* [Monograph]. Pittsburgh, PA: Research Institute on Preschool Mainstreaming, Allegheny-Singer Research Institute. Retrieved from ERIC database (ED388403).

Smith, B.J., & Rose, D.F. (1993). *Administrator's policy handbook for preschool mainstreaming.* Cambridge, MA: Brookline Books.

Smith, B., & Rous, B. (2008). Policy in early childhood education and early intervention: What every early childhood educator needs to know. In P. Winton, J. McCollum, & C. Catlett (Eds.), *Practical approaches to early childhood professional development: Evidence, strategies and resources* (pp. 247–262). Washington, DC: ZERO TO THREE.

Smith, B.J., Salisbury, C.L., & Rose, D.F. (1992). Policy options for preschool mainstreaming. *CASE in Point, 7*(1), 17–30.

Snow, K. (2007). *Revolutionary common sense: Great expectations.* San Antonio, TX: Disability is Natural. Retrieved from http://www.disabilityisnatural.com/~k061480m/images/PDF/grtexpect.pdf

Snyder, P., Hemmeter, M.L., & Fox, L. (2011). *Coaching to support fidelity of implementation of evidence-based practices in inclusive early childhood settings.* Presentation at the International Society on Early Intervention Conference, New York, NY.

Snyder, P., Hemmeter, M.L., & McLaughlin, T. (2011). Professional development in early childhood intervention: Where we stand on the silver anniversary of PL 99-457. *Journal of Early Intervention, 33,* 357–370.

Snyder, P., Hemmeter, M.L., McLean, M.E., Sandall, S.R., & McLaughlin, T. (2013). Embedded instruction to support early learning in response to intervention frameworks. In V. Buysse & E.S. Peisner-Feinberg (Eds.), *Handbook of response to intervention in early learning* (pp. 283–300). Baltimore, MD: Paul H. Brookes Publishing Co.

Soukakou, E.P. (2010). *Inclusive Classroom Profile.* Retrieved from http://webcache.googleusercontent.com/search?q=cache:PE6yxRJ-sjcJ:inclusioninstitute.fpg.unc.edu/sites/inclusioninstitute.fpg.unc.edu/files/handouts/ICP-handout-2013.pdf+&cd=1&hl=en&ct=clnk&gl=us&client=firefox-a

Soukakou, E., Winton, P., & West, T. (2012). *The Inclusive Classroom Profile (ICP): Report on preliminary findings of demonstration study in North Carolina.* Chapel Hill, NC: National Professional Development Center on Inclusion, Frank Porter Graham Child Development Center.

SpecialQuest Birth to Five: Head Start/Hilton Foundation Training Program. (2008). *Inclusion Planning Checklist: Center-Based Early Care and Education Programs.* Retrieved from http://www.specialquest.org/sqtm/inc_plan_chklist_center.pdf

Spouse, J. (2001). Bridging theory and practice in the supervisory relationship: A sociocultural perspective. *Journal of Advanced Nursing, 33,* 512–522.

Strain, P. (2014). *Inclusion for preschool children with disabilities: What we know and what we should be doing.* Retrieved from http://www.pyramidplus.org/sites/default/files/images/STRAIN%20PtrYC%20what%20we%20know%20%282%29.pdf

Strain, P.S., & Bovey, E.H. (2011). Randomized, controlled trail of the LEAP model of early intervention for young children with Autism Spectrum Disorders. *Topics in Early Childhood Special Education, 31,* 133–154.

Strain, P.S., McGee, G.G., & Kohler, F.W. (2001). Inclusion of children with autism in early intervention environments: An examination of rationale, myths, and procedures. In M.J. Guralnick (Ed.), *Early childhood inclusion: Focus on change* (pp. 337–363). Baltimore, MD: Paul H. Brookes Publishing Co.

Strain, P., Schwartz, I., & Bovey, E. (2007). Social skills interventions for young children with autism: Programmatic research findings and implementation issues. In S. Odom, S.R. McConnell, & W. Brown (Eds.), *Social competence of young children: Risk, disability, and intervention* (pp. 253–272). Baltimore, MD: Paul H. Brookes Publishing Co.

Teaching Tolerance. (2011). *Building blocks for civil discourse.* Montgomery, AL: Southern Poverty Law Center. Retrieved from http://www.tolerance.org/publications/chapter-2-building-blocks-civil-discourse

Tomlinson, C. (2001). *How to differentiate instruction in mixed-ability classrooms* (2nd ed.). Alexandria, VA: Association for Supervision and Curriculum Development.

Tomlinson, C., Brighton, C., Hertberg, H., Callahan, C., Moon, T., Brimijoin, K., . . . Reynolds, T. (2003). Differentiating instruction in response to student readiness, interest, and learning profile in academically diverse classrooms: A review of literature. *Journal for the Education of the Gifted, 27*, 119–145.

Trembath, D., Balandin, S., Togher, L., & Stancliffe, R. (2009). Peer-mediated teaching and augmentative and alternative communication for preschool-aged children with autism. *Journal of Intellectual & Developmental Disability, 34*, 173–186.

U.S. Department of Education. (1987). *Annual report to congress on the implementation of the Education of the Handicapped Act.* Washington, DC: U.S. Department of Education.

U.S. Department of Education. (2012). *2012 IDEA part B child count and educational environment.* Retrieved from https://explore.data.gov/Education/2012-IDEA-Part-B-Child-Count-and-Educational-Envir/5t72 -4535

U.S. Department of Education Office of Special Education and Rehabilitative Services. (29 February, 2012). *Letter on Preschool (LRE).* Washington, DC: Author.

VanDerHeyden, A.M., Snyder, P., Smith, A., Sevin, B., & Longwell, J. (2005). Effects of complete learning trials on child engagement. *Topics in Early Childhood Special Education, 25*, 81–94.

Watson, A., & McCathren, R. (2009). Including children with special needs: Are you and your early childhood program ready? *Beyond the Journal: Young Children, 64*, 20–26.

Wills, D., Darragh-Ernst, J., & Presley, D. (2012). *Quality Inclusive Practices Checklist.* Normal, IL: Heartland Community College, Heartland Equity and Inclusion Project.

Wolery, M. (2005). DEC recommended practices: Child-focused practices. In S. Sandall, M.L. Hemmeter, B.J. Smith, & M.E. McLean (Eds.), *DEC recommended practices: A comprehensive guide for practical application in early intervention/early childhood special education* (pp. 71–106). Missoula, MT: Division for Early Childhood.

Wolery, M., Brashers, M.S., Grant, S., & Pauca, T. (2000). *Ecological congruence assessment for classroom activities and routines in childcare.* Chapel Hill, NC: Frank Porter Graham Child Development Center.

Wolery, M., Brashers, M.S., & Neitzel, J.C. (2002). Ecological congruence assessment for classroom activities and routines: Identifying goals and intervention practices in childcare. *Topics in Early Childhood Special Education 22*(3), 131–142.

Wolery, M., Pauca, T., Brashers, M.S., & Grant, S. (2000). *Quality of inclusive experiences measure* [Unpublished assessment manual]. Chapel Hill, NC: Frank Porter Graham Child Development Center.

Wolery, R.A., & Odom, S.L. (2000). *An administrator's guide to preschool inclusion.* Chapel Hill: University of North Carolina, Frank Porter Graham Child Development Center, Early Childhood Research Institute on Inclusion.

Wong, C., Odom, S.L., Hume, K., Cox, A.W., Fettig, A., Kucharczyk, S., . . . Schulz, T.R. (2014). *Evidence-based practices for children, youth, and young adults with autism spectrum disorder.* Chapel Hill: University of North Carolina, Frank Porter Graham Child Development Center, Autism Evidence-Based Practice Review Group. Retrieved from http://fpg.unc.edu/sites/fpg.unc.edu/files/ resources/reports-and-policy-briefs/2014-EBP-Report.pdf

Woods, J.J., & Snyder, P. (2009). Interdisciplinary doctoral leadership training in early intervention: Research and practice in the 21st century. *Infants and Young Children, 22*(1), 32–43.

Resources

ACCOMMODATIONS AND MODIFICATIONS

Head Start Center for Inclusion: http://depts.washington.edu/hscenter

Play Modifications for Students with Disabilities by Susan Sandall (article): https://mymission .lamission.edu/userdata/mermelrd/docs/NAE50.pdf

Sandall, S., & Schwartz, I. (2008). *Building blocks for preschoolers with special needs.* Baltimore, MD: Paul H. Brookes Publishing Co.

ADDITIONAL PRESCHOOL INCLUSION BOOKS AND GUIDES

Buysse, V., & Wesley, P.W. (2005). *Consultation in early childhood settings.* Baltimore, MD: Paul H. Brookes Publishing Co.

Campbell, P.H., Kennedy, A.A., & Milbourne, S.A. (2012). *CARA's Kit for Toddlers: Creating adaptations for routines and activities.* Baltimore, MD: Paul H. Brookes Publishing Co.

Catlett, C. (2012). The right stuff: Evidence-based practices that support young learners in inclusive settings. Available at http://fpg.unc.edu/resources/right-stuff-evidence-based -practices-support-young-learners-inclusive-settings

Causton, J., & Theoharis, G. (2014). *The principal's handbook for leading inclusive schools.* Baltimore, MD: Paul H. Brookes Publishing Co.

Dinnebeil, L., & McInerney, W.F. (2011). *A guide to itinerant early childhood special education services.* Baltimore, MD: Paul H. Brookes Publishing Co.

Grisham-Brown, J., Hemmeter, M.L., & Pretti-Frontczak, K. (2005). *Blended practices for teaching young children in inclusive settings.* Baltimore, MD: Paul H. Brookes Publishing Co.

Gupta, S. (2014). *First steps to preschool inclusion.* Baltimore, MD: Paul H. Brookes Publishing Co.

Richardson-Gibbs, A.M., & Klein, M.D. (2014). *Making preschool inclusion work: Strategies for supporting children, teachers, and programs.* Baltimore, MD: Paul H. Brookes Publishing Co.

Rush, D.D., & Shelden, M.L. (2011). *The early childhood coaching handbook.* Baltimore, MD: Paul H. Brookes Publishing Co.

Sandall, S.R., & Schwartz, I.S. (2008). *Building blocks for teaching preschoolers with special needs* (2nd ed.). Baltimore, MD: Paul H. Brookes Publishing Co.

United States Access Board. (2010). Accessible play areas [PDF, text or recording]. Available on the ADA National Network's Accessibility Online web site at http://www.accessibilityonline .org/Archives/index.php?app=4&type=transcript&id=2010-12-02

Wolery, R.A., & Odom, S. (2000). *An administrator's guide to preschool inclusion.* Chapel Hill: University of North Carolina, Frank Porter Graham Child Development Center, Early Childhood Research Institute on Inclusion. Available at http://fpg.unc.edu/sites/fpg.unc .edu/files/resources/reports-and-policy-briefs/ECRII_Administrators_Guide_2000.pdf

ASSISTIVE TECHNOLOGY

Assistive Technology for Young Children: Creating Inclusive Learning Environments by Kathleen C. Sadao, Ed.D., and Nancy B. Robinson, Ph.D., CCC-SLP.

CONNECT: The Center to Mobilize Early Childhood Knowledge, Assistive Technology Module: http://community.fpg.unc.edu/connect-modules/learners/module-5

Supporting Early Education Delivery Systems (SEEDS): http://www.scoe.net/SEEDS/ resources/at/at.html

DATA COLLECTION

Gischlar, K.L., Hojnoski, R.L., & Missall, K.N. (2009). Improving child outcomes with data-based decision making: Interpreting and using data. *Young Exceptional Children, 13,* 2–18.

Hojnoski, R.L., Gischlar, K.L., & Missall, K.N. (2009a). Improving child outcomes with data-based decision making: Collecting data. *Young Exceptional Children, 12,* 32–44.

Hojnoski, R.L., Gischlar, K.L., & Missall, K.N. (2009b). Improving child outcomes with data-based decision making: Graphing data. *Young Exceptional Children, 12,* 15–30.

DIFFERENTIATED INSTRUCTION

McGee, L. M., & Richgels, D. J. (2014). *Designing early literacy programs.* New York, NY: Guilford Press.

FISCAL STRATEGIES

Early Childhood Technical Assistance Center—Financing Strategies: http://ectacenter.org/ topics/inclusion/funding/funding.asp

The Ounce—*Blending and Braiding Early Childhood Program Funding Streams Toolkit*: http:// www.ounceofprevention.org/national-policy/Blended-Funding-Toolkit-Nov2013.pdf

GENERAL INCLUSION RESOURCES

Division for Early Childhood (DEC) Recommended Practices: http://www.dec-sped.org/ recommendedpractices

Early Childhood Inclusion: A Joint Position Statement of the Division for Early Childhood (DEC) and the National Association for the Education of Young Children (NAEYC): http://npdci.fpg .unc.edu/resources/articles/Early_Childhood_Inclusion

Early Childhood Technical Assistance Center—General Inclusion Resources: http://ectacenter .org/topics/inclusion/default.asp

National Professional Development Center on Inclusion: http://npdci.fpg.unc.edu

Quality Rating and Improvement Systems Compendium: http://qriscompendium.org/

Research Synthesis Points on Inclusive Practices (National Professional Development Center on Inclusion): http://npdci.fpg.unc.edu/sites/npdci.fpg.unc.edu/files/resources/NPDCI -ResearchSynthesisPointsInclusivePractices-2011_0.pdf

LEGAL RESOURCES

Early Childhood Technical Assistance Center—Federal Laws: http://ectacenter.org/topics/ inclusion/legis/fedlegisl.asp

Education Law Center: http://www.edlawcenter.org/assets/files/pdfs/publications/ PreKPolicyBrief_InclusionChildrenWithDisabilities.pdf

U.S. Department of Education IDEA website: http://idea.ed.gov/explore/home

POSITION STATEMENTS

Additional Division for Early Childhood Position Statements and Papers: http://www.dec-sped .org/papers

Early Childhood Inclusion: A Joint Position Statement of the Division for Early Childhood (DEC) and the National Association for the Education of Young Children (NAEYC): http://npdci .fpg.unc.edu/resources/articles/Early_Childhood_Inclusion; http://www.dec-sped.org/ papers

RESPONSE TO INTERVENTION

Buysse, V., & Peisner Feinberg, E. (2013). *Handbook of response to intervention in early childhood.* Baltimore, MD: Paul H. Brookes Publishing Co.

Center for Response to Intervention in Early Childhood (CRTIEC): http://www2.ku.edu/ ~crtiec/aboutcrtiec/JuniperStaffPhoto.shtml

Frameworks for Response to Intervention in Early Childhood: Description and Implications: http:// www.naeyc.org/files/naeyc/RTI%20in%20Early%20Childhood.pdf

Technical Assistance Center on Social Emotional Intervention for Young Children (TAC-SEI): http://challengingbehavior.fmhi.usf.edu

SOCIAL-EMOTIONAL DEVELOPMENT AND CHALLENGING BEHAVIORS

Center for Early Childhood Mental Health Consultation: http://www.ecmhc.org

Center on the Social and Emotional Foundations for Early Learning: http://csefel.vanderbilt.edu

Pyramid Model Consortium: http://www.pyramidmodel.org

Technical Assistance Center on Social Emotional Intervention for Young Children (TAC-SEI): http://challengingbehavior.fmhi.usf.edu

SELECT STATES INCLUSION RESOURCES

Delaware Health and Social Services, Birth to Three Early Intervention System, and Delaware Department of Education—*Promoting Inclusion in Early Childhood Programs*: http://www.dhss.delaware.gov/dms/epqc/birth3/files/guidetoinclusion2013.pdf

Delaware, MAPS, Meaningful Access Participation and Supports: http://www.dhss.delaware.gov/dms/epqc/birth3/files/de_maps_inclusion.pdf

Early Childhood Inclusion for All Children in Louisiana: http://www.louisianabelieves.com/docs/early-childhood/brochure---early-childhood-inclusion.pdf?sfvrsn=7

Early Childhood Inclusion for Each and Every Child in Illinois: http://www.starnet.org/pdf/EC_Inclusion_Brochure_4pages.pdf; http://www.isbe.net/earlychi/html/ec_speced_lre.htm

Maine's Expanding Inclusive Opportunities Inclusion Toolkit: http://umaine.edu/expandinclusiveopp/ec-settings-inclusion-toolkit

Oregon Early Childhood Inclusion Collaborative Professional Development Workgroup (OECIC-PD), resources for establishing teams and supporting inclusive preschool programs: http://www.centeroninclusion.org/OECIC.htm

WEB SITES WITH TRAINING MODULES AND MATERIALS

Building Inclusive Child Care, video of how inclusive child care addresses universal design for all children and families: http://www.northampton.edu/early-childhood-education/partnerships/building-inclusive-child-care.htm

Center on the Social and Emotional Foundations for Early Learning, training materials, videos, and print resources to help early care, health, and education providers implement the Pyramid Model: http://csefel.vanderbilt.edu

Center to Mobilize Early Childhood Knowledge CONNECT, learning modules with content and videos about inclusion: http://community.fpg.unc.edu/connect-modules/learners

Child Care and the Americans with Disabilities Act (ADA), video about how child care centers can make sure that they understand and respond to the ADA law: http://www.adainformation.org/ChildCare

Coaching in Early Childhood, web site with content, training modules, and resources about coaching in early childhood (EC) settings: http://www.coachinginearlychildhood.org/cpractices.php

Delaware Meaningful Access Participation and Supports (MAPS), guide to high-quality inclusion of children with disabilities and their families: http://www.dhss.delaware.gov/dms/epqc/birth3/files/de_maps_inclusion.pdf

Embedded Instruction for Early Learning, learning materials about embedded instruction: http://www.embeddedinstruction.net/node/18

Head Start Center for Inclusion, training materials, tools for teachers and coordinators, as well as other resources: http://depts.washington.edu/hscenter

Kids Included Together (KIT), training modules to understand the laws supporting inclusion: http://www.kitonline.org/html/about/publications/2013_understanding_the_laws_supporting _inclusion.html

National Center on Quality Teaching and Learning, resources and videos regarding Head Start teacher personal development: http://eclkc.ohs.acf.hhs.gov/hslc/tta-system/ teaching

National Professional Development Center on Inclusion, federally funded center that has developed products and worked with states to ensure that EC teachers are prepared to teach young children with disabilities: http://npdci.fpg.unc.edu

Research Synthesis Points on Quality Inclusive Practices, short descriptions of practices associated with high-quality inclusion and their research citations: http://npdci.fpg.unc .edu/resources/articles/NPDCI-ResearchSynthesisPointsInclusivePractices-2011

Results Matter, videos of practices associated with quality inclusion: http://www.cde.state .co.us/resultsmatter/RMVideoSeries.htm#top

SpecialQuest, library of resources related to high-quality inclusive preschool programs: http://ncoe.pointinspace.com/trainingmaterials

Supporting Early Education Delivery Systems (SEEDS), resources about assistive technology for infants, toddlers, and preschoolers with disabilities: http://www.scoe.net/seeds/ resources/at/at.html

Index

Tables, figures, and notes are indicated by *t, f,* and *n,* respectively.